THE MOTHER OF ALL CAR BOOKS

Ladies and Gentl

THE MOTHER OF ALL CAR BOOKS

How To Get More **Fun & Profit** Buying, Showing & Selling Vintage & Classic Cars

By

Rod & Sherry Reprogle
with Charles Browning

duncliff's international

3662 Katella Avenue
Los Alamitos, CA 90720
1-800-410-7766

Published by:
DUNCLIFF'S INTERNATIONAL
General Publishing Division
3662 Katella Avenue, Dept. 226
Los Alamitos, California 90720
Phone   (800) 410-7766
Fax   (310) 799-6657

FIRST EDITION

Library of Congress Cataloging-in-Publication Data

Reprogle, Rod, 1945-
   The mother of all car books : how to get more fun & profit buying,
  showing & selling vintage & classic cars / Rod & Sherry Reprogle,
  with Charles Browning. — 1st ed.

   ISBN 0-911663-78-9 (pbk.) : $14.95
   1. Antique and classic cars—Purchasing. 2. Selling—Automobiles.
I. Reprogle, Sherry, 1945-   .   II. Browning, Charles, 1944-
III. Title.
TL 162.R47   1995
629.222'029'7——dc20   91—58795
                                                                              CIP

*Copies of this book may be ordered directly from the Publisher at $14.95 (paperback)
plus $4 postage & handling (California residents add 7.75% sales tax). For assistance
promoting private car events and charitable fund raisers, car-event products, author
interviews, and for discount terms on quantity orders, please contact the Publisher.*

Dedicated to —

YOU, our reader,
and the pleasure and the profit
we hope this book will bring into your life.

And to those fabulous cars of yesterday.

Long live the memories!

Table of Contents

Table of Contents   1
Here's To The *Real* Heroes   7
Why "The Mother" of All Car Books?   11

1. CAR SPEAK! Getting A Handle On Words Car People Use 13
   Car-Speak-To-English Glossary of Terms   16

2. How To Choose The Car That's Right For *You*   25
   The "Nostalgia Method" For Choosing The Right Car   29
   The "What's Hot Method" For Buying The Right Car   31
   The "Budget Friendly Method" For Buying The Right Car   34
   The "Swinging Door Method" For Choosing The Right Car   35
   The 4 Methods For Choosing The Right Car   38

3. How To Avoid The Pain, Aggravation, Misery & Regrets
   of Buying The *Wrong* Car   39
   Beware Of The LAFS — "Love At First Sight" Trap   41
   Beware Of The "You Have A Right To My Own
       Opinion" Trap   43
   Beware Of The "Perfect Color" Trap   44
   Beware Of The "Twilight Zone" Trap   45
   Get The Advice Of A "Fruit Inspector"   45
   Beware Of The "Slight-Of-Hand" Seller   47
   Any Leaks? — The Garage Floor *Speaks!*   48
   Color Chart To Troubleshoot Problem Leaks   49
   Beware of the "Shoulda-Woulda-Coulda" Trap   49
   Final Inspection Checklist   51

4. Twelve Ways To Save Hundreds, Even Thousands Of Dollars
   When You Buy Your Car   55
   1. Stay Cool, Calm And Collected   57
   2. Get The "Asking" Price   57
   3. Stay Positive   58
   4. Comment On Obvious Glitches   58
   5. Do A Ballpark Estimate Of What Fixing The Glitches
       Would Cost   58
   6. How To Talk To The Seller To Get Your Price   59

7. Don't Even Look At Cars You Can't Afford 60

8. Don't Let The Seller Pressure You 61

9. Don't Let The Seller's Personality Influence
   Your Decision 61

10. Be prepared To Pay The Right Way 63

11. How "Car Savvy" Is The Seller? 64

12. How "Car Savvy" Are You? 65

Twelve Ways To Save Hundreds, Even Thousands of Dollars
   When You Buy Your Car 67

5. How To Show And Shine! The Art Of Displaying
   Your Car: Tips That Give Your Car That Special
   Winning Edge 69

Timing Is Everything — Arrive Early! 72

Finding The Prime Parking Spots: Positions That
   Can Give Your Car Center Stage 73

To Show, Or Not To Show Your Engine? 75

To Show, Or Not To Show What's Under The Trunk 72

Should The Doors Be Left Open Or Closed? 75

What To Show, And What Not To Show?
   The 7 Guidelines 77

A Special Trick To Use With Your Windows 77

A Key Point About The Keys 78

"Look But Don't Touch Signs" — Use Them 78

Showing Your Car During The Day: The 5 Secrets
   That Really Pay Off 79

Showing Your Car At Night: The 3 Secrets Most
   People Never Discover 80

The Best Place To Place Your Lawn Chairs 81

You Don't Need A High-Dollar Car To Win
   Awards 82

Show Your Car, But Don't Be A Show-Off 83

How To Make Your Car Look Unique And Stand Out 84

The Right Distance To Park From Other Cars To Make
   The Best Impression 86

How To Make Decorative Touches The Right Way 87

Try This *Under* The Car To Get Big Attention 88

Some Special Tricks To Knock Their Eyes Out 89

When You Should NEVER Polish Your Car   89
Using Graphics To Make Your Car Look Super-Special:
   Some Do's And Don'ts   90
What To Do If Your Car Has Flaws: How To
   Minimize Them   92
One Little Trick That Makes Your Wheels
   Make The Best Impression   92
The Show & Shine Top 20 Checklist   94

6. How To Have A True Car Show Attitude: Car Show
   Etiquette, Good Manners, & How To Avoid
   Making Stupid Mistakes   95
Mistake #1: The Show-Off, "Me 'N My Car Are
   Best By Far" Attitude   98
How To Avoid Making Mistake #1   99
Mistake #2: The "Winning Is Everything" Attitude   99
How To Avoid Making Mistake #2   100
Mistake #3: The "Hit Or Miss" Attitude   100
How To Avoid Making Mistake #3   100
Mistake #4: The "Let Me Tell You What's Wrong
   With Your Car" Attitude   101
How To Avoid Making Mistake #4   102
Mistake #5: The "Buy The Judges" Attitude   102
How To Avoid Making Mistake #5   103
Mistake #6: The "Take All The Glory" Attitude   104
How To Avoid Making Mistake #7   104
Mistake #7: The Attitude of Ingratitude   104
How To Avoid Making Mistake #7   105
Mistake #8: The Bad Loser Attitude   105
How To Avoid Making Mistake #8   106
Mistake #9: The "Party Animal" Attitude   106
How To Avoid Making Mistake #9   107
Mistake #10: The "Crude-Rude-Dude" Attitude   107
How To Avoid making Mistake #10   108
Mistake #11: The "Who Needs A D.J. Attitude   108
How To Avoid making Mistake #11   109
Learn From The Experts   109
Good Manners & Etiquette Checklist   111

7. How To Convert Your Car Into Cash: Smart Strategies
        For Selling Your Car To Make The Biggest Profit   113
    The "Would You Take My Huzwatzit In Trade For
        Your Car?" Offer   117
    Made In The Shade Handling Trades: The Smart
        Way To Win At This Game   118
    Five Key Ways To Determine The Best Asking Price
        For Your Car   119
    Using The Shotgun Technique To Bring The Serious
        Buyers Out Of Hiding   122
    How To Save A Bundle Writing Classified Ads
        In Newspapers   123
    How To Write Ads That Save You Money And
        Sell Your Car Faster   124
    How To Use Emotional *"Trigger Words"*   125
    Trigger Words That Hook Potential Buyers   125
    A Way To Save Money With Classifieds   126
    Another Trick To Get More Calls On Your Car   127
    A Little Tip That Will Give Your Ad A Big Edge   128
    A Great Source Of FREE Local Advertising   129
    A Simple Way To Let Your Car Advertise & Sell Itself   130
    Using Word-Of-Mouth Advertising To Sell Your Car Fast   131
    A Powerful Way To Reach The Real Car Buff   132
    FROM FAME TO FORTUNE; How To Give Your
        Car A Reputation That Will Increase
        The Selling Price   132
    Selling Your Car In Free Shopper Papers   132
    How To Successfully Sell Your Car At Swap Meets:
        Step-By-Step Guidelines   134
    Practical Tips On Getting Your Price   136
    The Smart Way To Talk Price & Get The Price You Want   137
    The One Sure Way To Know If A Buyer Is Serious   139
    How To Answer the Question: "How Did You Determine
        The Price You're Asking For This Car?"   141
    How To Get Twice, Even Three-Times What Your Car
        Is Worth Using The "Trolling For Big Fish Method"   141
    How To Spot The Phony-Baloney Idea-Collector Vs. The
        Real-McCoy Car Buyer   142

The Attitude That Works Best To Win Over The Buyer   143
How To Answer The Question: "Why Are You Coming
    Down On Your Price?"   144
Use The Display Board To Grab The Attention Of
    The Serious Buyer   145
The Thrill Of The Sell!   145

8. How To Plan, Organize & Run Your Own Car Show
        Or Cruise Nite: An Interview With Lee McCullough   147
    All About The Basics   150
    Tips On How To Set Up Your Own Cruise-Nite   152
    How To Handle Money Issues   156
    The 7 Rules For Running A Successful Cruise-Nite   159
    Where *Not* To Put On A Car Event   160
    Where To Set Up A Successful Car Event   161
    A 16-Step Mini-Course On Creating A Good Flyer
        For Your Car Event To Bring In Big Crowds   161
    Where To Go To Get Quality Help For Your Event   163
    More Tips On Getting People Excited About
        Your Car Events   164
    What About Swap Meets To Promote Successful
        Car Events   166
    How To Use Direct Mail Marketing To Attract
        The Crowds To Your Car Events   167
    How To Successfully Use TV, Radio &
        Newspaper Advertising   168
    Putting On Your Own Fund-Raisers   170
    How To Get A Non-Profit Group To Back Your Events   173
    How To Get A Local Radio Station To Back
        You (And Provide The D.J. Free)   174
    How To Conduct An Exciting Raffle   174
    What To Do When The Party's Over   175
    A Great Sport For Great People   176

9. The Step-By-Step Ingredients For Putting On a Successful
        Fund Raiser: An Interview With Bob French   177
    The Magnetic Power Of Car Events   180
    What Attracts So Many People To Car Events?   180
    What Makes Car Events A Good Fund Raiser?   181

How To Make Your Event Attract More People   182
Some Unusual Car Show Themes   182
How Does An Organization Make Money Doing A Show?   183
A Description of One Of The Most Popular Car Events   184
How To Find A Sponsor For Your Car Show   184
How To Approach A Sponsor Or Vendor   184
Step-By-Step Basics For Organizing Your Car Events   185
The Most Important First Step   185
Where To Get Awards And Dash Plaques   187
How To Select Judges For Car Shows   188
How To Get City Permits   189
How To Get People To Enter Their Cars For Display   189
What Is The Best Way To Distribute Event Flyers   190
Perks That Make People Excited To Enter Their Cars   191
Money Matters   191
Ways To Raise Money For Your Event   191
The Mechanics of Handling The Raffle Or Drawing   193
The Best Place To Set Up Your Raffle Or Drawing   194
Ways To Handle Venders Profitably   195
How To Handle Money Safely   195
What Car Shows Mean To Business Organizations   196
The Impact Of Car Shows On Drawing New Customers   196
Handling Potential Problems   197
What Happens If The Event Is Rained Out   197
How Do You Handle Liability Insurance   198
Ten Key Do's & Don't For A Successful Car Event   198
One Final Word Of Advice   199

What's In The Trunk? *(Also Called the Appendix)*
Car Club Finder — National & International Clubs   205
Sample Promotional Flyers For Attracting Big Crowds 225
Directory of America's Top Car Publications   265
So You Think You Know Cars? Classic Slogans I.Q.Test   269
Special Gift & Raffle Copies Order Forms   273

Here's to The *Real* Heroes*!*

When you see one car get the top trophies at car shows, and attract the biggest crowds at cruise-nites, and cause near accidents on the highway because it's turning every head in sight, the owner of that special car is not the only one who deserves special honors. There are usually several other important people -- gifted people -- behind the scenes who worked together to make that car get so much attention.

These talented people do body work, engine work, chassis work, electrical work, glass work, paint jobs, graphics, and inside upholstery work. Without such key team members the car not only wouldn't be winning awards and attracting crowds, it probably would be abandoned somewhere in some weed-infested junk yard.

And like those special people behind the scenes who resurrect that car and make it shine, you probably wouldn't be reading this book if it were not for our own super team working together to make this book happen.

So, here's to those unsung heroes behind the scenes who deserve a ton of thanks ...

Here's to Lee McCullough. You'll find pictures and stories about Lee in many of the best car magazines. And if you look under the word "mentor" in Webster's Dictionary you'll find his picture there. Well, not really, but it should be -- because Lee was there to help us when we first got into the hobby of cars, and as the definition of "mentor" goes, he was a "wise, loyal advisor, a teacher and a coach." Thanks to Lee McCullough for sharing with you a wealth of wisdom about cars in the interview on setting up and running cruise nites.. His sample flyers in the back of the book for promoting cruise nites are true gems! And thanks for being a super-friend as well!

To Bob French — a man of many talents, a gifted magician and entertainer, and the promotor of some of the biggest and most popular car shows and fund raisers in California. Bob generously gives his time and skills in making top car events "work", and we are grateful to Bob for sharing with you the secrets and little-known tricks to make your fund raiser a big hit. You'll find his interview fascinating! And Bob's sample flyers for promoting car shows are real works of art! You'll find them at the back of the book. It's no wonder he is able to draw such huge crowds to his car events!

And here's to those dear members of our family who have been by our side giving of their love and support, and getting more excited with every passing day about this book. Our deepest heartfelt thanks to them ... Wynema Ferguson, Steve Baldry, George and Ann Mayo, Ray and Lillian Mayo, Edmond and Sheri Maggiora, and Steven Reprogle. Jennifer Browning for her diligent car-club compiling assistance. Beverley, Faith, David and Seth Browning for their patience and support during the preparation of this book. And Mary DeGiacomo for her faith and encouragement. We are richly blessed to have such a wonderful family.

And we owe special thanks to Jason Knight, who became paralyzed playing high school football at age 15. His life and spirit were an inspiration to us and helped remind us what car events as fund raisers can really mean -- people caring about people, having a blast celebrating life together. And sincere appreciation to all those car buffs who gave of their hard-earned money to help Jason.

Without the almost daily assistance of Peggy Oquist, Stephanie Smith, Linda Wong, Uyen Nguyen, and Sally Guess, this book would still be in the making. Their special talents are a God-send.

Car-loads of thanks to Mark Kelly and Marion and Gary Nixon for their expertise, suggestions and wisdom, along with Lee McCullough — all helping us put together the chapter on Car Speak! What a great team of consultants!

And to Randy Dubb, for his enthusiasm, his good advice, and his skillful editorial contributions to the final version of this book. Randy is the kind of guy you meet at a car show that makes you glad you're into cars simply because it gives you the opportunity to meet people like him.

To Dorothy Pilone, whose editorial eagle-eye has helped make this book reader-friendly. We thank Dorothy for bringing New-York-publishing excellence to the west coast — and with a sweet spirit to boot!

And in memory of the late Dr. Francisco Trinidad, our lives have been changed by his inspiration and example.

And last but not least, we want to thank you for showing the good judgment buying and reading this book! We hope it will fill your evenings, weekends, holidays and vacations with countless hours of fun and profit as you buy, sell, show and just plain enjoy those nifty things on wheels we call *cars!*

Here's to one fantastic team! God bless you all!

Why "The MOTHER" of All Car Books?

Is this book called *"The Mother of All Car Books"* because it tells you everything under the sun about cars? — Nope.

Is it because it tells you everything you ever wanted to know about cars but were afraid to ask? — Nope.

Is it because this book makes all other car books obsolete? Nope.

Is it because this book covers cars from A to Z? — Nope.

Is it because it covers cars from front to back? — Nope.

Is it because it covers cars from top to bottom? — Nope.

Is it because this is the BEST car book ever written? — Well, we'll leave that up to you, but that's not the real reason it's called *"The Mother of All Car Books."*

Then if it's not all these things, why in the world is it called *"The Mother of All Car Books"*?

Simple. It's because it's like a mother!
It's a sweet and friendly book.
It cares about you and what you care about.
It will give you things good for you.
It understands what's important to you.
It's a book you feel good being around.
It's a book that will give you good advice so you
    don't end up doing something dumb or stupid.

And it's a book that's totally concerned about helping you have more fun and saving you more money in your passion for those memories on wheels.

No, it can't bake you a cherry pie or babysit the kids for you while you do some serious bench racing at next week's cruise-nite — or show 'n shine at next Saturday's car show. But it will for sure make those events a lot more enjoyable and rewarding for you and your family. That's a promise!

Yep, you have in your hands a real "mother" of a book!

"The Mother of All Car Books!"

11

Chapter 1

Car Speak!

Getting A Handle On The Words Car People Use

CHAPTER ONE

Car Speak!

Getting A Handle On The Words Car People Use

"Man, that T-bucket is really tricked out" ... "Check out that cherry lead sled" ... "Park over there by that resto rod parked next to the low rider just behind the kemp" ... "Who owns that shoebox over there by the spotted beater?"... "That worm-burner is really down in the weeds!"..."I go for these big balonies!"... "Who owns that nifty garage queen over there with the Hollywood chop?"... "Personally, I think those weenies look outrageous on that thing!"

Now, if you've been hanging around rod and custom people long enough and spending time at the right car events, you could probably translate what you just read into English. If you're just getting into customs, vintage and classics you look at that stuff and scratch your head and say, "huh, what in the world are they talking about?"

We don't want anybody coming across a term in this book they don't understand, or feeling like a fifth wheel at a car event, because they don't understand some term they run across. That's why we are not going to do what the typical book would do -- they put the glossary definitions at the back. We're going to put it up front, like headlights, to shed some light on "car speak", to help you get a handle on all those terms most commonly used at cruise-nites, car shows, swap meets, and other car events. After all, who wants to be bench racing, comparing their favorite slope-back with some other guy's flat-back or garage queen and not knowing what in the heck they're talkin' about?

If you understood immediately what that last statement means and know precisely what kind of cars were referred to -- year and all -- and if you can translate the first paragraph of this chapter into plain English -- you might want to jump to Chapter 2. Because if you can easily handle all this, you probably could have written this chapter yourself!

But if you stumbled the least bit over "bench racing," "slope-back," "flat-back," "garage queen," "worm burner," "kemp," "balonies" or "weenies," stick around. You might find something helpful in what's coming up.

Car Speak-To-English Glossary of Terms:
Car Lingo Made Simple

When people get together to talk cars, there's a certain lingo that you'll hear that is the jargon comfortable to the car buff, like the lingo you hear on CB radios, it's unique to that circle of people -- car people have invented their own special words. Here's a list of some of the most commonly used words and what they mean.

ANTIQUE — any car from the '30s on back.

BEATER — an unfinished car usually painted in primer. It may or may not be beat up.

BENCH RACING — gathering around to talk about the good old days, old cars, engines, cars you've raced against —, swapping stories till they close the place!

BIG BALONIES — see STEAMROLLERS .

BILLET — large solid chunks of aluminum or steel used to make custom car parts .

BONDO — a product trade mark for the filler used to fill in dents for painting preparation.

BONDOMOBILE or BONDO-MACHINE — a car with a lot of dents in it that could use a few gallons of Bondo. You don't want to call someone's car a bondo-machine unless you're trying to start trouble!

BOTTLE BABIES — engines that boost horsepower by bottle-fed nitrus oxide (laughing gas), also called "jungle juice."

BURN-OUT — where the engine is highly revved and thrown in gear to squeal the tires. In the old days it was done to be macho or "cool", but now people at car shows and cruises won't put up with it.

CAR SHOW — an event held to display cars for the purpose of competition, social enjoyment, and for supporting charitable causes.

CHANNELED — a frame cut for purposes of lengthening or shortening the car .

CHERRY — a really nice body job, block sanded and painted with a real high-quality gloss to it.

CHOPPED (DROPPED & CHOPPED) — a section of the roof is cut and the roof is dropped and lowered.

CHOP TOP — a few inches is whacked off the top of the car to give the car a lowered appearance.

CLASSIC — an era or period car, like a '55 through '57 Chevy or Ford, or the '64 through '67 Mustang, or the GTO from '64, or '55 through '57 T-Bird, or the '53 through '67 Stingrays.

COLLECTABLE — usually this refers to a car out of the '50s, although it could refer to any car that people get excited about at car shows and cruises.

COMMERCIAL VEHICLE — pickup trucks, ice cream trucks, some station wagons, Rancheros, El Caminos.

COUPE — a 2 door .

CRUISE — nowadays it means to meet at a specific place to enjoy cars. In the old days it meant riding around from place to place.

CRUISE-IN — a group of cars starting at one place and ending up at another, turning a lot of heads along the way.

CRUISE-NITE or CRUISE-NIGHT — the place where the cruise or the event is held. It's not competitive like a car show, but is for fun with family and friends that's really low-profile.

CRUISER — people who attend cruise-nites on a regular basis.

CUSTOM — basically this has four or more body modifications, such as louvers, or lowering, changes in the grille or body, or a custom paint job.

DEUCE COUPE — '32 three-window coupe. In 1932 they would take a '32 frame and put it under an earlier model body (like a '23 T) to make the car stronger and longer.

DIECER — a dragster, a car built for attaining high speeds.

DOWN IN THE WEEDS — a car lowered way down.

DROP SPINDLES — modification of the front axle with a downward off-center so the chassis rides way low down to the ground .

DROPPED — see CHOPPED .

FAT FENDERS — any car from the mid '30s to late '40s that you can unbolt the fenders off of them. It's round-looking.

FLAT-BACK — basically a '35 through '37 Ford two-door sedan. It's a fat fender car.

FUND RAISER — events held for the purpose of raising money and gaining attention for worthy causes.

GARAGE QUEEN — a car you generally don't see on the road because they keep it in the garage or put it in a trailer and hardly ever drive it because they don't want dirt or grass on their tires.

GRAPHICS — artistic designs painted on cars (but not including pinstriping).

HAMMERED — the top of the car is lowered, chopped and dropped.

HEMI — hemispherical shape of combustion chamber over cylinder bore.

HI TECH — using the latest technology on the market in the mechanicals of the car, like using tuned port induction (TPI) instead of a carburetor.

HOLLYWOOD CHOP — a few inches is whacked off the front portion of the roof only to give the car that low-down look in the front.

HOT ROD — in today's circles it might be a coupe or a roadster of the '20s, '30s, or even the '40s. Most don't have fenders. It might have large tires in the rear, small tires in front. No hood. It's the name of a magazine, but the term has been around since the '30s.

INDEPENDENT SUSPENSION (front & rear) — each wheel's ability to act independently of the others in responding to road conditions. IFS - independent front suspension; IRS - independent rear suspension (not to be confused with the *InFernal Revenue Service!*)

KEMP — a custom or lead sled that's a 1949 or '50 Merc, chopped and lowered and really tricked out.

KEMPER — another name for a custom car.

LEAD SLED — the opposite of a low-rider, it's a pre-'65 car all the way back to a '39. Before the days of Bondo they had to use lead when preparing a car body for painting. In the old days calling someone's car a "lead sled" was an insult. Nowadays it's a high compliment since there are probably no more than 300 or 400 lead body men in the United States that do that type of work. You can do a car using Bondo in 1 hour, where it would take 30 to 40 hours to do the same job using lead!

LOUVERED — originally factory installed. In modified cars, slots are punched or perforated into the sides of the hood and other places on the car, typically done on Model As and Model Ts, but also in a wide variety of other cars.

LOW-RIDER — a custom car from the mid '60s up through the current era cars, having fat tires on real skinny rims and hydraulics.

MODEL T & A — 1928 — 1931 Model A Ford, and 1911 through 1927 Model T Ford.

MOUNTAIN MOTORS — engines over 500 cubic inches .

MUSCLE CAR — '64 through '73 factory-built car with a large engine in it, like the Corvette with the 427 motor, the big Dodges and Plymouths with the 426 wedge or hemi. Also included the Pontiac GTO. Most muscle cars are about 400 horsepower.

PINSTRIPING — stripes of various thicknesses painted on various parts of the car for decorative purposes .

POWDER COATING — electromagnetic powder   that gives paint a durable, film-like surface.

PRESTO ROD — is when an old car is modified to make it safer, faster, pleasing to the eye, and fun to drive, but not spending a fortune doing it.

PRO-STREET — is professionally built, or gives the appearance that it is professionally built (having a lot of magnesium, aluminum, or a hi-tech look), it may have tub fender wells, big tires on the back and lowered to beat the band!

RAIL — a digger or dragster, a car built for speed.

RAKED — the front end of the car is lowered way down.

RAT MOTORS — big block Chevys.

REPRO — reproduction replicas of classic, antique, or custom cars usually made of fiberglass.

RESTO-ROD — a restored rod or a kit-car, a copy-cat car that you can buy from a supplier (like a pre-fab job), like a copy of a '67 Cobra. Most of them are made out of fiberglass, not metal.

ROADSTER — an open-top car, ranging anywhere from a Model T to an early-'40s car.

ROD — see STREET ROD

RODDER — someone interested in the street rodding phenomena with any type of vehicle and someone who is very active in car events.

ROD RUNS — a group of car buffs making long drives together as a group for social or charitable purposes .

SCALLOPS — straight-back or swept-back lines, or flames, appearing like they are blowing in the wind painted on the car .

SEDAN — a 4 door.

SHOE-BOX — a small sedan or coupe, terminology used basically in drag racing. The term is used a lot on the streets because of the disappearance of many drag strips. It's basically a '49 to '51 Ford, or a '55 to '57 Chevy that may or may not have a big motor in it for cruisin' around in.

SHOEHORNED — taking a big engine and putting it into a car not made for that engine with not much room left over.

SLAMMED — the top or the whole look is lowered way down to give it the pro-street look.

SLICK — originally comes from drag racing, which identifies tires with no grooved treading, and are made of softer compounds that give them better traction. The term can also means a sharp, nice looking car.

SLICK RIDE — a real nice-looking car that's finished off well (the opposite of a beater).

SLOPE-BACK — a torpedo fastback '49 to '52 Chevy sedan. It used to be called a low-riders.

SMOOTHIES — a custom car with all the chrome, door handles; hood ornaments removed and tail lights inset and smoothed out; typically done on '50 and '53 Mercs.

STEAMROLLERS (also called BIG BALONIES) — big, fat, wide back tires .

STREET ROD — is a car that is made prior to 1948 that has later-model running gear.

SUB 'N TUB — narrowing of rear sub-frame with wheel tubs so the car can take big, wide tires to give it the pro-street look .

SUICIDED — the doors on the car are reversed so they open out toward the front, like the '32 three-window coupe.

SWAP MEET — a place where people go to sell or buy used parts or cars. Nowadays they also sell new parts at good prices.

T-BUCKET — a roadster that's normally associated with an old TV program that had Norm Brabowski's kookie car in it.

TRICKED OUT — a car that has a lot of easily-identifiable modifications on it, like hi-tech machining, aluminum billet material under the hood.

TUCK 'N' ROLL — a diamond - shaped , pleated interior .

TURN-KEY CAR — a car that is professionally built by someone, you just add gas and car keys and off you go. It could be any car someone has an expert (or different experts) build for him. The buyer may not have the knowledge or time to build it himself, but he sure will have the fun!

WEDGE — elongated, wedge - shaped combustion chamber for high performance for Fords, Dodges and Plymouths.

WEENIES — very thin, skinny front tires.

WHEEL STANDS — the car gets so much traction on slicks that it can accelerate and lift the front end off the ground.

WOODY — a factory-built car with wood sides, built from 1910 through the early '50s.

WORM BURNER — a car that is so lowered and so close to the ground that it "burns worms."

Okay, now that you have mastered "Car Speak," let's speak about the excitement of buying, showing and selling those cars we speak about ...

---

* *You can become a contributor* to the next edition of *"The Mother of All Car Books."* If you come across any words we missed, or you discover some newly invented addition to the car speak vocabulary, send them to us with a good, simple definition. If we use it in the next edition, we'll mention your name.

Chapter 2

How To Choose The Car That's Right For *You*

Personal Notes & Ideas

CHAPTER TWO

How to Choose the Car
That's Right for *You*

The Bill of Rights is a wonderful document when it comes to people, but it certainly doesn't work when it comes to one of man's favorite pastimes -- *cars.* Just as all cars are not created equal, the same can be said of the car lover. All men, and women, who are fascinated by cars, are created quite unequal .

All you have to do is spend an hour or two at a local car show or "party" at the next cruise-nite and you'll see how very different car buffs really are. One person drools over a slick '57 Chevy, while someone else thinks that a '66 Mustang is the best thing since the wheel. A third guy says they're both wrong -- "you can't beat a '21 Model A with a rumble seat," he says. And then there's the Model T lover, who would cut off his mother-in-law's right arm to own one.

And then you take a group of people standing around "oooing" and "ahhhing" over the same '57 Chevy or '66 Mustang or Model A or Model T. One guy says that the "perfect" car is black. The guy next to him says , "no way, cherry red is the only way to fly." Then a third voice chimes in and disagrees, "you can't beat hot pink." Two other guys swapping Model A stories argue about chrome and pinstripes.

So, who's right?

They are *all* right!

It's like chocolate, vanilla and strawberry. Bacon and eggs, ham and eggs, sausage and eggs. The 49ers, the Giants, the Raiders, the Broncos. The A's, the Reds, the Dodgers, the Mets Who's right?

They're all right because each person has the "right" to his or her own opinion.

So just as no one can tell you what to order from a menu at your favorite restaurant, and no one can tell you which football or baseball team to go nuts over, the same thing applies to which rod,   classic, or custom car is right for you.

You are the expert about you.   And what may be one man's pleasure might be another man's poison.   What may be one man's dream car might be another man's nightmare.

So there is no way we can tell you in this book which car to buy and which car not to buy.   But what we will do is give you a few tips and suggestions to help you make the best decision for you.   After all, we're not talking about buying a $10 gizmo that, if it doesn't work, or you don't really like it, so what, who cares?   We're talking about shelling out literally *thousands* of dollars of your hard - earned money.   When you use the tips in this book, you should save money — a lot of money!

Let's just say that someone earns $15 an hour on the job.   He decides to buy a beautiful '32 Ford and the price tag is $17,500 .   Do you know how many hours he has to put out the blood, sweat and tears on the job to park that beauty in his garage?   He spends 1,167 hours in the salt mines!   That's more than 29 working weeks!   That's January, February, March, April, May, June, July, and part of August on the job!   Not to mention the countless, endless hours on his back on a cold concrete floor, while Ethel screams, "Come to bed!" *(At the end of the book you'll see Ethel in action!)*   Ouch! There's a lot of *you* poured into that car!

So the decision you make about which car to spend your money on is a biggie.   Let's spend some time carefully considering *the right car for you* .

The "Nostalgia Method " For Choosing the Right Car

If you are the cool, calm, and collected, no-emotions type who wants to get into rods, custom, classic and antique cars to use as an investment, then you may want to skip this section and move on to the next. If you have no intention of spending hours and hours enjoying memories of "the good old days," and you simply want to buy a car that you can turn around and re-sell for substantially more than you bought it for, then skip to the next section.

But if a flood of happy memories rush into your head just at the sight of a particular car from out of the past, stick around. This method is just what you may need to make the best choice.

Buying a classic, custom or vintage car involves a lot of money and a lot of time to upgrade and maintain the car the way you want it

And you spend enough time working during the week, and you don't want owning a special car to be all work and no fun. So to make sure that the car you buy will give you the most pleasure, fun and enjoyment, the car should trigger images of those free, wild and crazy days gone by. Creating nostalgia is what makes your car worth so much. So be sure the car you buy creates plenty of nostalgia for you .

How can you do this? Simple. Ask yourself: What was the "car of your dreams" during those Clearasil days when you were in your teens? _____. What was the make and model and color of the car you longed to have, but at that time you couldn't afford it ?_____
Back in those days the guy who owned that "dream car" was living your dream. It was all you could do just to afford a soda and a movie. Now things are different.

Now you can *live your own dream.*   Now you can afford to own that car. Because people have a love affair with cars, that car is probably worth more years later than it was when it was brand new. Now it's back to the future for real. Now you can drive that car right out of your memories into your own driveway!

Try this.   Close your eyes. Let your thoughts wander back to the most happy and carefree time in your life. What is the car that comes to mind first and most strongly? The car that brings a smile to your face?_____

What memories do you associate with that car?_____
_____

What people who were special to you during those days come to mind?_____

What things did you do during those younger days, things that you haven't done since then, but that make you feel great just thinking about them?_____
_____

When you talk to friends about those happy days gone by, what year or years come to mind?_____ What car did you admire most during that time that comes to mind above all others?_____ What car did your best friend or friends own during that time that you loved to ride in?_____

Think back on those special dates you'll never forget. Drive-ins. Proms. Cruising. And maybe even those back-seat adventures! What special cars are linked to those special memories?_____

Or maybe it was the car your brother owned that you longed to own. Or perhaps it was the car that turned all the heads in high school, but someone else owned the pink slip. What car comes to mind?_____

You are going to spend a lot of money, a lot of time, and tons of energy with the car you select, so spend some time now closing your eyes and going back in time in your imagination. Pay careful attention to the *one car* that keeps flashing upon the screen of your mind's eye. Odds are, that's *your dream car!* And the search for the right car for you may be over.

The "What's Hot" Method
For Buying the Right Car

Now let's suppose you are not particularly the back-to-the-future romantic type and you don't have many of the good-old-days memories linked to cars. You might be more comfortable taking the "What's Hot" road to finding your special set of wheels.

You want to know what people are really getting excited about these days. What makes, models, years, styles, colors, and custom touches are drawing the crowds at car shows and cruise-nites? How can you get this information fast?

The best way to find out what's "in" or "hot" right now at this particular time is to check out good car magazines. The people who publish classic, custom, antique and street rod magazines have their finger on the pulse of what cars are turning on the crowds right now. Their staff reporters attend all the shows, big and small, and talk to the people who matter. They give you photos, facts, and tips galore on the cars winning all the trophies and getting the most attention. These magazines also give you a feel for what makes a car hot and why, as well as what to expect to pay for cars that turn heads.

At the end of this book you'll find a directory of some of the best magazines in the country to help you do your homework. These are monthly publications put together by people who spend their lives and careers finding out what's hot, why, and sharing that knowledge with you. Using their expertise, you can make wise decisions about buying a car that will bring top dollar.

Another way to find out what's hot is to resist the temptation to go to the fridge for a cool one during TV commercials and stick around and watch them. Why? Because those fat cats on Madison Avenue who create the commercials have their finger on the pulse of what excites the American consumer and they know just how to arouse his or her attention, interest and desire in order to get you to lighten your wallet and buy their products.

One of the things they use in those commercials is cars. Not just any cars, but the "in"*cars*. Watch a few. Take notes. Not just those ads trying to get you to buy a new car; watch ads about clothes, soft drinks, beer, cosmetics, fast-food restaurants, and even toothpaste. The cars in the ads may have nothing at all to do with the products they are trying to unload on you, but you can bet everything in the ad has been carefully, *very carefully* planned to get you to whip out that wallet. After all, they are spending hundreds of thousands and even millions on that 30 or 60 second ad. And if you see a '57 Chevy or a '58 Corvette in one of those ads, they've done their research. They know what kind of cars stir up and turn on your emotions. In short, they know *what's "hot."*

And you can do the same thing at the theater or at the video store. If you think they spend a bundle on TV ads, what about the millions spent on movies? And what you see in those movies and on those videos, you will be seeing the same look at car shows soon after the movie is drawing the crowds. The Hollywood types know what's in, what's hot, and what's setting trends. And, they know how to *start trends*, too. For example, after *"Driving Miss Daisy"* hit the big screen you saw Packards just like the one in the flick at most all the car shows and cruises. No accident, folks .

So, get your popcorn, pop some bonbons, and do your research while enjoying the movie! You can have a ball while finding out what the most popular car is now -- what cars are hot -- riding the crest of the wave. And that may be the perfect car for you. And if you use this method, you can bet you'll get plenty of attention at cruises and car shows. Yes, and maybe a few trophies to boot. And when you use this method to choose the right car you'll be more likely to pick a car that will gain in value as an investment .

Another way to take the pulse of car buffs is to go to car shows. Who wins the awards? Which cars get the ooo's and ahhh's? What models stir up the most excitement? And what models get the most pictures taken of them? Talk to people. Listen to people. Watch people. You'll find out pretty quick what's hot and what's not.

And then there's car videos. Most video stores now carry videos that take you on tours of various cruises and car shows throughout the country. You'll get an up-close look at several hundred cars so you can check out what's in them. You can see how many Model A's and '32s are in those shows, how many '51 Mercurys, how many '57 Pontiacs, or Chevys or Studebakers. And you'll see them at their best -- great paint jobs with all the trimmings to please the car buffs and the judges and the investors. This is a really good way to research what's hot now.

But keep this in mind. Like fashions that can change overnight, something is "in" and "hot" now, and tomorrow it might be "out" and as cool as a cucumber. So when you research the temperature of what's hot, don't rely on magazines or videos or shows you've attended even a few months ago. Get the hot-off-the-presses latest stuff and visit the shows right now, today. Then you'll get the right reading on the really hot cars .

The "Budget Friendly" Method
for Buying the Right Car

A lot of people get so emotionally caught up in finding their perfect dream car that they go overboard and end up over their head in debt. It's like the couple buying their first home, who just *have to have* that "dream house" and buy the house they should have bought second or third, after investing in a smaller, starter home to build up some equity. Their fat mortgage is a whopping $2,000-plus a month, they both have to work overtime to make ends meet, and they end up hating the house, and begin feeling the same way about each other!

Don't let this happen to you! Don't let your dream car turn into your worst nightmare. Nothing, not even the "perfect" car, is worth adding stress to your life, or to those relationships most important to you and your family.

So make up your mind, *BEFORE* you start your search for the right car, make up your mind that you will buy *only the car that is budget friendly -- that fits easily into whatever money is left over after all your bills are paid.* If you've got some cash stashed away somewhere and the purchase won't take a bite out of meeting those obligations we all have each month, no problem.

But if you are going to have to pull some money out of your paycheck to finance the purchase, make haste slowly! Ask yourself: "How much can we afford to take out of our income each month to pay off this car? Will that amount make us cut it too close each month? Will it require so much that we don't have anything left over for fun, for vacations, for eating out, or for those will-happen necessary repairs on the car?"

If you cut it too close, you'll regret it when you can't meet some expense and those nasty letters from the collection agencies and those threatening calls from bill collectors come rolling in like a steamroller. Don't let that happen to you!

Get into something that you can *easily* afford now. A starter car. That's how we did it. We bought a '58 Impala for our son. I knew nothing about '58 Impalas, but we knew it was worth $2,000 at the time. So we bought it, took it home, fixed it up and when it was all fixed up real nice, he didn't want it. So we started playing around with it and got it looking really nifty. Next thing we knew, a gal from a nearby town saw it, loved it, and said she'd give us $3,200 for it. Almost a $1,000 profit after expenses. Sold! We were hooked -- real new-born car buffs!

Then we saw a '57 Chevy that we had always wanted but couldn't afford. Now we had enough money to buy that car, and we did. Now years later, we keep repeating the same strategy -- buy what you can afford easily, get it looking great, sell it for more than you bought it for, then turn around and buy another car that's (1) right for you, and (2) has good resale value. We're now buying and selling cars worth nearly $20,000 , but we started with a $2,000 car that was friendly to our situation at that time.

Getting into cars should always be fun, not frustrating . It should create memories, not cause misery. If you let your realistic budget determine what car is right for you today, you'll end up loving your cars, not hating them tomorrow! So, be good to yourself; keep it budget friendly.

The "Swinging Door" Method
for Choosing the Right Car

You've heard the expression, "the door swings both ways." Well, that old adage works real well for those who want to get into rods, antiques, classic and custom cars simply for investment purposes.

By "investment" we simply mean that you buy a car with the

single objective of turning around and reselling it for a profit later. And if you're patient, play your cards right, and do your homework, you'll probably be able to make a sizable profit reselling the car.

If this is your goal, you'll need to follow certain rules of the road in selecting just the right car, or, you could lose big-time. Here are some good guidelines to follow :

First rule: Do not let your emotions or feelings get in the way here. And you can forget nostalgia, too. We're talkin' hard numbers-crunching using this method, so you'll have to let the numbers lead you, period. A good rule of thumb is, *don't get emotionally involved in business decisions!* This is easier said than done, but it works!

Next, look in the local Auto Trader papers. You'll find them at most convenience stores and liquor stores. You'll get full descriptions of all kinds of cars, including what kind of equipment they carry and don't carry; most with photos and prices. Then compare the same make and model car you're considering in several of these publications, looking at price and what they carry. You'll get a good feel for the "going rate" of that particular car, comparing and contrasting prices.

You can also go to your local library and look up old newspapers, say 2, 4 and 6 years old. Check the classified sections of those papers and see what the car was selling for back then. This will give you some idea as to whether the car you're thinking of buying is appreciating in value, or not .

Some of the Blue Books go back all the way to 1948 and offer another good way to get a feel for price. Compare what the Blue Book shows and what you notice in the Auto Trader papers.

Also check out the free-ad type of papers. One Southern California paper is called the *"Recycler."* They take ads from sellers for free and are loaded with good buys and even better research info you can use.

Then, pick up the phone and talk to people. People selling cars similar to the one you're interested in. Go look at the type of car you're narrowing it down to. Then talk to people. Listen. Then talk to people and listen some more. The more you listen to people selling the type of car you're interested in buying for resale, (1) the more you learn about the car itself, (2) the more you learn about what makes one car of this type a great deal and another a dog, and (3) the more you educate yourself for the resale phase, because before long you may be running your own for-sale ad and talking from the sellers point of view. So listen, and then listen some more.

Before we turn to tips on how to avoid buying the "nightmare" cars, let's review on the next page the four key methods for finding the right car that fits you best.

The 4 Methods For Choosing the Right Car

1. *The "Nostalgia" Method* — you put that time machine inside your memory bank in reverse gear and let your mind's eye float to the surface that special dream car from the good old days. The car you always dreamed about owning .

2. *The "What's Hot" Method* — you study and research car magazines, car shows and cruises, videos and movies to take the temperature and the pulse of what's popular today.

3. *The "Budget Friendly" Method* — you make up your mind to buy only that car that easily and comfortably fits your income-outgo life style. If you have to start small, start small. Then you can move up to bigger and better things.

4. *The "Swinging Door" Method* — you buy to turn around and re-sell the same car at a profit. This is simply cool, calculated business. But if you go this route, watch out! You may get bit by the car-buff-bug. *It's contagious!*

Chapter 3

How To Avoid The Pain, Aggravation, Misery & Regrets Of Buying The *Wrong* Car

Personal Notes & Ideas

CHAPTER THREE

How To Avoid The Pain, Aggravation, Misery & Regrets Of Buying The *Wrong* Car

C all them dogs, lemons, turkeys, white elephants, a bad joke, junk-yard candidates, or your worst possible nightmares -- no matter what you call them, you don't want one of these cars anywhere near your garage! These are cars that look great on the outside, but give you nothing but trouble. And they may even be called "classics" but they're still "classic pains in the posterior!"

If you don't know how to spot these sour yellow duds with the green stem on top, you may end up with nothing but pain, aggravation, misery and regrets. We want to save you all that, and help you avoid losing a lot of money, too. So read and re-read this chapter with great care. You will be mighty glad you did!

If you follow the steps in the last chapter, your chances of finding the right car are greatly increased. Now, add to that knowledge the following strategic tips and you can avoid being stung. *So beware!*

Beware of the LAFS "Love at First Sight" Trap

The "love at first sight" trap can catch 8 out of 10 would-be car buyers when they first get into owning a custom, classic, rod or antique car. What happens is this. They see a beautifully restored whatever and this voice in their head says, "You've just got to have this baby!!!" Love at first sight, and they have never even sat in the front seat or driven the thing ten feet. But it's love!

And, as the old expression goes, "love is blind."

Unfortunately, we are talking from first-hand experience. Several years ago we went out to a Labor Day Cruise and we saw a car we *just had to have.* We just couldn't wait to buy it. Love at first sight all the way. So we gave the guy a $500 deposit, went home, and the next day we drove the car. A rude awakening! The car drove so fast we could hardly control the beast! Beautiful, yes, but drivable, no. So we backed out of the deal. We also lost our five hundred bucks! A painful lesson in love at first sight. We're glad we didn't go through with the deal, but that is an expensive way to learn to beware of the LAFS trap.

A good friend of ours tells of a similar experience. He bought a '68 Mustang for his daughter's 16th birthday. She just had to have a red Mustang with a white rag top. So he and his wife "fell in love" with the first one they saw, paid $6,000 and took it home. One problem. It had a 302 engine; too much muscle for a brand new driver. So like us, they learned the hard way. Fortunately, though, their story has a happier ending. In addition to learning a valuable lesson, they sold the car a week later for cash at a healthy profit to a guy who drove it straight to the dock. It's now turning heads and thundering down some crowded street in downtown Tokyo! But most people are not so lucky.

Many times this impulsive, love-at-first-sight trap does not have a happy ending and you get burned -- bad. So if you see a car you *just have to have,* do this first: Go home. Talk about its good points. Talk about its potential problems. Write them all down. The good, the bad, the pretty, and the pretty-ugly. WARNING: When you see a car you just love, it's tough to come up with *any* problems or drawbacks. But force yourself. Every set of wheels has *something* potentially wrong with it, or some possible headaches. List them, in writing. And before you put your money down, go and look at some other cars of the same type. Drive them. This will help you detach to the point of objectivity and will help you come down from the clouds, and get your feet on the ground so you can put emotions aside to some extent to help you get balanced on the thing. You will never regret doing this one important step, even though it's tough to do .

Then, if you still love it, go for it. And who knows? -- Since you didn't buy on first impulse, you may have added confidence to make a bold counter-offer and the seller may be more willing now to come down a little on the price. Congratulations! You just bought the right car and saved some cash in one simple move! Aren't you glad you found this book?

Beware of the "You Have a Right To My Own Opinion " Trap

There's a big audience out there. If you try to please them all you will go nuts. And every person out there has an opinion. They would love nothing better than to tell you how to live your life.

The same thing is especially true of some car buffs -- they will try to tell you what car is just right for you. It's like the used car salesman who tells you, "Look at this beauty! ... It's perfect for you! ... It's YOU!" The only thing it's perfect for is making him a fat commission. But how does he know it's "perfect" for you if he's never laid eyes on you until now?

You'll get all kinds of advice from well-meaning folks. They will tell you how a particular car is "the" best buy, "the" one that can't be beat, and "the" car that's right for you. And if they're true car buffs, they will be bubbling over with enthusiasm to persuade you saying, "don't let this puppy get away!"

Solution: Don't let their zeal or enthusiasm influence you one bit. Just say, "Thanks for your opinion" and keep your own enthusiasm under control. What may be perfect for them may be perfect pain for you. Go and look at many other cars. Sleep on it. Let your own emotions settle down. Then you won't be influenced to make a choice that is right for someone else and terrible for you.

And remember: There's only one car that's right for *you*. And there is only one person who knows what that car is. That one person is *you!*

Beware of the "Perfect Color" Trap

Why do so many sellers paint their cars red? Because research has shown that red is the color that sells more cars. It's simply good business. But it's bad business for you, as the buyer, to let color "color" your decision to buy.

Remember: You can have a car painted any color in the rainbow that suits your fancy. What you want is to buy *the car* that's right for you, and the car that is a solid, smart investment as well.

Like our friends who bought their daughter that '68 Mustang. They were lucky that the car didn't have major problems under that fire-engine-red hood, because they wouldn't even have noticed them. Why? Because it had a sensational, gleaming, fire-engine-red paint job. That's what sold them.

So, try to pay no attention to the color at first because you will get too emotionally involved in the car and you'll be too influenced by color if you do. First, go over that car like Sherlock Holmes on a case. Then, when you are satisfied that it's a real deal, and you've compared it to others of the same kind, go for it.

Then no matter what color it is, a hideous chartreuse, or putrid pink -- you can have your favorite shade applied. Even red!

Beware of the "Twilight Zone" Trap

The absolute worst time of the day to check out a car you are thinking about buying is just before sundown, twilight, evening or nighttime hours. Why? Because it may look great under the lights, all sparkling and glittering. But all that glitters is not gold.

The reason that this is the worst time to look over a car is that you can miss important clues, that you may be getting ready to buy a car with major body work required. Or, you may not be able to see some lousy body work that has been done on the car. The darkness hides the truth.

In the daytime you will see plainly, if you look, all the flaws and glitches. At night, they just blend in and escape your eye. So get the car out in the bright sunlight and then nothing is hidden -- nothing, that is, that might be on the surface.

Get the Advice of a "Fruit Inspector"

What is a "fruit inspector?"

A fruit inspector is a crack mechanic who knows cars. He also knows how to spot lemons. And the car you may want to believe is a real "cherry" may turn out to be in reality a real "lemon."

A good mechanic is not swayed by his feelings. What they look for are problems or potential problems that most of us can't spot. They have the trained eyes and ears and nose to zero in fast on those lemon symptoms.

How can you find a good fruit inspector? Got any friends who know cars like the back of their hand? Any brothers-in-law? Good-ol'-boys as friends? Friends of friends? Or boyfriends of your daughter who can tear any car apart on Saturday and have it running on Sunday? These are some good sources of mechanical expertise.

What about the auto shop teacher at the local high school who wants to earn a few bucks on the side moonlighting? He may be a great source of good advice, cheap.

Another great source for good, solid advice you will find at local cruise-nites and car shows. All you have to do is talk to people and listen to their recommendations. Everyone likes giving their opinion. "Hey, I'm looking for a good mechanic to look over a car I'm seriously thinking about buying ... Know anybody?" It's that simple. You'll get a good list of mechanics, body people, painters, — you name it — that you can choose from. Or you might even meet one face to face at the event showing his or her own car.

What if you're not so bad yourself at mechanical things? Great. Go ahead and check it out yourself. One caution, though: You still might be so enthusiastic and emotionally caught up in buying the car that you won't allow yourself to see potential problems because your feelings may blind you to the truth.

If you have already fallen in love with the car, you just don't want to see problems. If you're talking a high-priced car, our advice is this: Get someone in on helping you make the final decision; someone who is totally uninfluenced by emotions. A smart doctor will not treat himself. A smart lawyer (and there are a few) will not defend himself. So be smart. Get good mechanical advice.

And by the way, the same strategy for getting help works after you buy the car. A good example just happened a few months ago. The lights went out on our car. We looked at each other and realized that we didn't know an electrician in this entire world. So, we practiced what we're teaching here. We went around at the car show that weekend and told everyone our problem. We found a guy there, he followed us home and fixed our lights for us. It was just that quick. The really important thing about this was that we had a taped interview set up for the following day for the car, and without those lights working we couldn't have done the taping.

At another car show we were at we had a throttle cable break in the car and it wasn't even an hour later that the cable was fixed. We never even had to touch the car, because someone came over and said , "Let me in there and fix that thing for you." So don't be afraid to get the word out and tell everyone around you what the problem is. *Car people are great people!*

People into cars tend to be people who don't mind sharing their ideas and helping others out. Keep in mind that when you help someone out today, you never know how that will come back to help you tomorrow, just when you need it most. What goes around comes around. And who knows? -- The person you lend a helping hand to today may be one of the judges looking at your car tomorrow!

When you do bring someone with you to inspect the car, the seller should have no objections at all. If the seller is in the slightest bit reluctant to let your mechanic check out the car, or let you take the car to him, *BEWARE !* If the seller has nothing to hide, he or she will be glad for you to be completely satisfied with the car and will make it easy for you to get the car to the mechanic. If they resist at all, there's something rotten somewhere. Forget this deal and move on ... FAST! Remember this: Real car people get about as excited seeing you, the buyer, happy with the car as they do about getting the cash. Car people are great people!

Beware of the "Slight of Hand" Seller

The slight-of-hand magician can make his tricks work on you and pull the wool over your eyes because he uses distraction with great skill. If he can get you to look at what one hand is doing, he draws your eye away from what his other hand is doing. And if he can do that, he's got you.

The magician distracts your eye with his hands. The slight-of-hand seller does the same thing with *words*. Lots of words. He'll say, "Look at this chrome ... look at this paint job ... look at this pinstriping ... look at this, look at this, look at this ..."

As Shakespeare might have said were he here today, "Me thinketh he talketh too mucheth." All those words pointing out the frills and the tinsel are designed (1) to get you excited about some emotional aspect of the car, and (2) to distract your eye or ear from some flaw or problem he doesn't want you to notice -- not until he's got your money, that is. Beware of all those words!

Go ahead and let him talk on. But don't let that stream of verbiage distract you from going over the car step-by-step, detail-by-detail. You'll find some helpful tips and checklists in the next two sections.

Any Leaks? -- The Garage Floor *Speaks!*

What does the garage floor (or wherever the car is parked) have to say to you? A lot! Pay attention and save yourself some grief. There's more to the garage floor or driveway than just concrete.

Before you make up your mind about the car, take a look at the garage floor or driveway where the car has been sitting. If there are any leaks, you'll see signs of them clearly visible. You want to find out about all leaks *before* that pink slip changes hands so you can have *the seller* fix the problems, or so you can avoid big, costly problems later.

Have the seller move the car. Inspect the area underneath where the car had been sitting. If you do find spots on the concrete, pay attention to color. You can get a pretty good idea of what kind of problem the car has by the color of the spots on the floor or driveway (see chart on the next page.)

Color Chart To Troubleshoot
Problem Leaks

RED - PINKISH = Transmission oil

BLACK = Engine oil

BLUISH = Engine oil

GREENISH = Antifreeze

PUTRID BROWN = Transmission fluid in radiator

CLEAR = Air conditioner coolant fluid

METALLIC PINK - REDDISH = Metal shavings
from transmission

REDDISH - PINK - THIN = Power steering fluid

So, some problems are color-coded, and you need to know how to read the code. When the seller moves the car, carefully examine the ground where the car has been standing. Then check the underside of the car. Let the seller know that you assume that he or she will have any of these leaks fixed -- the bill is on them, of course. If they don't want to handle it, get an estimate on the repairs and negotiate the price down.

Beware of the "Shoulda-Woulda-Coulda" Trap

You don't want to have to say, "We shoulda' checked out everything before we bought this turkey!" Or, "I wouldn't have bought this dog if I had known that it runs like a tank!" Or, "We coulda' avoided having to pay for all these repairs if we'd checked this thing out before driving it home!" The shoulda-woulda-coulda blues.

We bought one car years ago for $12,000. We were so excited about the car, we paid the man, and were driving it home that night when we tried to roll the window up. Guess what? The window was cracked so bad you couldn't roll it up. $12,000 and we had not even thought to roll up the windows! A good lesson learned. So here we were trying to find somebody who knew how to fix a busted window on a '29 Model A. Thanks to a good friend, we got the window fixed all right, but the car ended up costing us $12,080. The seller would have paid for that window if we had had the benefit of reading the kind of book you are holding in your hands right now. We learned the hard way. And who knows ; maybe this book will save you $80! ... or more!

So before you put down your hard-earned cash, check out EVERYTHING. Every detail: Does it work properly? Smoothly? Quietly? Roughly? Works sometimes, doesn't work others? Check it out!

What follows is a checklist to help you go over the car with a fine-tooth-comb before you finalize the deal. Don't write the check or get out your money until you go through this checklist !

FINAL INSPECTION CHECKLIST

PROBLEM PAINT JOB -- flaws, cracks, chips, dull spots, pealing, bubbles, runs, mis-matched touchups, rust spots

RUST ON FRAME -- signs of under-rust, obvious or covered over

PATCHED PAINT -- areas where Bondo has been used for patching, rippley, uneven blending of finish

ELECTRICAL SYSTEM PROBLEMS --
Headlights
Spotlights (if any)
Brake lights
Tail lights
Turn signals
Interior lights
Dash lights
Ignition
Radio
Tape deck,CD
Speakers
Alarm system (if any)
Power windows (if any)
Power seats (if any)
Horn (and special-effects horns)
Cigarette lighter

HEATING SYSTEM -- Switches and levers
Vents and ducts
Proper temperature output

Continued on next page —

AIR CONDITIONING SYSTEM -- Switches and levers
Vents and ducts
Proper temperature output
Fan controls

TAPPETS & POINTS -- Start car and let it run a while,
then listen for sticking

SMOKING & EXHAUST PROBLEMS -- Let it run
a while, look and listen for
overheating, exhaust leaks,
muffler problems

MUSCLE CAR FAN SYSTEM -- Does fan system
cool car down properly

WATCH GAGES FOR OVERHEATING -- Let it run
a while, drive it, then see if
it overheats.Check other gages

CHECK FOR LEAKS -- Move the car and look under
where it's been sitting to check
for oil, fluid, coolant, or other
leaks

POWER STEERING PLAY -- Check to see if power
steering is too lose or too tight

POWER TOP PROBLEMS -- Does it easily move when
opened or closed, clamp down
properly, unlatch easily, any
snaps missing, window zipper
jamming, is top worn, rear window need replacing, tears in top

Continued on next page —

CHROME PROBLEMS -- any rust, lose or corroded chrome on bumpers, missing chrome

DOOR LOCKS -- Can car be locked, trunk lockable, gas cap, if any of these cannot lock, are they fixable, trunk and hood latches

FRAME ALIGNMENT -- watch it drive toward you and away from you to see if the frame is bent

ENGINE STALLING -- Check idling, restarting for stalls

TRANSMISSION PROBLEMS -- Shifts properly, gears slipping, not smooth, play in the clutch, grinding

SHOCKS -- If it's a car does it ride like a truck, tank, or a ride at the amusement park

PROBLEMS IN THE BRAKES -- adjustment problems noisy, worn

WINDOWS -- Do all windows work properly, any cracks, chips, discolored glass

UPHOLSTERY -- Tears, splits, patches, stains, discolorations, mats in front and back

DASH -- All instruments working accurately, easy to read, well lit, glass or plastic discolored, trim damaged, cracked

Continued on next page —

REGISTRATION & PAPERWORK --
Does registration have current date on it.?
Does VIN or engine number on the registration match that on the car?
Does body description on pink slip match the car?
Are tags current with DMV?
Does it have current and valid insurance to be transferred?
Is the smog check in order?
(If your state requires this).

How To Avoid Getting Lemon-ized

Some final words of warning to help you steer clear of those rip-off sellers who want to unload their classic lemon on you. When you read classified ads offering you those deals of a lifetime, "buyer beware!" Here, in straight and simple English, is what some of those ads may *really* mean:

WHAT THEY SAY	WHAT THEY *REALLY* MEAN
"Must sell"	Before it blows up!
"Must sell"	To some other poor sucker before it drives me into the poorhouse!
"Runs fine"	I was going to say, "Runs excellent," but I had a last minute conscience attack!
"Needs some body work"	Was blindsided by a Winnebago!
"Well maintained"	I changed the oil occasionally.
"Looks like new"	Just don't try driving it anywhere.
"All original"	I never had anything fixed, adjusted or replaced.
"Loaded with options"	Each one more troublesome than the next!
"Never smoked in"	Unfortunately, that's the best thing I can say about it!
"Project car"	Doesn't run.
"Lots of potential"	Doesn't run.
"Needs minor repair"	Doesn't run.

Adapted from Steve Salerno, *Los Angeles Times Magazine,* quoted in *Reader's Digest,* February, 1995

Chapter 4

Twelve Ways To Save Hundreds
— Even Thousands Of Dollars —
When Buying Your Car

Personal Notes & Ideas

CHAPTER FOUR

Twelve Ways to Save Hundreds
— Even Thousands Of Dollars — When Buying Your Car

L et's walk through the whole scene together. You find "the" car that you know is "your" car. You are ready to get to the bottom line, and you want the final bottom line to be as low as you can get it. But the seller wants that bottom line as high as he can get it. Here are some tips that can give you, the buyer, the edge over the seller, to save you hundreds, even thousands of dollars.

1. Stay Cool, Calm and Collected

As we pointed out before, whatever you do, do not let the seller sense your inner feelings about the car. Use the "poker face" method of looking cool, detached, and projecting a take-it-or-leave-it attitude. If you're looking at a car as a couple, be sure not to do too much oooing and ahhhing and drooling over the car. Control your enthusiasm until the deal is closed. The more excited you appear the less bargaining power you have!

2. Get The "Asking" Price

Get the seller to commit to how much "he's asking for the car". Put it this way so that you plant the idea in his head right off that we're talking about something here that is negotiable, not a price that's set in concrete. Even if the seller doesn't say "OBO" "or best offer" always assume that he means it anyway. And always assume that the price he's asking is well above the price he's after. Get him to state the "asking price."

3. Stay Positive

Don't knock his car. Don't make faces and run it down, even if you notice things that need work. Why? Because if you do you'll make him mad and you lose your leverage in getting him flexible on the price if you get his anger up. Be positive and respectful.

4.   Comment On Obvious Glitches

Although you don't bad-mouth his car, you do mention-in-passing any obvious defects or something that needs work as you walk around looking at the car. It needs a paint job. The upholstery is ripped. The tires are pretty bald. Needs new chrome. Needs a new top, window, dash, grille, carburetor, muffler, or something else. Go ahead and mention each point, but be respectful and friendly. You simply want to let him know that you know these things need fixing. This will help you leverage the price downward. Remember, if you don't mention them, the seller will think you didn't see them!

5.   Do a Ballpark Estimate Of What
   Fixing the Glitches Would Cost

As you notice and mention the various things that need work, keep a mental list of them. Then tell the seller you want to go sit in your own car or take a walk and think about it. Get out your pen and pad and write them all down, making a guesstimate of how much it would cost you if you had to repair or replace each item.

Now you're ready to go back and point out specifically to the seller what these problems would cost were you to have to do them yourself. This then gives you more leverage to bring him down on the asking price. So do a good job here.

6. How To Talk To The Seller To Get Your Price

With a positive, friendly, non-competitive attitude, here's a sample of a smart, easy-going but powerful way to talk turkey with the seller after inspecting the car and giving it careful thought:

> "Well, we had time to think about your car, and we took
> a good look at it. I think you've got a real nice car here.
> I do notice some flaws though -- nothing serious -- but
> some flaws that need to be corrected, and I'm going to
> have to make some repairs on it.   So, I'm willing to
> make you an offer of what I think the car's worth to me."

Let's say he's asking $17,000 . You continue by saying :

> "Well, with upholstery, tires, and a new paint job, I think
> $14,000 is what I'm looking at. Yep , fourteen."

The seller may come back and say, "No, I think I have a good thing here and I'm firm at seventeen." Then you make a decision whether you want to pay seventeen -- plus the repairs, or go on to another car .

Now, suppose he comes down, but not all the way to the number you are offering, which is very likely. How can you handle this without paying his second asking price?

Most sellers are prepared to come down a bit on their price. A good rule of thumb is this: If the seller won't come down at all, let it go and move on to another car. If the car is "perfect," however, meaning that it doesn't need any work done on it, and the price is fair, buy it. Otherwise, pass.

Let's say he comes down from $17,000 to $16,000. Your strategy should be to again bring up the things that you will have to pay for out of your own pocket to get it right. For example :

> "OK, we'll forget about the chrome work and tires, but
> I'll have to take care of the tune up, the transmission
> work, fixing the leaks, and all that will run me so
> much , not to mention the whining in the rear end that
> will need work -- I'll tell you what -- I'll split the
> difference with you and give you $15,000 . I'll meet
> you half way."

Using this technique you let him know why you can't pay his second asking price, point by point, and offering to "split the difference" lets everyone save face. A true win -- win deal. Sure, he may say no, but your chances are at least better using this method . Try it.

Let's say you want to buy a car that is offered at $12,000, but it is in need of new chrome, new brakes, and a good paint job, then you had better find out how much doing those will run you. If you check and find out that they will cost about $2,000, then make up your mind not to pay more than $10,000. Be prepared to walk if the seller won't come down.

7.   Don't Even Look At Cars You Can't Afford

WARNING: Don't play with temptation. Don't even look at cars that you obviously cannot afford. Because if you do, you will definitely see the perfect car you just can't resist.

And if you see it, guess what? You will fall in love with it. Then you will buy it. Then guess what? You will regret it for a long, long time when the bills, and the bill collectors come rolling in. So the smart thing to do is, don't even look at cars that aren't budget friendly!

8. Don't Let The Seller Pressure You

One common trick some sellers use to pressure you to make a decision now, and not to give you time to think about the deal, is this. They will see that you really like the car and want it. The phone rings, they go inside, come back out and tell you,

> "That's another guy who is really interested in the car
> and he wants to come over in about an hour.....Now
> I can't guarantee that the car will still be available.
> First come, first serve, ya know, and if he gives
> me a deposit, what can I do? So if you want the car,
> you better jump on it now."

He may be telling you the truth, or he may be just blowing smoke, trying to squeeze a decision out of you. Either way, don't be influenced one bit by this maneuver. If you can't have time to think it over carefully, don't be pressured. You buy the car on your terms and your time, not his.

If you find nothing whatever wrong with the car and someone else is on the way over to see the car and you would buy it anyway, go for it. But never buy a car when the seller is pressuring you. You want to buy a car using your head, never letting fear of losing it to someone else control you.

9.   Don't Let The Seller's Personality   Influence Your Decision

Remember Columbo? He always got his man by playing the "good old boy" and making himself so likable and innocent that nobody ever noticed that he was giving them the third-degree. So beware of the good-ol'-boy, the country-boy, that sweet-and-innocent soul who seems like he just came off the farm. It may be a slick maneuver designed to get you to believe everything he tells you. And he may be hiding something you need to know. So ignore the personality, pay attention to the car!

And then there's the guy who can talk a blue streak, able to chit-chat about anything and everything under the sun. The kind of guy who can talk to anybody about just about anything. Likable. Friendly. Seems like he's known you forever. Talks about his kids, his dog, his house, his job, his neighbors, the weather, local politics, the pennant race, or the Super Bowl. He's so good at talking that you never notice that you've just spent two hours shooting the breeze and haven't even discussed one important thing about the car he wants to sell you. The talk may be interesting, but you had better remember that it may also be a smoke screen. He knows that if he wins you with his wonderful personality, that you won't want to offend him later by bringing up the details about what's wrong with the car. BEWARE! The wolf wears sheep's clothing.

Then there's the intimidator. He's just the opposite of the smooth talker. He is the hard-sell type. He tries to control you with his overpowering personality. He talks loud, fast, and cocky. He wants you to feel so threatened by him that you are afraid to (1) point out the problems with the car, and (2) you don't dare walk away without buying his car -- whether it's right for you or not.

With the intimidator, remember this: He's all bluff, all show, like the guard dog behind a fence. He has no power to make you do anything, including being intimidated. So, don't let his bark influence you one bit. Even if you want the car, pass it by. Why reward someone who abuses and misuses people? Buy the right car from someone who treats people with respect.

Then there's the laidback, novice type. He or she comes across as if they have never sold a car in their life, they have no idea what this car is really worth, and they're just trying to get a reasonable price for it but have no idea what it's true value is. The idea with many of these types is to lure you into thinking that you are taking advantage of someone who just got off the boat. Many times they even use their problems speaking English as a scam. They want you to feel one-up on them. Why? So you will feel so good about being in control of them that you won't keep your mind on the business at hand -- the specifics about the car.

Don't fall for this trap. They probably know more about that car than most experts. And they also know how to set you up and empty your bank account real fast.

Even though we have been talking about some of the lowlifes who sell cars for the wrong reasons out of motives of sheer greed, remember that most people selling rods, custom, classic and antique cars are fine people. We don't want you to feel paranoid or overly suspicious about buying a car. You just need to be well informed and able to spot these types when they crawl out of the classifieds. Most people you meet buying and selling cars are truly great people and may become good friends.

10. Be Prepared To Pay The Right Way

If you know how much you are willing to pay, have that amount ready in cash or in the bank. The seller will probably not take a personal check. So you will need to have the green stuff or a cashier's check for the entire amount.

Toting thousands of dollars in cash around with you and visiting strange neighborhoods in strange garages, is not smart. You'd be better advised to go to the bank and get a cashier's check.

If the seller insists on cold cash, fine. Take him or her with you to your bank or credit union and make the transfer of money and pink slip right there in public. Most sellers will be happy to accompany you, smiling all the way to the bank.

If it's a Sunday, give him a deposit and make arrangements to meet on Monday morning. You don't want to say you'll be back in a few days for the car, because someone with cash or a cashier's check might show up before you get back and you lose your car. So be prepared.

But if you decide to take a great deal of cash to their house to pay for the car, take a few friends with you when you lay out the bills. You'd be better off playing it safe than being sorry later.

Most sellers are honest, trustworthy, good people, but when you are dealing with thousands of dollars, you have to use your head.

11.   How "Car Savvy" Is The Seller?

It will help you to try to get a feel for how much the seller really knows cars. Has he owned and sold cars before? Is this the first custom, classic, or street rod he's owned or sold? Is he selling his own car, or selling it for a family member? Is this a car that's just been hanging out in his garage for years and he wants to get rid of it? Is he a collector? Does he buy custom cars, fix them up, turn around and sell them at a profit? Do you get the feeling when you meet him that you are dealing with a used-car salesman on furlough?

You're in luck if he's just had this car sitting in his garage for ages and just wants to get rid of it. He's not likely to be car-savvy and you've probably got yourself a real good deal.

Or he may be selling the car for a loved-one who has passed away. He is not a serious car buff, and just wants to settle the estate. You'll probably get a fair price there.

However, if he's into cars, you will have to use all your wits and all the tips in this section to get yourself the best deal. You'll also have to be more on guard if he's car-wise so you don't get taken. The point is this. If he's smart about cars, you had better be, too, or even a little bit smarter! And if you're not, take somebody with you who is!

One final tip. To get inside the head of the savvy seller, you might want to read chapter 7, "How to Convert Your Car Into Cash." It will help you think like the seller and buy smart. You'll always get a better deal if the seller knows that you know what you're doing -- and what he's doing!

12. How "Car-Savvy" Are You?

Suppose you haven't been into cars much yourself and are just getting started. If you haven't bought and sold rare cars over the years, then you may not be able to spot the wheeler--dealer car-savvy seller or know when you are being told the truth, being led down the garden path, or are being dealt with honestly. You need help.

You need the skilled eye and ear of the car buff to protect your interests. So, this is what to do. When you go to see the car, or to make your final decision: Take along a trusted friend who has been into cars for years. If you don't have such a friend in the circle you hang with, make a new friend. Cruise-nites, '50s diners, car clubs, and car shows are excellent places to meet and make new friends. Or hire a car buff. Find someone who you trust and who knows cars and offer to take them to dinner, or offer them $20, to go along with you as your expert agent to keep you from making mistakes and who will ask all the right questions for you.

Put your pride aside, because we're talking big bucks here. If you need help with your taxes you hire an accountant. If you need help with your engine, you hire a good mechanic. And if you haven't been involved in the business of buying and selling cars for long, you need the "nose" of the car buff. They can smell a great deal -- or a dog! His or her experience could save you a fortune!

One more point here. Remember this: if the seller is car-savvy and you're not, he'll know it. He'll then use his skills to get the most money he can out of you for the car. On the other hand, if he senses that you brought along with you a person who knows the moves as well as he does, he'll be more reluctant to try his tricks on you. And, you may even get your best price, not his, because he   respects the savvy of your expert-friend.

Remember this:

"In the multitude of counselors there is safety,"

Twelve Ways To Save Hundreds, Even Thousands of Dollars When You Buy Your Car

1. Stay Cool, Calm And Collected
2. Get The "Asking" Price
3. Stay Positive
4. Comment On Obvious Glitches
5. Do A Ballpark Estimate Of What Fixing The Glitch Would Cost
6. How To Talk To The Seller To Get Your Price
7. Don't Even Look At Cars You Can't Afford
8. Don't Let The Seller Pressure You
9. Don't Let The Seller's Personality Influence Your Decision
10. Be prepared To Pay The Right Way
11. How "Car Savvy" Is The Seller?
12. How "Car Savvy" Are You?

Chapter 5

How To Show & Shine!

The Art Of Displaying Your Car:

Tips That Give Your Car
That Special Winning Edge

How To Show and Shine!
The Art of Displaying Your Car:
Tips That Give Your Car That Special Winning Edge

T here's a lot more to showing your car at car shows than just giving it a nice wax job, parking it wherever you can find a spot, and sitting back in your lawn chair to see if the judges happen to like it.

When the fisherman goes after those prize-winning catches, does he just throw anything on the hook that might be laying around? Not likely, especially if he knows fish. What does he do? He comes at it from the point of view of the fish, right? His whole strategy in getting those rascals to bite is this: *Bait the hook to suit the fish.*

He'll also choose his spot very carefully. Where is the most likely spot that fish tend to be attracted to? He doesn't just head for the middle of the lake and drop his line. No way. He tries to think like the fish. He finds some shady cove where the fish are patiently waiting for breakfast. His strategy is this: *Place the bait to suit the fish.*

And the skilled fisherman doesn't dangle the bait in front of the fish's nose just any old way. He bounces it along the surface for some, he lets it sit near the bottom for others, he uses a simple hook tucked neatly inside a worm for some, and shows others a fancy silver-blue gadget with feathers and rattles for others. His strategy here is: *Display the bait to suit the fish.*

Now, that's what to do if you're after fish. But suppose you're not after fish but after something else, like the excitement, the fun, and the satisfaction of displaying your car at car shows? We can learn a lot from the expert fisherman. The only difference is that at the car show (and cruise-nite) you are interested in *judges*, not fish.

In this chapter we'll show you what gets attention and why. How to prepare the car to get the "Would you look at that!" reactions. And we'll show you the whens, the wheres, and the how-tos of making the judges -- and everybody else -- smile when they lay eyes on your car.

In short, you'll learn *how to get a special edge at car shows using simple, easy-to-do tricks that work.*

Follow these tips and you'll win friends and influence judges, and you might even find yourself in one of the top car magazines! And even if you could care less about showing your car competitively, using these tips will help you display your car in its best possible light to show its stuff. Or you might want to sell your car. Using the methods you'll find here can give you the best possible image for your car to get the best possible price.

Whatever your goal may be, the people who get the most ooo's and ahh's, the cars that draw the biggest crowds, and the rods that win the most awards do certain smart things to make that happen. Read on and you'll see what they do.

Timing Is Everything — Arrive Early!

Next time you go to a car show, notice who wins awards and special honors. Odds are, this guy or gal probably is a consistent winner at many of the car shows. If you talk to them you'll find out that they always *arrive at the site of the show very early* the day of the event. If you arrive early yourself at the next show, you will no doubt find the regular winners arriving early with you.

Why arrive early? It's simple. You get the best opportunity to choose a good spot that will help your car grab attention and make the best impression. The winners at car shows, and the cars that get the most attention at cruises are almost never parked at random. A lot of thinking goes into where that car is parked. You want to park your car in a spot that will make it most pleasing to the eye, and that will take certain environmental conditions into account. If you arrive late, someone else has already thought about these tricks and you can't park two cars in the same spot. So the early bird gets the worm -- and the best display position, too.

So, let's talk about what to look for and what to do when you arrive early.

Finding The Prime Parking Spots:
Positions That Can Give Your Car Center Stage

When you arrive at the site of the cruise or show early you have an important advantage over others. What advantage? Position.

Position or location is of the utmost importance because your car will either be lost in the crowd, or it will stand out and shine above the rest. Selecting the prime spot for positioning your car makes the difference between being lost or being noticed.

There are four important things to keep in mind when you decide where to park your car:

1. Think like the person handling the publicity for the event or reporting on it for a car magazine. He or she wants to get some great photos of the show for the magazine, right? What do they want to appear in the picture? Sure, cars, but also a sign announcing the show and perhaps the place where it is being held. If the event is being held at a diner, a good shot of the front of the diner and its sign will be what the photographer wants in the background. Look at the

photo at the top of the page to the left of the title page of this book. Notice that the photographer covering this car show got the sign clearly featured, showing where the show took place and when. Remember that the establishment or group sponsoring the show may be the one responsible for getting the photo taken. Naturally, they will want their sign featured up-front. Also notice which cars stand out in this picture?

There are approximately 35 cars in this picture. Which ones stand out most? The cars that got there early, parked up front, in front of the sign, on an angle that would show most of the car -- they get the exposure. The '56 Chevy gets the prime spot. The owner of that car showed up early, knew where pictures about the event would likely be taken, and maneuvered his car just right. Later he saw his car with prime publicity in *Street Rodder Magazine,* (February, 1990) — 650,000+ people saw his car!

2. Here's a really important tip. Scope out the site of the show the day before. You'll know well in advance the specific day of the show or cruise. Try to go to the location before the event takes place. The purpose is to look over the site from all kinds of different angles. You want to get an idea of where to find those "prime spots" when you arrive the day of the event. Remember, you will have to show up very early -- sometimes at 5 or 6 a.m. -- for some shows. And it's not easy making those kind of decisions in the dark! So walk around the area keeping the ideas you find in this section in mind and decide on the best locations.

3. Choose more than one strategic spot to park your car. Why not just "the" one best spot? Because right now, at this very moment, someone who is smart enough to have gotten their hands on this book may be reading it, too. They may show up 5 minutes before you, and may take your "perfect" spot, so you had better have an alternate spot in mind.

4. Keep in mind when you're scoping out the best parking spots that there are some crucial differences showing your car during the day vs. showing it at night events. Check out the following key points to think about:

To Show, Or Not To Show . . . Your Engine?

In most car shows and cruises you have the choice whether to show what's under the hood or not. So you need to use your head when making that decision.

Rule of thumb: If you do not have any chrome or special features on your engine, *do not show it.* If it's got the original engine, don't show it. If it's "just another engine," don't show it.

Rule of thumb: If your car is parked next to another car that's loaded with special work done on the engine, *don't show yours.*

Rule of thumb: If you've got a good-looking engine, chromed to the max, and your car upstages cars parked nearby, *open the hood and show it off.*

To Show, Or Not To Show What's Under The Trunk

The big factor to keep in mind here is this. A sloppy, messy, or ugly trunk only detracts from the overall image and the impression you make on the mind. The key rule is: *If the interior of your trunk is not A-1, perfectly neat and clean, don't show it.* If the spare tire and tools in the back are neatly displayed, show it. If you have a flat spare tire, or an open hole where the spare used to be, don't show it.

If you've stored the rags and cleaning supplies you've used on the car in your trunk, don't show it.

If you show your car and the trunk is the slightest bit messy or cluttered, it will take points off the car and people will come away with a tarnished image of your car. It's like wearing a nice clean shirt or blouse. If you have one spot on it, or a lot of wrinkles, that's what people see -- not the clean shirt. So, make the inside of the trunk as sharp as the outside; otherwise, keep it closed, tight.

Should The Doors Be Left Open . . . Or Closed?

The first consideration here is: Does the appearance of the interior of the car add or detract from the overall image or appearance of the car? Is the upholstery in good condition? Does the color of the upholstery and interior trim coordinate well with the exterior paint job? Is the dash in good shape and make a positive appearance? Are the carpets well maintained? If all these things look sharp, open the doors.

The type of car show you are in also determines whether you leave doors open or closed. If you are showing in a high-dollar car show, open the doors and show what you've got. The more you show, if it looks nice, can help give you an extra edge. Some cars that win awards win because of interior, some because of what's under the hood, and some for overall general appearance. You want to show everything that can add points to your car and to your chances. The flyer promoting the show will tell you what classes of awards will be given -- for example, engine, under-carriage, interior, paint job, flame paint job, pinstriping, chrome, original features, customized features, and so on.

If you see that they are only giving awards for the best sedan, there may be no need to show the interior of your car. If it can't benefit you or add to the overall image, don't bother to show it. If it enhances the image, and if you think what you show can give you even a slight edge, or it makes your car stand out above others in its class, show it.

What To Show, and What Not To Show?
The 7 Key Guidelines

There are seven basic questions you need to ask yourself when trying to decide what to show and what not to show:

1. Is it necessary to show it? If it is, show it.
2. Does it benefit the overall image or appearance of the car? If it does, show it
3. Does it make my car distinctive or make it stand out over others of its class? If it does, show it.
4. Is it so-so, ho-hum, or just like other cars? Don't show it.
5. Don't show anything I don't have to show to win.
6. Is there something about my car that's a conversation piece, a crowd-stopper? If there is, parade it ... flaunt it!
7. Am I showing off what's special about my car, or am I showing off? Yes, show off the car, but no, *don't show off!* People -- and judges -- can't stand show-offs. Read very carefully the next chapter, *"How To Have A True Car Show Attitude: Car Show Etiquette , Manners & The Important Do's & Don'ts."*

A Special Trick To Use With Your Windows

Here's a little technique that will help people get a better look at your interior when the doors are closed, and that will help keep people's hands from smearing your windows or leaning on the car.

Roll the windows half-way up. This way people admiring your car can easily look in and see everything without even touching the car. Many people, trying to keep people's hands out of the car, will mistakenly roll the windows all the way up. But when this is done people will put their hands against the windows to shield out glare to see through window tint. After hundreds of folks do this, the windows are a mess.

Another benefit besides these is that it discourages those people who want to see if the windows crank up and down from cranking them up and down.   And you don't want anyone playing with anything on the car.

A Key Point About The Keys

This may seem too obvious to even mention, but you would be surprised how many people make the mistake of leaving their keys in the ignition during car events. Obvious or not, here goes:

Be sure to take the keys out of the car after you get it parked just right.   Otherwise, you put temptation in the way and many people will just *have to* start your engine to see how it runs. And you may even have some lowlife start it up and put it in gear and drive it away before the show is over. You don't want to end the cruise or show having to report grand theft auto! That kind of spoils the day, know what I mean?

"Look But Don't Touch" Signs — *Use Them*

Most shows will provide signs you can put in the side and front windows of the car. But just in case they don't, carry them with you.

And try to make the signs cute or humorous, not rude and obnoxious. Don't say, "KEEP YOUR FILTHY MEAT-HOOKS OFF THIS CLASSY MACHINE!" Do say something like, "THIS CAR IS LIKE ANOTHER MAN'S WIFE -- YOU CAN LOOK BUT BETTER NOT TOUCH!" Or a sign with kids on it saying, "IT'S OK TO LOOK, BUT THANKS FOR NOT TOUCHING!"

Another sign that shows that you care about people and have "class" might say, "THANK YOU FOR BEING THOUGHTFUL ENOUGH TO HELP KEEP LITTLE FINGERS FROM TOUCHING THE CAR!", with a cartoon of a mom and dad holding onto the kids' hands (or handcuffing them!). Remember this when making a sign: You want everything about your car to create positive feelings in those who see it. So make your signs gracious, kind, gentle, and firm.

Showing Your Car During The Day:
The 5 Secrets That Really Pay Off

1.   Be sure to scope out the site of the event during the time of day the upcoming event will be held. This way you'll be able to see from which direction the sun moves across the sky, shading from trees and buildings, where signs are, traffic from nearby streets and shops, etc.

2.   Keep visual effects in mind. During the day your car will either be in bright sunlight or be in the shade. Background buildings, signs, fences, parking lots, dumpsters and other things will be noticed behind your car. Take all these visuals into account. You don't want your car parked in front of a billboard for some politician you don't want to be associated with. If your car is white, you don't want it positioned up against a white building; it just fades out, not stands out, and looks totally blah. And the same thing goes if your car is black; you want to park it with something light behind it for contrast. And you don't want dumpsters or trash cans in plain view when people check out your car. Most people forget all about the psychological aspects like this. So this gives you a special edge to make your car really shine!

3.   If you think the show will take place during a very hot day, park your car near a shady tree. Not under it, but near it. Why? So people can cool off by standing in the shade and at the same time get an eye full of your car. It adds to the positive impact people come away with about your car -- even though they aren't aware of why (it's a subliminal or subconscious effect). It's a little like car dealers

who serve coffee and doughnuts to customers. Park your car on an angle facing the shade of the tree that is the most flattering to the car. As people feel good in the shade, getting out of the hot sun, that "feel good" gets linked to guess what? *Your car!*

4. Use a large canopy during hazy or drizzly days. Position the canopy to cover the car, giving people a good place to view your car free from the glare or wet. Some folks use canopies during sunny days if they don't have much chrome to show off in the sun. You can even tie balloons to the corners and center of the overhead covering to draw more attention (refer to the information on decorating).

5. As you select the location and angle to park your car, ask yourself: Which direction will the sun be shining from, and how can I position my car so that the sun highlights the best features of my car? You don't want the sun to cast dark shadows over nice-looking chrome on the body or the engine. You want the sun to shine directly on those areas to show it off. Remember, if you're parking your car early in the morning and you position your chromed engine facing east, you'll get the best exposure during morning hours. But all afternoon that good-looking engine will be shrouded by shadows because the sun is behind the car. The better method is to park on an angle facing north-to-south or south-to-north so the engine gets the direct rays of the sun all day long. So, carry a special tool in your glove compartment --- a compass!

Showing Your Car At Night:
The 3 Secrets Most People Never Discover

You are concerned with the direction of the light during the day, and likewise, you need to keep in mind the location of lights when showing at night.

1. Try to look over the site at night, but if you can't do this, if you look over the site during the day, look for light poles and position of various floodlights around the area. Position your car under or near this lighting. You don't want to end up having your car hidden in shadows.

2. Don't park your car in a position where bushes, fences, trees or other obstructions will cast a shadow on your car because it obstructs the light.

3. If possible, try to park in such a way that people will stand with their backs to floodlights as they look at your car. The floodlights are bathing your car in light, making it gleam real pretty!

The Best Place To Place Your Lawn Chairs

Never put your lawn chairs too close to the car. People need plenty of room to move freely around your car to get the best unobstructed view of it. You don't want them to have any irritation from chairs and other things they have to climb over or walk around.

The best thing to do is place your chairs and other items close to the chairs in the rear of the car, with plenty of walk space between the chairs and the car. Keep ice chests and other items close to and between the chairs for a neat appearance. Remember that everything adds or detracts from the total impact of your car.

Why position the chairs in the rear of the car? Because you don't want chairs to get in the way of people's clear view of the front of the car, where most pictures will be taken.

Some key rules to keep in mind when setting up are: (1) Set up everything near and around your car to give the most flattering appearance; look at it like a photographer would see it. (2) No clutter. (3) No obstructions to easy movement all the way around the car. (4) Keep the area free of trash, cans, and cigarette butts.

(5)   Be thoughtful and inconvenience no one to enhance the appearance and the lingering memory of your car. Remember: The way you conduct yourself around your car, and the way you present yourself personally, reflect on the overall evaluation of your car.

You never get a second chance to make a first impression!

You Don't Need A High-Dollar Car To Win Awards

Next time you go to a car show, check it out. You'll notice that many of the most expensive, big-money cars are not among those who win the praises of the judges and the trophies. Sure, sometimes a high-priced car will win, but the price of the car, or how much money is poured into restoring it, does not determine success. If you want to show and shine, you simply need to be meticulous about details.

For example, we paid $15,000 for our '34 Ford coupe, and won first place over a beautiful '35 Roadster. The Roadster is one of the top ten cars in California. It is valued at over $40,000!

Now, let us give you an example of how it worked the same way for someone else whose less expensive car beat out ours. Their '57 Chevy was worth maybe $7,000, at the time and it beat our $15,000 Ford. You should have seen the super paint job and the attention to detail on that Chevy.

When people look your car over, and when judges rate your car, they are looking for a lot more than how much you paid for it. Just stand nearby people and judges at the next car show or cruise. What are they talking about? "Look at that chrome work on the engine," "What a beautiful paint job," "Those pinstripes are matched perfectly with the interior," "Look at that chromed beer keg he's using as a fuel tank!" and so on.

Remember when Madonna celebrated her divorce by selling her '57 T-Bird-wedding-present for $60,000? You don't have to compete with the $20,000, $30,000, $40,000, or the $60,000 boys (or girls). Don't sweat it. It doesn't matter one bit what your car is worth on the open market. What *does* matter is that you make your car sparkle with excellence in every detail of the car that is open to plain view.

Show Your Car, But Don't Be a Show-Off!

We deal with this in chapter six, *How To Have A True Car Show Attitude,* but it deserves mentioning here to drive the point home. If there's one thing that really turns people off fast it's someone who brags and boasts. "My car is the hottest thing on wheels" ... "Everything else at this show is also-rans and can't even come close to my rod" ... "Look at all the awards and trophies my car has won, and it's even on the cover of the best car magazines." Even if his car is hot, he'll turn people — and judges — cold with a puffed up and arrogant attitude like that. Don't make that mistake!

If you have won one trophy or one hundred trophies, that's great. But don't offend people by displaying them around your car or inside the car during car shows.

If your car is on the cover of top car magazines, that's great, but don't leave a copy conspicuously positioned on the front seat of your car during the show.

First of all, people are instantly offended and turned off by someone who needs to flaunt his successes.

Secondly, judges will look at all those trophies and might just say to themselves, "Why give this guy the top prize, he's already got 18 trophies, what's he need another one for?" They will probably give it to someone who deserves to win more than you do, and someone who doesn't need to bribe them with past successes.

So what should you do? Let the car speak for itself. No need to gild the lily. If it's hot, people will love it. If it deserves another honor today, it will win another honor today like it did last week. Show off the car, but don't show off past victories. Like the old proverb goes, "Don't praise yourself, let others praise you."

And never forget this:

A good reputation is hard to get, but so very easy to lose!
A bad reputation is easy to get, and so very hard to lose!

There are times when it's appropriate to display honors you've won with your car. For example, some months back we won first place at the National Hot Rod Association and received a beautiful plaque. The following weekend we were invited to drive our car down the runway at the Winternationals and appeared on national TV. There were about nineteen other top cars displayed that day before the race. So we waited to see if others were displaying their awards before making the decision to show ours. Since we were only displaying the car and we were not in a competitive show, it was appropriate to put the plaque in the center of the front window. But if others had not done the same thing, we would have kept it out of sight. Use good discretion when making this decision and you won't offend anyone.

How To Make Your Car
Look Unique And Stand Out

Think about displaying your car the same way you would try to make the best possible appearance you can when displaying yourself. You wouldn't, for example, have one shirt tail tucked in, the other hanging out and all the rest of you looking great. That hanging-out shirt tail would or could ruin your whole appearance, right? The same thing applies to showing your car.

Try to give your car a balanced appearance. You don't want your left door open and the right side of your hood up (if you are showing an antique car, let's say), or your right door open and the left side of your hood up. Somehow that throws everything out of whack. What's better? You could have both doors open and both sides of the hood open as well. Or, you could open the right door to display the interior, and have the same side open on the hood to show off the chromed engine. Or vice versa.

Now let's suppose the sun is shining from the right side of your car. That would help determine which side you open. You might therefore open the right side of the hood and the right doors to display both interior and engine in bright sunlight. You would keep the opposite side closed. Simple.

Having one side open and the other side closed also allows people to walk around one side and get the feel for the inside-aspects of the car, and they can walk around the other side and get the over-all outside perspective view.

There are times when your car is out in the open with no cars up close to you, you may want to open both sides of the hood and all doors open. Or you might want to leave the hood closed and leave all doors open. This is done typically where cars are parked with plenty of distance between each car. People can easily move about without feeling crowded, and you can have doors all the way open without risk of scraping someone else's car.

Of course, when making the decision whether to open the hood you must ask yourself this question: Does the appearance of the engine add to or detract from the overall positive impact of my car? And similarly, ask yourself: Does opening the car doors enhance the appearance or tarnish the look of the car? Is it *fragrance or odor?* If the engine or the interior are *odor*, that is, they make a negative impression on people viewing your car, don't show them. Keep the hood and doors closed. But if they are *fragrance* and like perfume, they give your car a little something extra special, then show them off.

Oh yes, by the way, you would be surprised how many people forget one important thing when showing their interior, and lose points because of it. And that one thing is this. They have a great paint job, sparkling chrome engine, perfect upholstery and dash ... but the floor mats are filthy dirty and there is trash and clutter all over the floor. Bad mistake! Somehow that one negative feature sticks in people's minds, including the judges -- like a sour note in an otherwise beautiful song. Attention to detail: Remember to do the "little things" right and big things can happen.

Is all this just nit-picking? No way. No matter how good or attractive or special something may be, people are drawn to the flaws, aren't they? So, since life isn't fair, and since this is a fact of life, look at your car with the critical eye and give the people only the positives to remember you by.

The Right Distance To Park From Other Cars
To Make The Best Impression

It's easy to forget that how close you park to other cars can make a big difference on the angle people see your car, and how comfortable they are at those different angles. When you park the car you want to be sure people can get far enough away from the car to see its best features clearly. A good rule of thumb is to allow at least 6 to 8 feet of walk space all the way around, with perhaps more space in the back for lawn chairs, if you use them.

You want plenty of space for doors to be opened and still allow for others to walk around it. You want enough space so that baby strollers don't have to sideswipe your car to get by!

The person running the car show will probably have some idea of how close they want the cars. But if you simply ask, "Hey, can I get over a couple of more feet here?" they will almost always let you and you'll give yourself a better chance of giving your audience easy access.

How To Make Decorative Touches The Right Way

Those "little things" can make a big difference in making a good impression. But you have to use good judgement when selecting decorative touches. For example, dice hanging from your rear-view mirror look great on a '57 Chevy. But suppose you see dice hanging from the mirror of a '32? Somehow, they just don't seem to fit, do they?

Venetian blinds in the back window look sensational in a '49 Ford, don't they? How do they look in a classic T-Bird? Not so hot.

The same thing goes for raccoon tails, mirror warmers, Brody knobs, and other interior-decorating ideas. *Make them period pieces, appropriate to the time period that your car represents, and the era when they were popular.*

If you have a car from a given period and you're not sure what little touches people used to dress them up during that era, do some research. Talk to people who have similar cars as your own at cruises and car shows and swap meets. What are they using? What do they remember as some of the neater things people did to outfit cars at that time? Walk around cruises and shows and take notes. What looks really sharp to you, and then make sure it's appropriate to the era or time period. Go to the library and pull out some of the car magazines from back then. Check out the little things. Some used book stores have older magazines and you can browse to your heart's content, writing down good ideas. And even some of the old movies, now on video, offer good sources of info and ideas.

Why bother with the little touches like dice, raccoon tails, Brody knobs on the steering wheel, or mirror warmers? Here's why: Suppose someone is checking out your car, and there just happens to be another car there that's just as hot as yours. Great paint job. Perfect interior. Chrome that will knock your eyes out. Everything on both cars is just right. Then, suppose a person (or one of the judges) at the show sees, say, a raccoon tail hanging down from your mirror. That's not just a raccoon tail. It's a memory trigger. That little touch may trigger the memory of his or her own favorite car, some hot dates enjoyed in that car, the happy recollections of cruisin' up and down their favorite strip with someone special sitting real close next to them. Special memories -- warm fuzzies -- you want linked to *your car!*

So don't neglect adding those special little touches. Just be sure they "fit" the period represented by your car, and you may get an important edge in making the best impression.

A Special Touch *Under* The Car
To Get Big Attention

There are some axioms or truths about showing cars that are worthy of repeating over and over again. One of them is this: If there's something special or unusual or just great-looking about your car, find a way to show it off.

We've talked about the outside, and we've talked about the inside; now let's talk about the under-side. Yes, that's right, the underside. Many car buffs take pains to make every visible part of their car look its best. Many have the under-side chromed from front to rear. If you've spent the money to show off the part nearest the road, why not try this. Get some full-length mirrors and lay them under the car the long way. People can then easily get an eye-full of your chrome. And like those other touches, this may give your car that something-special-touch to make it stand out. Some people have even hooked up small fluorescent lights along with the mirrors. Try it, if that turns you on.

Some Special Tricks You Can Use To Knock Their Eyes Out!

Be sure to carry some good car polish with you to the event. Some good polishes that are on the market include: *Carnauba, Turtle Teflon, Blue Coral,* and *Eagle One.*

What's the best thing to use to buff in a shine that will knock their eyes out, and that will leave no streaks and lint? Believe it or not, it's diapers. That's right, baby diapers! But not just any diapers will do. To get the best results, you'll need old, cloth diapers that have been washed hundreds and hundreds of times. They're the softest and most free of lint. So you'll have to find someone with a toddler who still uses the old-fashioned cloth diapers. They'll have some great "rags" to donate to your cause. However, these may be hard to find in the 90's and the 21st century, with all the disposables on the market. But don't give up--call diaper services and see if they can help.

When You Should NEVER Polish Your Car

Is there ever a time when it is bad judgement to rub out smudges or rub in a super shine? Yes there is.

You should never work on making your car appear more attractive when the judges at a car show are looking over your car. Why? Because it looks as if you are trying too hard. Remember our rule of thumb: Just let the car speak for itself when people -- and especially when judges -- are checking out your car. If you want to improve the shine, there's plenty of time when the judges are looking over someone else's car.

Using Graphics To Make Your Car
Look Super-Special: Some Do's & Don'ts

We bought a beautiful '30 Model A, black, and had it looking almost perfect, with plenty of chrome and a great interior. We were surprised to find that although people liked it quite a bit, it never won any awards at car shows or cruises. We couldn't understand it. But we noticed that at the various events there were several cars similar to ours and none of them really stood out above the others, including our own.

So we decided to try something. We had a hot pink pinstripe put around the car that tied in really well with the interior. And that's the only change we made.

Results? Our '30 Model A started getting all kinds of reactions from people at the car events. More people asking questions about it. People complimenting us on it. Yes, and even more offers to buy it! And what made it even sweeter, is that we started winning consistently at car shows, and have a shelf full of trophies and plaques because of that little decorative stripe.

Before you go hog-wild and pinstripe your car, or put flames all over it, or have fancy graphics painted on the sides, go slow! *Make haste slowly!* The thing you don't want to do is to overdo it, making your car look gaudy or garish. You've seen cars that lay on the glitz. They look just plain cheap. Just enough perfume gets the right kind of attention. But too much perfume makes people wonder if the lady wearing it is maybe trying too hard?

Like our car, yours may profit from a little bit of dressing up. But before you spend the bucks to have it done, do some investigating. Attend all the cruise-nites, shows and meets you can. Spend some time with good car magazines. Visit a paint shop that specializes in customizing and look over photos they may have to show off their work. Gather all the ideas you can to see what fits your car. When you find a few ideas you like, run them by some friends and people you talk to at shows and cruises. Watch and listen carefully to their reactions.

And keep in mind that in addition to pleasing others, whatever design you come up with has to also please someone else. *You.* There should be a nice fit between your own personality and the special touches you add to your car. The thin pinstripes worked great for our personalities. But exotic flames on the sides would not have been right for us, but okay for someone else. When we sell the '30 Ford, no doubt someone else will customize it to reflect something about their own style or personality. That's what makes car events so enjoyable -- you see as many different unique expressions on, and in the cars themselves as there are different personalities of the owners.

Try this little experiment. Next time you go to a show, try to notice how similar the special customizing touches are to the personality characteristics of the owner. See if you can predict what this person is like before you meet him or her. It's a lot of fun!

And let us warn you of one thing before we leave this section, please. When using graphics on your car, use good taste. Keep in mind that car shows and cruises are *family events.* You wouldn't want anything you have painted on your car, any decorative knob inside, or any other custom touch, to offend anyone. There will be children there, and there will be women there, both groups may be offended by, let's say, some nude painted on the side or hood of a car or van, or a Brody knob with a nude prominently displayed on the steering wheel. Such things may be items of interest to some groups of guys, but they definitely don't belong at shows and cruises. Again, use good judgement.

What To do If your Car Has Flaws:
How To Minimize Them

You want to accentuate the positive, and you want to play down or minimize the negative. No car is perfect. Every car has "something" that can spoil its overall impact. It's a rare car that you can't find some little thing wrong with it.

But if you have obvious little things that you haven't yet corrected, here's how to handle them "smart."

First of all, if there are imperfections in the paint job or in the body work that are noticeable, you need to keep them out of direct sunlight. The sun will magnify problems in body or paint work that people will remember. So if the car show or cruise is being held during the day, be sure to get there early and park your car so that it will be in the shade throughout the day, if possible. Park it under a canopy, in the shadow of a building or fence or sign, or under a tree. There are risks, however, parking under a tree. You may have some fine, feathered admirers up in that tree who have lousy bathroom habits. You get the point!

If your interior is not so hot, keep the doors closed and locked. Keep windows rolled part-way down to keep people's handprints off the windows. And even if it's not the greatest upholstery job, be sure it's at least neat, and free of all litter and trash.

If the engine is nothing to look at, nothing to talk about, keep the hood closed. And unless the trunk is really neat and sharp, keep it closed.

One Little Trick That Makes Your Wheels
Make The Best Impression

Many people spend hours and hours getting the outside and inside of their car looking fabulous, then once they get to the cruise or car show, they forget one important part of the car that people notice. The wheels.

You wouldn't spend hours getting all dressed up in your finest duds, hair looking great, smelling good and head out for a party with filthy shoes. Right?

Yes, it's true: Not too many people spend much time drooling over your tires, unless they happen to work for Goodyear, perhaps. But if everything about your car is clean and sharp and your tires are dull and dirty, this can make a subliminal or subconscious impact. And that impact will not do anything to add to the overall good reaction to your car. You don't want anything taking points away from your car -- you've put too much blood, sweat and cash into it to let that happen.

So stick some rags, a wire brush and some Armorall in the trunk and take them along to the event. Put them in a canvas bag or sack to keep the trunk looking neat. When you have the car parked just where you want it, look over the tires. Many times you will notice dirt or mud caked on the tread or even on the outside of the tires or rims. Clean it off real good. Then Armorall all exposed parts of the tires. Shine up the rims too. And check to be sure that no dirt or mud has been thrown up on the lower part of the car.

Next time you walk around a car show, notice how many people have overlooked this one, important point. They've come to the party, but have they shined their "shoes"!? *But you have!*

So now you have the step-by-step how-to's so you can show your car in it's best light, and *make it shine.* Do what you've learned in this chapter and you ought to have to make another special investment — a new and much bigger trophy shelf!

The checklist on the next page will help you quickly and easily be sure you've touched all the bases before each car show or cruise, so you get the results you want ... *as you show and shine!*

The Show & Shine Top 20 Checklist:
Giving Your Car That Special Winning Edge

1. Plan to arrive at the show very early to get the best location.
2. Scope out the best parking spot the day *before* the show.
3. Choose a spot where publicity photos will likely be taken.
4. Check out the location during the day or at night, depending on when the event will be held.
5. Choose 2 or 3 good spots to park.
6. Showing your car during the day or after dark is very different -- know the differences.
7. Show only those things that add to the positive impression you want to make with your car.
8. Keep your windows rolled half-way up.
9. Don't leave your keys in the car!
10. Put "Look But Please Don't Touch" signs up.
11. Show off your car, but don't be a show-off!
12. Know how to make your car stand out by doing special little things that others don't think to do.
13 Leave plenty of walking and looking room around your car.
14. Decorate your car with things appropriate to its time period.
15. Use mirrors to show off your car.
16. Use old diapers to shine your car.
17. Don't polish your car when the judges are watching!
18. Use good taste when painting graphics on your car.
19. Hide your car's flaws in a shady place.
20. Make sure your tires are clean and shine like the rest of the car.

Chapter 6

How To Have A True Car Show Attitude

Car Show Etiquette, Good Manners, & How To Avoid Making Stupid Mistakes

How To Have A True Car Show Attitude

Car Show Etiquette, Good Manners, & How To Avoid Making Stupid Mistakes

C ar shows and cruises are as much about *people* as they are about cars! Anyone can buy a car, park it at a special car event, and proceed to make a total fool of himself or herself, make people mad, and very quickly build a reputation for being a you-know-what. But those people don't enjoy the real benefits of getting into rods, classics and antique cars, and they almost never win awards. And for sure they *never* win any friends.

What we are going to share with you in this chapter is as important as anything else in the book, and it is just as practical. What we're going to do is introduce you to and let you follow one of our "friends" around and let you get a look of what he does at car shows and cruises. Then, we will advise you how to *do exactly the opposite of what he does.* Why the opposite? Because he has a reputation as the person people most want to *avoid.*

We've learned a lot from him over the years, and we've followed him around and observed his methods. It wasn't pretty, but brother, did we learn a lot! So let's follow him and see how he makes all the wrong moves so that you don't make the same mistakes yourself.

He is known as "Mr. Obnoxious" around Southern California car events, so we'll change his real name to protect the guilty, and we'll just call him Mr. O. B. Noxious, "O.B." for short.

Here we go ...

Mistake #1: The Show-Off,
"Me 'n' My Car Are Best By Far" Attitude

First off, Mr. O.B. Noxious is into cars for all the wrong reasons. He's not really a car lover or a car buff. He's not even concerned about learning about cars or bench racing and talking about cars over a good burger and Coke. Nope. What he is interested in is proving to everybody at the event that he is the *greatest.*

You see, at car shows and cruise-nites there are a lot of people gathered in one place. He sees this as a good place and a golden opportunity to impress others. If his car can get more attention and win more trophies and awards than others, he can hang them on the wall and fill up his shelves with proof of his greatness.

What he's really trying to do is convince himself that he's "OK." Deep down inside in his private thoughts he feels very insecure and very lonely. Anyone who needs all this "proof" that he's a good human being has a lot to hide -- and a lot to learn.

So O.B. goes around bragging and boasting. Telling people how much he spent on his car. Telling people how many top awards he's won and major shows he's been in. Telling people how many TV shows and magazines his car has been featured in, and how many videos have used his car.

He always has to be one-up on everybody. His car is always a little better, has something that the other guy doesn't have.

And you'll never hear him complimenting someone else's car. No way. If he talks to them at all it's to point out some defect or flaw in their car. Why? Because that makes him and his car look better. He lifts himself up by putting others down.

How To Avoid Making Mistake #1

Get into cars for the fun and for the people. Don't let yourself have a competitive spirit.   Never brag or boast. Give others compliments and give sincere, positive praise. Find something special about their car and complement it. Form a new habit -- catch people doing something right!

Mistake #2: The "Winning is Everything" Attitude

Because O.B. has to prove that his car is best by far, he must find ways to make sure he gets the top awards and trophies at car shows. How does he do this?

Simple. Pick up stacks of slips to use to vote for his own car. He doesn't just cast one vote for his own car, oh no, that would be fine. He grabs a whole stack of voting slips to pad the vote real good.

How does he get away with this? Easy. He goes to the nearest pay phone. He gets out his handy-dandy address book. He calls all his kids, his in-laws, his out-laws, his cousins, his aunts, uncles, granddad, grandma, ex-wives and their present husbands, old girlfriends, people he knows from work, people who owe him a favor, neighbors, and anyone else who may be on his Christmas card list.

Next, he persuades all of them to come down to the car show, fill out a ballot -- voting for *his car*, of course -- and then they are free to go. It works like a charm!

Then, when all the votes are tallied, guess who wins? You guessed it. Good old O.B. Noxious himself. And you hear about that victory for the next six months. And he feels good about himself because his car is best by far. And that means, to him, that he is best by far. How sad. But that's O.B.

How To Avoid Making Mistake #2

Realize that you are special just because you are you. Winning or losing isn't what it's all about. Having fun and enjoying life is what it's all about. Let your car speak for itself. It's OK to vote for your own car, but only one vote. If your car deserves some honor or award, you'll win it; if not, so be it. And if you do invite everybody on your Christmas card list, tell them to vote for their choice of cars, even if it's not yours!

Mistake #3: The "Hit or Miss" Attitude

To O.B. it doesn't matter much whether he shows up regularly to the various car events. If he feels like it, he'll go. If not, who cares. After all, he's only going for what *he* can get out of it. He's not going for the enjoyment of meeting people, talking and sharing ideas and stories.

He's interested in showing what he knows or showing off what he has. You never see him offering to help someone set up, park cars, giving advice to those who may not know how things are done at a show, or offering a friendly compliment to others.

There's no loyalty with old O.B. Noxious. No sir. He's all for O.B.; nothing else matters (after all, that's how he got his name and his reputation).

How To Avoid Making Mistake #3

There are two big words in cruise and car show circles. They are: *Loyalty* and *Consistency*. You'll get a reputation pretty fast for being one of the "good guys," one of the regulars, if you make every effort to attend most of the local events. Be there, and offer to lend a hand when people need help. Get there early. Help whoever is putting on the show or cruise set up. Ask what you can do to help out. Be friendly. Offer helpful advice. Give sincere compliments and praise. Notice special little things about people's cars, or about their families, and comment on it. Help clean up when the event is over, including leaving the parking lot and restaurant neat and cleaner than when you arrived. Offer to hand out flyers for the next show or cruise-nite. Be a faithful, reliable, participant. You might be surprised at how many people win awards and make friends because of their loyalty to be there! Park cars. Take registrations. Help out with the raffles. You'll not only get awards, but free passes to future shows! And you'll build a positive reputation for yourself that will follow you around like your own shadow.

Mistake #4: The "Let Me Tell You What's Wrong With Your Car" Attitude

This actually happened to us some time ago. O.B. came up to us at a Southern California car show and looked at our new car and said, "Is that your car?" I said, "Yeah." He replied, "God, that's sure an ugly color!" He tried to soften the blow, being a gentleman and a man of such gracious manners, so he added, "I mean, that's a beautiful car, if only it was a different color."

You see here another example of how he got his name!

On another occasion he said to a friend of ours about their car, "That would be a nice car, but you've got the wrong kind of rims on it -- the wheels are all wrong."

One other time he offered this good advice: "You know, if you put some pinstripes on this car it might look nice; it just doesn't look good the way you've got it."

And then he told us what was wrong with our '30 Ford, trying to be helpful, I'm sure: "You know what's wrong with this car? It has no rumble seat in it. Without a rumble seat in it, you've ruined the looks of it!:"

And at other times he's not so direct. He's more subtle in his "helpful" advice. He uses questions instead. Like, "How come you put *this* kind of grille on your car?" Or, "You changed something on this car; why did you change it and make it look like *this* ?"

Or he might tell you that he doesn't like a '30, if that's what you have. He says, "I prefer the '34, it's a lot better." Or he's been heard to say, "Why'd 'ya buy a post model and not the hard top, because the hard tops are the most popular model?"

He just knows what to say to make people want to run the other way whenever they see him. But, if you ever want to know what's wrong with your car, or how you blew it, just call old O.B. over -- he'll tell you all you need to know, and some more besides.

How To Avoid Making Mistake #4

The old saying is still true. If you don't have something nice to say, don't say anything at all. Find what's good, what's special, what's hot about someone's car, and tell them you noticed it. If you like another model or color or style better, keep that preference to yourself. Find something — anything — that is positive about their car and say so. If they have something on their car that doesn't fit the period or the year or the model, stuff it. Don't say anything about it to the owner of the car, and don't say anything about it to anyone else, either. Remember, if you bad-mouth other people's cars you'll get a reputation *fast* for being a jerk. You're not a jerk, right? So be positive, be sincere, and *never criticize or give negative advice!* Then you'll be a good guy, not a jerk, like O.B. Noxious.

Mistake #5: The "Buy the Judges" Attitude

This little tactic is very simple. You just try to buddy up and make friends with someone who does a lot of judging at car shows. Do him or her some favors here and there, always keeping in mind, however, that someday soon you will call for repayment on those favors, a little like the Godfather principle. Then, at a big show let this person know that since you are friends, or since they "owe you one," after all, you'll appreciate their voting for *your car.*

Ask them repeatedly about your car's chances of winning. Ask them what odds they give your car of beating others.

And when you do win, ask them what they think your chances are of winning at the upcoming car show next month. Drop some hints that you are still counting on repayment on the favors you've done for them. Yes, the idea here is to *own* as many judges as possible. That way you don't have to work as hard keeping your car looking great or spending the money everyone else does to keep it sharp. Why bother when you have the judges in your hip pocket?

That's O.B.'s philosophy. And believe it or not, he wins some shows using these tactics. But he also makes a truckload of enemies, too. Once you get a reputation for buying judges, you're dead. You're about as popular as a thunder storm in the middle of a car show, or an invasion of mini-trucks at a cruise-nite!

How To Avoid Making Mistake #5

Once again, let your car speak for itself. Don't buy judges. Don't try to manipulate judges. And if the only reason you do favors for people is to control them so you can get pay-backs later; keep your favors to yourself. Do good deeds for people because you care about people. And don't ask about the odds of your car winning next month's car show. Nobody knows and nobody cares. Just have a blast and forget about winning. Win true friendships and be a friend. Go ahead and buy judges -- buy them a Coke and a hamburger and have someone take it to them *anonymously!* Now you're talkin'!

Mistake #6: The "Take All the Glory " Attitude

Car people are givers. They enjoy sharing tips and ideas that have worked for them and others. They don't like "secrets" that seem to give one person the edge over everybody else. There is a kind of give-it-away attitude that makes the whole car scene more of a fellowship than a sport (although it certainly can be considered that, too). But as you know by now, old O.B. is only concerned about one thing: Winning, looking good, and upstaging everybody. So when he picks up good ideas from people and uses them, does he give anyone credit for helping him? No way. He simply looks down his nose at those who don't have his "secrets" and never bothers telling others who may just be starting out, how to improve their car, or how to do better at car events. "Me, my, and mine" ... that's his only motto. His 3 favorite words.

How To Avoid Making Mistake #6

It's so simple. Give credit where credit is due. If someone gives you advice or tips that work and help you, let others know how that person helped you. Let them share the glory. "I couldn't have done it without So-and-So's good know-how." "I want to publicly acknowledge the help I received from So-and-So -- I have gotten a lot of great ideas from him and his cars." "You know what, this trophy belongs as much to So-and-So as it does to me; he's been a true inspiration." Build other people up in the eyes of other people. Share the spotlight. Share ideas and tips to help others. People will admire you for it. And remember:

"It is more blessed to give than to receive."

Mistake #7: The Attitude of Ingratitude

The words "Thank you" are Greek, or some other foreign language, to O.B. Noxious. The last time he said these two magic words was when he saw his own reflection in the window of his own car, and gave thanks for being such a gift to mankind!

No matter how generous people may be with ideas and tips that help him, he never bothers thanking them. No matter how many times people come up to him and compliment his car, he never says "Thanks;" no sir. He just says, "Yeah, that's right, there's nobody in these parts with a hotter car!"

How To Avoid Making Mistake #7

Use those two, little magic words every day. They make people feel good. They make people know that you care. They show people that you have class, manners, and that you appreciate them. And they demonstrate that you are not a selfish know-it-all. And they encourage people to want to get to know you better, and perhaps to become your friend. And who knows, those two little words may even help you win your own awards at car shows. But the most important thing about the words, "Thank you" is this: You recognize the importance of something the other person has gone out of their way to do for you. "Thank you" is like the oil you put in your engine -- without it, you're dead.

Thank you!

Mistake #8 The Bad Loser Attitude

What happens when our boy, old O.B. Noxious, doesn't win first place at a car show, or when more people gather 'round someone else's car at a cruise? He immediately has a trunk load of reasons why he lost. And he makes it known that a "crime" was done to him.

"This show is nothin' but politics, if you ask me!"
"I bet he paid off those judges."
"They must be in tight with the owner of this restaurant."
"These people are idiots! They wouldn't know a hot car if they
were run over by one!"

When O.B. doesn't win, it's not because somebody else had a hotter car. It's because something shady's going on -- to O.B.'s way of thinking.

And if you want to find out what your friendship is really worth to old O.B., just vote for some other car, if you happen to be one of the judges at the next car show. You'll find out pretty quick that you're on his black list

If you want him to like you, just praise his car above all others, and promise to always vote for his car for first place. He'll love you!

How To Avoid Making Mistake #8

When you lose, and everyone does once in a while, show some good old-fashioned maturity about it. Be a gracious loser. Find something positive to say to others about the winners. Find something positive to say, with sincere praise, to the winners personally. Don't accuse anyone of "rigging" the event, or "buying judges." The judges did just what they were asked to do: They selected the cars that deserved special honors. Your turn will come -- be patient. And try to learn from the fortunate ones who win; don't criticize them. Ask them questions. Look at their cars carefully and pick up tips that can help you. And once again, get involved with people and put them at the top of your priority list. Put winning down the list somewhere. You'll have a whole lot more fun and make a whole lot more friends.

Mistake #9: The "Party Animal" Attitude

O.B. loves to have a good time. But the only way he can relax enough to enjoy himself and talk to people is to pound down a few brews. He figures that if it helps him unwind, why not share the fun with others.

So what does he do? He brings a cooler full of beer to every event. So as not to offend anybody, he discretely hides the cooler in his trunk. He also brings some good-sized plastic cups along so the sight of beer cans won't upset anyone.

When he finds a few guys who are like-minded, he breaks out a few and says, "This brew's for you." Translated into English, this simply means, "I hope you will like me now that I am giving you something you can't buy here." Or, "When you vote for the hottest car today, remember who gave you this beer."

As the day wears on you see why almost all car events have a no-drinking policy and enforce it. Old O.B. Noxious starts living up (or down) to his name. He gets louder and more argumentative all the time. He picks fights. He gets more negative as the day wears on. And his language gets uglier and uglier. Not a pretty sight.

How To Avoid Making Mistake #9
There's nothing wrong with partying or having a cooler full of your favorite brew. But there's a lot wrong with having them at a car event. NEVER, ever do any drinking at car functions! If you want to get the left foot of fellowship fast, and find yourself banned from future events, get the reputation for drinking at car get-togethers. So, whatever you do, remember this simple phrase:

ALCOHOL AT CAR EVENTS WILL KILL YOUR REPUTATION!

Mistake #10: The "Crude-Rude-Dude" Attitude

If we follow old O.B. around at a car show or cruise-nite, we'll learn the fine art of bad manners practiced with great skill. Crude and rude, that describes O.B.'s style the best.

He breaks all the rules of good taste as he walks up and down each row of cars. He opens other people's car doors. He plays with their windows. He puts his hands and finger prints all over their windows and paint jobs. He sits on their fenders. He opens and slams their hoods. And he even gets into people's cars and makes himself right at home.

He plunks himself down, without even asking, in people's lawn chairs. He leaves cups, cans, and other litter around their cars. And he puts out his cigarette butts on the ground next to whatever car he happens to be closest to. A real charmer, our O.B.!

How To Avoid Making Mistake #10

Just try to live by the old proverb that says, "Do unto others as you would have them do unto you." Respect the property of others. Treat their cars the same way you would like them to treat yours. If you're tempted to touch, stick you hands into your pockets, hook your thumbs through your belt loops, or handcuff your hands behind your back! Whatever works. And if you see litter around someone's car, pick it up and throw it away for them. And if you have an irresistible urge to get inside someone's car go ahead and ask their permission. Treat their car the way you want your car treated!

Mistake #11: The "Who Needs A DJ" Attitude

O.B. has himself a great set of speakers attached to his tape deck. He's mighty proud of that boomer. It's got the Dolby equalizer and the works. And he's got some great tapes, too. And, of course, if *he* likes that kind of music, doesn't everybody?

So to keep things lively, old O.B. decides to share his sounds with everybody at the show. Not just those next to his car, but those at the other end of the parking lot!

He cranks it up real good. It doesn't matter if the show or cruise nite has hired a DJ to do the music. The DJ won't play O.B.'s kind of music. So old O.B. rattles the windows of everybody's cars with his sound machine — whether they like it or not.

He might turn down his system if someone protests too much, but after they walk away, he simply cranks her up again -- this time even louder!

How To Avoid Making Mistake #11

If you must play music, keep it soft and low. Respect the ear-rights of those at the event. Make your sound system heard only when people get close to your car. People parked near you should not have to turn their music up to compete with yours. If the show has a DJ, let him do his job. Turn your sound system to the position with those three letters — "OFF." And if you do want to use music at times, remember: Keep it in style. Make it 50's or 60's rock classics. People are in that mood anyway, so "when in Rome," play stuff that fits the mood. If you have any doubts, the best choice is "OFF!"

Learn From The Experts

What we've given you here are the "classic" mistakes you need to avoid like the plague. Thanks to our good old buddy, O.B. Noxious for teaching us so well to watch what he's doing, and go the other way.

But these 11 Classic Mistakes are the key mistakes -- they are not all possible stupid moves that can be made at car events. To get a real education, do some research on your own. Try this: At the next car show or cruise, find one of O.B. Noxious' relatives. Who are they? He has people just like himself — clones — at most car functions. Now, O.B. is a master of all the wrong moves, as you've seen in this chapter. But some of his kin may have perfected bad taste and poor judgement to an even finer art still.

When you find such an expert, follow him around. Observe carefully his ways and moves. Watch what he does and listen to

what he says. See how he blows people away with his rudeness.
Hear how he offends everybody in earshot. Carefully note his
arrogant bragging and boasting.

Then, convert everything you've observed to it's exact opposite
and make up your mind to do just that.

Then jot down your new discoveries in the realm of bad taste
and send them to us! We'll put them in our next edition and give you
credit as one of our researcher contributors. And thanks for your
help, helping the rest of us avoid those classic blunders, making car
events more pleasant for everybody!

If you put the following tips into action, you will be one of the
"good guys" (or gals) at any car event. You'll make lots of friends,
you won't offend people, and you can bet nobody will be following
you around trying to learn how to make the same rude, crude
mistakes O.B. Noxious made! Carefully study the list on the next
page, and have the family go through it, too.

Good Manners & Etiquette For Car Shows & Cruises: 20 Do's & Don'ts Checklist For The Family

1. Don't touch anybody's cars!
2. Don't stand on the running boards.
3. Don't roll the windows up and down.
4. Don't put hands on the windows.
5. Don't get inside the cars.
6. Don't slam doors or open doors.
7. Don't beep the horn.
8. Don't kick the tires.
9. Don't pull up a chair next to a car.
10. Don't run strollers too close to the cars.
11. Don't sit soft drink cans down near the cars.
12. Don't litter near the cars.
13. Don't sit on fenders, bumpers, hoods, trunks, or running boards.
14. Don't lean up against a car where zippers, buttons, belt buckles or cameras hanging around your neck can scratch the car.
15. If you bring a pet, keep it under control and on a short leash. Better yet, don't bring them!
16. Don't play your radio or tape deck loud.
17. Keep your lawn chairs, cold box, etc. neatly close together & behind the car, allowing easy walking distance all around.
18. No alcoholic beverages.
19. No profanity.
20. If your car is for sale, make the signs small and tasteful, have it painted on the back window, or lay a small sign in the inside front seat -- don't plaster it on the window.

Chapter 7

How To Convert Your Car
Into Cash

*Smart Strategies For Selling Your Car
To Make The Biggest Profit*

Personal Notes & Ideas

How To Convert Your Car Into Cash

Smart Strategies for Selling Your Car To Make the Biggest Profit

W alk up and down the aisles of any sporting goods store and count the number of different items to choose from. This vast array of items represents the many different sports activities, hobbies, and leisure time "fun" activities that people enjoy every weekend of the year. You'd better take a calculator with you, because the number is staggering!

How many of these activities that people get into offer the opportunity not only to have a ball enjoying the sport, but offer the ability to *make money, to make a profit when you decide to sell the gear or equipment you used while you enjoyed the sport?* On the contrary, most hobbies or sports activities suck up a ton of money, and return nothing on the investment, except the fun of the sport.

Not so with cars!

When you get into customs, classics, rods and antiques, you can add to the fun and enjoyment of the sport the very real possibility of selling your car for more than what you paid for it. A double-win, sweet deal, isn't it?!

There aren't too many things in this world that *pay you for having fun!* But when you own the right kind of automobile, well, you've found the exception to the rule. Of course, this assumes that you have done your homework, as we discussed in the chapter on buying the *right* car. If you did, you own a car that is worth more now than the day you bought it. Not only that, but if you own the right car, that car brings you more money today than the dealer got for it when it was driven off the lot brand new! Not a bad investment, especially since we're talking 20, 30, 40, 50, or even 60 years or more later!

For example, here's just a sample of what some classic and vintage cars sold for new, and what the same cars sold for in 1994 and 1995. An amazing testimony to their staying power, and why these cars are so near and dear to people's hearts -- many of whom weren't even alive when these cars rolled off the assembly line and were on display in showrooms. Take a look at this:

Car Make & Model	Year	Original Dealer's Price	1995 Asking Price
Model T Ford	1915	$375	$5,000-$30,000
Deluxe Roadster	1932	$500	$15,000-$50,000
Buick convertible	1955	$3,225	$11,000-$18,000
Pontiac convertible	1956	$2,857	$11,000-$18,000
Chevy Bel-Air 210	1957	$2,299	$11,000-$20,000
Corvette Stingray	1964	$4,252	$18,000-$34,000
Chevy Impala (conv.)	1965	$3,212	$12,000-$28,000
Pontiac GTO	1970	$3,267	$12,000-$24,000

This is only one key reason that classic and antique cars fascinate American families -- and people in Japan, Germany, and many other parts of the world, as well. Many of the cars in the list just shown have *increased in value more than 600%,* while today a brand new Cadillac, Chevy, Mustang, or sports car is worth 30% less as soon as it is driven off the lot brand new!

The point is clear. Now that you are involved in the *right* kind of cars, you are involved in a major business transaction when you go to sell that car. In this chapter we will help you sell that car *smart, strategically, and thereby helping you get the biggest return on your sweet investment.*

Using the tips in this chapter you'll get lots of calls when you put your car on the market. Let's start with some of those calls which you might not be prepared for -- callers who try to get you to sell your car on *their terms.*

The "Would You Take My Huzwatzit In Trade For Your Car? " Offer

First of all, a "Huzwatzit" is anything under the sun that people think is worth something, and they won't hesitate to try to get you to take it in exchange for your car. It may be another car, or it may be a boat. It may be a truck, van or RV. It may be their big screen TV, their VCR, or maybe their mother-in-law. It may be worth quite a bit, or it may be a piece of junk.

Regardless of what they offer you, remember this: They are asking you to take something as a substitute for *cold, hard, cash.* And their Huzwatzit may or may not be worth money to you. But the point is that you need to be prepared for those "trade ya" offers.

The first thing, therefore, that you want to ask yourself is: "Am I interested in receiving cash, so that I can either cash-out of my car, or upgrade?" If you need the money, then you should make up your mind before you put the car on the market, that you *won't consider any trade offers, no matter how tempting.*

If the person making the trade offer says, "Hey, this is a good deal! After all, my Huzwatzit is worth at least $10,000!" Fine. If it is, let him convert the Huzwatzit into ten grand and turn the ten grand over to you -- in cash! If you accept the trade, you have added a new headache to your head -- having to put out all the time, money and effort trying to sell the thing. Is it worth it? Probably not.

If you want the cash and are determined not to get into any trade offers, do this: At the bottom of your ads or signs state flat out,

"No Trades," or "Cash Only." You'll cut out a lot of nuisance calls that only eat up your time. And when some persistent souls don't take the hint, or can't read English, just say politely, "That's a nice offer, but as I said in the ad, I'm not interested in trades, I prefer cash."

If you write this statement down somewhere, it will really help:

You take control, or someone will control you!

Made-In-The-Shade Trades:
The Smart Way To Win At This Game

If you are open to trades instead of cash, or trades plus cash, the most important thing is to *know exactly what you will accept in trade, and what you will not.* Let's say you and the family have been thinking about "someday" owning a motor home. You know some friends who have been doing it for years, love it, and save a fortune in motel bills they don't have to pay. So, you will consider a trade for a motor home.

This means that the only item you'll consider as a trade is a motor home. You are not interested, and will not consider, a boat, motorcycle, dune buggy, van, truck, or Huzwatzit. A motor home, period.

When callers call and offer everything or anything else, you simply say, "Thank you for calling, and that's a nice offer, but I'm looking for a motor home, and if you don't have that, I would prefer cash." And don't let them go on and on about their Huzwatzit. Repeat your "Thanks, but no thanks" decision and say goodbye.

Let's suppose that someone does call and just happens to be offering you a trade deal involving a motor home just the right size for your family. What should you do?

You have to do your research. Look through the newspaper to see what comparable motor homes are going for. Check out the RV magazines to compare features and prices. Call people in the classified ads selling similar vehicles and see what they are selling for. Go to dealers and see what similar models are going for on the lot.

Then, if you like the offer and the deal looks good, find out what mechanical shape it's in. Take it to a friend who knows such things, or to a trusted local mechanic. Or take it to a dealer and have them check it out for you to be sure it's working good and no big repairs are just on the horizon. You don't want someone unloading his lemon on you!

Then, consider the add-ons. How much will you have to pay for licensing, tax, registration, etc., etc., etc. Add this to the trade offer so you can then determine how much additional cash the buyer will have to come up with. This homework is your protection. The buyer is not likely to spell all this out for you, so *be careful, go slow, don't get emotionally involved in the offer, and do your homework!*

Remember, don't get involved in trades to have to turn around and re-sell what you accept in trades unless you have all kinds of time to push the thing to sell it, or unless it's a real "steal" and the thing is obviously worth a heck of a lot more than the naive person offering it to you knows it's worth. Otherwise, *get cash.*

Five Key Ways To Determine
The Best Asking Price For Your Car

Okay, now you know how you are going to handle people who will try to give you what they want, and not necessarily what you want. You now want to set a price for your car that is (1) realistic, (2) in line with other cars of its class and condition, and (3) comparable to the going price of similar vehicles for sale in your particular community, neck of the woods, or part of the country.

You can't base this price on the price you paid for the car. When you purchased it you may have been influenced by many factors, and the person who sold it to you may or may not have priced the car at a smart price. Plus, time has passed since your purchase of the car, and, as you know all too well, time changes value. So you cannot rely on the original price paid.

You also cannot follow your feelings or emotional issues about the car to set the price. You may be so carried away with this particular model and year car, but that doesn't mean other people will see it that way. If you use raw emotion as your guide, you will probably overprice the car and you'll have it on the market for a long time. Then you'll have to go through the discouragement of bringing the price down little by little, giving people who know about the car the edge when it comes to negotiating your price down.

Here are the 5 best ways to set a price for your car that will get the car sold at a price that puts the most money in your pocket.

1. CLASSIFIED ADS: This is the first place most people list their cars for sale, and one of the first places prospective buyers look to find the right car. If your city has more than one large daily paper, get a copy of each one. Go through the appropriate section and circle all cars that are the same make, model and year as yours. Circle cars that are close in type and year, even though they are not exactly like yours. This will enable you to do some comparing and contrasting, to get a good idea of the going price. You'll get some extremes, but for the most part, you'll find some consensus or agreement on the accepted value of your particular car and its features. This method will give you a feel for the upper and lower price limits.

2. AUTO TRADER MAGAZINES: You'll find these in most liquor stores and convenience stores. Many of them have pictures along with descriptive copy under the photo. These papers are very

popular places to list cars because they reach the serious car buyers, and because the ads are relatively inexpensive (sometimes even free). Take careful notes, as you did using the classified ads. Compare prices and look for patterns in what people ask for their cars. Again, you'll need to weed out the extremes and come up with an average going price. If you find a car that looks a lot like yours, go ahead and call the seller and get some idea of how he/she determined their price. Ask a lot of questions — and listen.

3. CAR SHOWS AND CRUISES: Here's a great source of first-hand free information. You'll find cars similar to your own at shows and cruise-nites. Talk to the owners of cars that have "For Sale" signs on them. See how they are determining the price and what equipment they have. Also, talk to people who have cars like yours that are not for sale. Ask their opinion. For example, you might say something like this, "Nice car you've got. It's a lot like mine. I'm in the process of selling mine, and I'm curious if you're selling yours (or if you were thinking of selling yours) what kind of price range would you be using, so I can get an idea?" You'll get a lot of good input this way. Even if his car does not have all the equipment yours has, it will give you a good base of comparison to determine a fair price from. On the other hand, if his car has a lot more stuff on it than yours does, that will help you get a feel for what you can realistically expect to get for yours.

4. CAR SWAP MEETS: People who display their cars at auto swap meets have done their homework. They want to sell their car, the same way you do, and they are serious about it. Many times, they have had their car offered for sale at many such swap meets and shows, in the classifieds, and in the auto traders. They've been down this road a lot longer than you have with their car, and so they've found out what price doesn't work. This is good info for your cause. So you check out all cars similar to yours and see (1) what price they are asking, (2) what equipment does the car have on

it that makes it similar or different from yours, and (3) how long has the seller had it on the market at this price? And don't forget to pick up those important little touches that he or she is using to display the car. You want to make yours look as sharp as possible when you put it up for sale. Pick up ideas. They'll come in handy! And pick up flyers that people hand out on cars for sale. This is a good way to borrow some good ideas for your own flyer.

5. CAR CLUB EXPERTISE: If you're a member of a car club, you've got a wealth of good advice right at your elbow. If you're not a member, do some asking around and find a club that knows your car better than anyone else. After all, that's why they exist, right? Tell them all about your car and ask what price they would suggest. People love giving their opinions, so don't be afraid to ask. You'll find a good list of car clubs nationwide at the end of the book. You can contact them for help. Great people!

This gives you plenty of good ideas on how to set a price to give you the maximum profit, and hopefully to help you sell it as fast as possible. Now let's talk about how to make people aware that your car exists and that it's for sale, and how to get them excited about buying *your* car.

Using The Shotgun Technique To Bring
The Serious Buyers Out of Hiding

The "Shotgun Marketing Technique" for selling your car simply means that you shoot out the message that your car is for sale in as many different directions as possible. You don't just rely on one method, like the classifieds. Many would-be car sellers make the mistake of running one ad, in the same paper, over and over again. They spend a fortune for the ads and get little or no results. Like fishing, the more lines and the more different kinds of bait you have in the water, the better your chances are of having fish for dinner.

There may be someone out there who has been looking for a car just like yours for weeks or months, but doesn't even read the paper you are advertising in. In fact, he may not read any newspaper! So, how do you reach him?

You reach those potential buyers by advertising your car in all directions. Yes, the classifieds are fine, but you don't stop there.

Let's list the best places to market your car to get the best possible exposure, and sell your car *fast.*

How To Save A Bundle Writing
Classified Ads In Newspapers*

People read them. Especially the larger daily papers. But these ads tend to cost you a bundle. So when you write the ad, go over it and use the "bacon principle" on the ad before you call it in. Like bacon, the more you cook it down to its basics, the better it is. You have to cut out all the "fat" from your ad so you don't end up paying for words you don't need (remember, you pay by the word, so every word you can cut out without ruining the message, saves you money!).

Let's take an example of an actual ad. Look at the first rough draft of the ad, and then look at the same ad after we applied the "bacon principle" on it to boil it down to its basics.

Rough Draft

This ad has all the info, but it'll cost you a bundle:

> 1964 Chevy Corvette Stingray, new paint job, red, black interior, original, great condition, $18,500 or best offer. Please call 876-5432 after 6 o'clock p.m.

---

* Be sure to review "How To Avoid Getting Lemon-ized" on page 54 so you don't make the same mistakes!

Money-Saving Boiled Down Version
64 Stingray, FAST! Nu red paint
Rare & Original. $18,500 OBO. 876-5432.

You'll pay a whole lot less, and probably get more calls with this punchy version that's 7 words shorter, and seventy-seven times more effective!

**How To Write Ads That Save You
Money & Sell Your Car Faster**

Someone once said, "To catch a mouse, you've gotta make a noise like a cheese." That says a lot. Advertising is like that. To get the attention of prospective buyers -- serious buyers with the money to buy -- you need to know how to make the right kind of "noise" to get them to pick up their phone to call you.

There's a lot of advertising that makes all kinds of noise, but doesn't do much to stir up the interest and desire of the prospective buyer. It simply, and boringly, announces a car for sale. Take a look at the list of cars for sale in any classified or auto trader paper. Dozens and dozens. All those ads trying to flag down that potential buyer. Pretty stiff competition, right?

So, to make your ad stand out among all the others, and to get someone to call *you* and not someone else, you need to do some strategic thinking about writing those ads.

Here are a few guidelines to help you make your ad pull in more buyers, and more ideas to help you save money at the same time on the cost of those ads.

**How To Use Emotional *"Trigger Words "*
To Sell Your Car Faster**

Sometimes it pays to add special words to your ad, even if it costs a little more. For example:

What's the difference between these two descriptions?

Ad #1   "66 Mustang convertible with V8 in good condition, $8,000, OBO, call 987-6543

Ad #2   Classic '66 Mustang, hot, cherry red, white powertop, 302, turns heads! 987-6543

Big difference between these two ads, isn't there? They are advertising the same car, so what makes #2 pull *ten times* the number of inquiries as #1? *Trigger words* .

Ad #2 uses words that arouse the emotions and desires in the reader, and trigger positive pictures in their minds. Works like *"classic ... hot ... cherry red ... powertop ... 302 ... and turns heads."* Ad #1 is about as boring as mashed potatoes with no salt! Ad #2 has some real zing and appeal to it, doesn't it? Which one would you respond to if you were in the market for a classic Mustang?

We took a recent issue of the *L.A.Times* Classified section and circled those ads that really hooked the reader's attention the best using emotional trigger words. Here is a list of some of those words. See if you can use them in writing your own ad -- if you do, you'll get more calls and sell your car faster:

needs nothing	collector's choice
must sell	must see
1st place winner	like nu
boss	mint cond

beautiful!	beautiful & strong
1 owner like nu,	1 owner
runs great	HOT DEAL!
very rare!	Like nu in & out!
moving, must sell	nu red paint
xlnt	rare & all original
everything nu!	nu interior, nice car!
mint orig	Classic!
Persian red leather	porthole, awesome!
FAST!	classic beauty
looks & runs great!	it's hot

A Way To Save Money With Classifieds

Most newspaper classifieds will charge you either by the word or by the line. Either way you pay more for every word you use to describe your car. So the trick is, make the ad as tight and short as you can and still get the point across. Like the old saying goes, make it like a good-looking skirt on a classy lady — long enough to cover the subject, short enough to be interesting.

You need to tell enough about your car to hook the attention and interest of the prospective buyer, but you don't want to use excess-baggage- words in doing it.

Sometimes the people who take your order for the classified ads are helpful in showing you how to shorten your ad down to its basics, using nifty abbreviations that save a lot of space in the ad, and in the process save you a lot of dough. But be careful! The ad-taker may be good at shortcuts, but in most cases, they are not savvy when it comes to using trigger words or other descriptions that arouse a buyer's appetite for your car.

For example, it's a wise move to say "nu" instead of "new,"

"xlnt" instead of "excellent," "nu pnt" instead of "new paint job," "orig cond" instead of "original condition." Using these shortcuts gets your point across fast. But they don't lose the meaning, and *they save you a bundle!* After writing your ads, go through them and see how many words you can abbreviate without causing confusion.

However, here's some bad advice you should ignore that many classified order-takers recommend: "Runs good" instead of "FAST!" "$7,500 obo" instead of "HOT DEAL!" "$12,000 obo" instead of $12,000 must sell." "'66 Mustang" instead of "'66 Mustang classic beauty!" "'53 Chevy, 4 dr" instead of "'53 Chevy, very rare!"

You get the point. Sure, it would save you money at times to cut your ad to the bare bones. But those trigger words are an absolute must! They are like a bright feathered lure with a noisy and shimmering bauble bouncing and rattling slowly along the top of the water. All that fancy stuff will attract more fish than a bare fish hook. *Trigger words attract big fish!*

It makes sense to try your best to cut the ad down to the smallest size that will send the message correctly. Do it. But don't let anybody tell you to cut out the trigger words. They are worth their length in gold!

Another Trick That Will Get You More Calls On Your Car

Look through those classifieds. Notice that some of them have special symbols just in front of the first word, or bookending the top line of the ad. They are called *bullets*. They may be stars, large dots, big checkmarks, or some other symbol. You pay extra for these. Do they work? As a gambler would say, "You bet!" The trick is to pick the one that is the *BOLDEST AND DARKEST*. Many people are what is called "lazy readers." They want to get in fast and get out fast. They are not patient enough to work their way through all those ads. So they take the easiest route to finding a car. They skip all the "routine-looking" ads and zero in first on the ones with the big symbols. Use them to stop the reader at *your* ad; like neon signs saying, "Pull in here!"

A Little Tip That Will Give Your Ad A Big Edge

If you don't want to go all out and pay for those stars, check marks, and other symbols, try this. You can have them put the first few words in BOLD PRINT, ALL CAPITAL LETTERS. This usually costs less than those symbols, but still hooks the reader's eye fast.

You can also have other words in the body of the ad set in BOLD CAPS. It costs you more, but it can pay off by increasing the reader's desire to see your car. For example, look at the '66 Mustang ad again. We put a couple of the most important trigger words in bold to jump out at the prospective buyer as he or she skims over the column of ads:

CLASSIC '66 Mustang, HOT, cherry red, white powertop,
302, TURNS HEADS: 987-6543

What happens many times is that as someone is skimming through all the columns of ads looking for the right heading, their eye is caught or hooked by those bold trigger words. Your ad has an immediate edge over all the other cars lined up there screaming, "Please buy me !!!"

So if you have to spend a little extra on the bold type, go for it. Remember, you are not spending extra money for bold ink: you are spending extra money for results -- for more rings on your telephone, more messages on your answering machine saying, "Hi, I'm calling about your car," and for more money in your pocket!

A Great Source of Free Local Advertising

A lot of people pause in the midst of their day's activities to read the messages on bulletin boards. You'll find them at supermarkets, car washes, laundromats, yacht clubs, country clubs, health clubs, and even at the employee coffee room at work. And there are dozens of them at local colleges and universities.

The great thing about these bulletin boards is that they are FREE! You can't beat the price. You also reach lots of people.

They are not as powerful in drawing the serious car lovers to ring your phone because the only people reading classified ads are people who already have some interest in cars. But since the bulletin board price is right, if you only get one hot buyer in a week, fine. After all, you only need *one person* to turn your car into cash!

Take a 3 x 5 index card to write your ad. Don't use ho-hum white like everybody else. Get yellow or pink or blue cards. Then print your ad in dark, felt-tip pen. Print, don't write. Underline those trigger words and make them BOLD. Use the same tips we gave you for writing classified ads. But try not to use too many abbreviations. Say "new" and not "nu." Say "power steering" and not "PS." But most of all, use those emotional hooks, the trigger words — link pleasure to the purchase!

Then make up a good-sized stack of cards and hit all the places in town where you find bulletin boards. If you're too busy to do it yourself, hire a few of the neighborhood kids to do it for you. Give them some Scotch tape, thumb tacks, and push pins and send them out on their mission!

A Simple Way To Let Your Car
Advertise and Sell Itself

When people see your car they look twice -- maybe even three times. There's something about classics, rods, customs, and antique cars that captivate people's imagination and kindle memories of those good old days.

Since one of the most important principals in good advertising is to capture the attention of the person you are trying to persuade to buy your car. It's no problem for what you are trying to sell. The car does it all for you. All you have to do is let people know that this car could be parked in *their* garage .

Make a small sign to place in your car's window. A straightforward message: "FOR SALE -- 987-6543." You don't want to make the sign too big or gaudy, because that would detract from the image of the car.

An even better way to let your car advertise itself is to hire a good graphics artist to paint the sign on your window. You can use a color to match the paint job on your car, its trim, its pinstriping, or even the interior colors. Just be sure that it's bright and grabs people's attention .

You can find a good graphics artist to do a class job on your sign at a good car show. Also, talk to people at cruise-nites and car swap meets. They'll know who to direct you to. At swap meets you'll see many people selling their car who have good signs painted on their windows. Talk to them.

Some people who want to sell their car do not want their sign to take away from the special look of the car. They have an easy-to-read sign printed up and lay it on the seat of their car during shows and cruise-nites. Subtle, laidback selling, but effective. Anyone really interested in your car will spot that sign. This approach can also give you a slight edge in the selling and price-negotiation process, since you come off as not too hungry or eager to sell, since your sign is small and a class act. Try it.

Using Word-of-Mouth Advertising
To Sell Your Car Fast

There's another way to get the word out that your car is for sale that will cost you nothing. It's word-of-mouth advertising.

It's the simplest form of marketing. You tell people your car is on the market, and they tell someone else, and they tell someone else. One of the people in the message chain may be the one with the cash, just itchin' to buy your car.

In addition to using all the other forms of selling your car mentioned so far, you should make it a habit (without being obnoxious) to tell people about your car. At cruise-nites, at car shows, at gas stations, at parking lots, out in your driveway while washing the car, at stoplights when people admire your car, at conventions, at car clubs, anywhere you meet people.

Start telling people about the car even before it's on the market. Say something like, "I'm thinking of possibly putting it on the market in the near future," or "If you're interested in the car you might want to give me your phone number, because I'm thinking about possibly selling it in the near future." If it's already for sale, just tell people you meet at car events or anywhere, "If you know of anyone looking for a so-and-so car, I've just put mine on the market, it's in great shape and it's hot. Have them get in touch with me if they'd like to see it ."

Car people are helpful people. They will pass the word for you and will thank you for doing the same when they put their own car up for sale. You won't find a greater bunch of people in any kind of sport or leisure time activity anywhere topside of Mother Earth!

and will thank you for doing the same when they put their own car up for sale. You won't find a greater bunch of people in any kind of sport or leisure time activity anywhere topside of Mother Earth!

A Powerful Way To Reach The Real Car Buff

Some of the major car magazines have classified sections where they list cars for sale. These ads are not free, but they are worth paying for. Why? Because they get results!

The thing that makes them worth so much is this. Who is reading the magazine in the first place? Not your typical man or woman on the street who doesn't know a rod from a roller skate. Oh no. The person reading a car magazine has spent a few hard-earned bucks of his or her money to get hold of this magazine. And even if they are borrowing the magazine from a friend or from the library, just the mere fact that they are reading it shows that they demonstrate a well-above-average enthusiasm for special cars. They're hot prospects.

What this does for you is bring in calls from people who mean business about cars. They are serious when it comes to quality cars. Your chances of getting a good prospective buyer by advertising in car magazines are much improved over other types of ads. So go ahead and spend the money on the ads in these specialty magazines. They're worth it.

You'll find a directory of some of the best magazines at the end of this book with complete information about how to contact them.

FROM FAME TO FORTUNE:
How To Give Your Car A Reputation
That Will Increase The Selling Price

Try this little trick and add hundreds or even thousands of dollars for what you get for your car!

magazines and get ideas. What makes the magazine editors choose to feature some cars over others? What features do they highlight in the photos? What special touches do they describe in articles? Take notes!

Then do things that will make your car stand out and grab the ooo"s and ahhh's and attract the crowds.

Then find out who the magazine reporters are and tell him that his or her readers might be interested in your car. If they like it and spotlight it in the magazine -- pictures and all -- you've got a great selling tool . Or call people featured in articles and ask their advice.

Winning trophies at car shows can also help. Your car's fame can lead to your good fortune!

How To Sell Your Car in "Throw-Away" Free Shopper Papers

Most neighborhoods have one or more of these multiple listing, no categories shopper papers. They have item after item all listed together so that the reader has to plow through everything to find what he or she is looking for.

The benefit of this kind of classified paper (usually a free-bee) is that even if you don't catch the eye of the car buff personally, someone who knows about their love of cars might say, "Hey, did you see that classic car in the Pennysaver?" (or whatever the paper is called where you are), "It looks like a great deal."

These ads aren't cheap, but they do reach thousands and thousands of homes and a lot of people read them. And remember to use those trigger words when you write the ads!

How To Successfully Sell Your Car
At Swap Meets: Step-By-Step Guidelines

People who visit a car swap meet are ripe to buy. They tend to be people who have done a lot of thinking about the car they want, and have spent hours fantasizing about owning the right car. Yours may be just the car they are looking for.

There's plenty of competition for the buyers attention and his car-buying dollar at these swap meets. So, you will have to do all you possibly can to make your car get both the attention and the dollars. Here are step-by-step guidelines that will help you do both:

Step 1: Carefully review the chapter on *How To Show and Shine.* Everything that you'll learn in that chapter about how to help make the best impression at shows and cruises will help your car stand out from the herd at swap meets as well.

Step 2 : Make sure that everything about your car is neat and clean in appearance.

Step 3 : People love the sight of seeing their own faces. Let them see the reflection of themselves in your car. Put the best wax job you can on your car just before the swap meet. Or have it professionally detailed. Polish it real good just before the meet with an old, well-washed diaper, and periodically during the day of the meet. And use a glass polish to get the best shine on the windows.

Step 4 : Make the interior look sharp. ArmorAll the interior to make it look its best. Do the dash, seats, side panels, and even the floor mats. And appeal to the sense of smell with a vanilla scenter.

Step 5 : Don't forget the *tires!* Who cares about the tires?! Most people don't know that they notice tires, but they do. Your tires can add to the overall neat appearance of the car, or they can hurt it. After you get the inside and body of the car sparkling and nifty-neat, check out the tires. Get all the mud or dust or dirt off of them. Then ArmorAll them real good. After all, you don't want to go to a party with dirty-dog shoes!

Step 6 :   If you've got good-looking chrome, show it off. If your engine gleams with chrome, open the hood. The rule of thumb is this: Show off all good things about the car. That chrome might help put someone over the edge when it comes to deciding between buying your car and someone else's that has all the goodies yours does, but it doesn't have the chrome. If it gives your car even the slightest edge in terms of looking good, show it off!

Step 7 :   If you've got a classy car to sell, make sure your "FOR SALE" sign is just as classy. Have you ever seen a real hot-looking, outrageous car with a crummy, beat-up, old and faded "FOR SALE" sign taped to the window with masking tape? Not cool! Pathetic. Or a cheap sign someone put together with the phone number scrawled across it in pencil? Not cool! Dumb.

Not only is it uncool, but it will make your car, *and you*, look like you just got off the boat and have no class at all. Your sign, like everything else visible to the eye of the potential buyer, should be first rate, and a class act all the way.

The best method is to hire a pinstriper or a graphic artist at a paint shop and have your sign painted on the side windows or the lower right corner of the windshield. Use a color to coordinate with some color on the car, either inside or outside. This should cost about $20 per window. The big money cars do this, why not do it on any car you're selling if it's really special? Incidentally, on one car we sold, the sign we had painted on the window was so nice a guy took a picture of *the sign!*

Or you can use a clean, neat sign of any type that looks new, no bent corners, the color is not faded out, and everything written on the sign is printed carefully and is easy to read.

The sign should give the basics, such as:

FOR SALE
PHONE #(321) 987-6543
$12,500 (obo)   No Trades

Be sure to put your area code with your phone number. Also, if you don't want trades, save yourself a lot of hassle with those "Hey, I'll trade you my mother-in-law for your car, what-a-ya say?" calls. If you don't want all those trade proposals, say so, "No Trades."

Practical Tips On Getting *Your* Price

Put the price clearly on the sign with "obo" under it -- "or best offer." Does putting the "obo" mean that you probably will not get your asking price? Yes, but it also will help some people who are reluctant to talk to you and make them feel more comfortable approaching you with an honest offer you might not want to pass up. So it's best to use it, unless your price is at rock-bottom, that is.

Let's say you don't want to put a price on the car, but want to feel out what the market will pull. Instead of a money figure, put "Best Offer." Then see what people think.

When you use the "Best Offer" approach someone will come up to you and say, "How much do you want for it?" You then say, "Make me an offer, because what I'm going to do, fella, is at the end of the day I'm going to take all the offers and the one at the end of the day with the highest offer, that's the one I'm going to call back." Using these words may motivate the potential serious buyer to give you a better and bigger offer.

But let's say someone comes up to you and makes you such a

good offer that it's pretty close to what you want to get for the car. Then you can say, "Tell you what, that's probably one of the best offers I've had right now on the car, so if you're really interested, why don't you give me a deposit now on the spot." If he's serious, he'll give you the deposit so he won't risk losing the car. If he won't give you the money, he's blowing smoke ... keep looking for the right buyer.

Have some neat, attractive flyers printed of your car. Show a picture of the car that shows off its best features. Give the list of all the goodies and features, and be sure to use those trigger words! Put the price, "obo," or "Best Offer" on it, and give your phone number. Sometimes it helps to give a person's name to ask for when they call. This makes some people feel more comfortable calling when they have a name to use -- "Just ask for Dave."

The Smart Way To Talk Price
& Get The Price You Want

There's more to getting the money you want for your car than simply putting a price tag on the car and someone handing you the cash . Remember, the person interested in owning your car wants to pay *the least possible amount he can get away with.* On the other hand, you, the seller, want him to own the car, too, but *at the greatest possible amount you can get him to fork over.* But you can't have it both ways. Someone, either you or him, will end up getting the edge in the deal.

We want it to be *you*, of course, unless you are the buyer. But we have already covered that in an earlier chapter.

The person who knows how to smoothly and confidently talk price will win at this game. Here are some tips that should help give you that edge you need.

Remember this rule of negotiating:

YOU SET THE LIMITS FIRST — OR
THE BUYER WILL SET THEM FOR YOU !

Before you even say one word about price, you must have fixed in your head three things :

1. What you want to get for the car.
2. What you feel is fair to get for the car.
3. The range of reasonable offers in between.

Remember those three key points!

If you have these figures nailed down beforehand, you will be able to quickly spot offers that are worth bothering with, and those you don't want to waste time with. If you don't have clearly set in your mind what you want, what's fair, and the range in between, then the would-be buyer can get the advantage over you -- especially if he's savvy at getting the price down in the weeds to where he wants it. If he senses that you already have the price range firmly fixed in mind, he will be more likely to stay within *your* price range, and you will not be led down the garden path. You get the best end of the deal when *you set the limits in advance.*

Let's say you have a sign on the window of your car at a swap meet that says, " FOR SALE -- $18,900." It's unlikely someone will walk up to you and say, "Sold, here you go, here's $18,900 cash." What's more apt to happen is this. Let's say a guy walks up and says, "How much cash do you want for that car, what do you need to get for it?" Your response should be, "I've got some offers ... are you interested in making one yourself?" You already know (1) you want to get $18,900 for the car, and (2) that a reasonably fair price is

$17,000, and (3) that you will seriously consider any valid offers in the middle.

So he comes back and says, "I'll tell you what, I'll give you $17,500 for the car." But don't be too hasty to take that money just yet . Get a deposit from him, and if his offer ends up the best offer, it's sold.

And be careful of the slick low-ball question that a lot of experienced car buyers will try to use on you. They "innocently" ask you, "I'm interested in buying your car; what's the least amount you'll take?" See the hook? He's trying to find out your bottom line so he doesn't have to spend one penny over it. Notice in the example we just gave, your bottom line was $17,000 and you ended up getting $17,500. You wouldn't have received that extra $500 if you had answered his "What's the least amount you'll take" question, would you? So *don't answer that question!*

What should you answer instead? Simply say this when he asks what's the least amount of money you'll take for the car:

"How much is the car worth to you? Make me an offer." If he continues to stall and keeps pressing you for your lowest acceptable figure, just do the broken record routine on him and say, "I'm open to all good offers -- what's the car worth to you?" Don't let him move you off of this tactic and, guess what? YOU WIN! This one little tip could put hundreds of dollars in your pocket that you would not have gotten otherwise. Aren't you glad you got hold of this book!?

The One Sure Way To Know
If A Buyer is Serious

The old expression is " earnest money." We call it "a deposit" in today's lingo. The old term is a good one because it meant that if a person is earnest or sincere about going through with the deal, and not just blowing smoke, he'll put his money where his mouth is.

When you're selling a car, you are dealing in one thing, and one thing only -- *business.* You don't care about personalities. You don't care about how professional or well dressed a person looks. All you should be interested in is, does this person have the money to buy my car, and is he or she genuinely interested in completing the deal, or just window shopping or playing games and wasting my time? They can shop and play games somewhere else. What you want is to close this deal.

So if someone makes you an offer and says that they really want to buy your car, don't believe it until you see the color of their $$$ - earnest deposit money.

Make it $100, $200, $500 or whatever amount you want. Tell him that you are willing to take the car off the market if he gives you a deposit. And a good rule to follow is that you will only give someone a ride in the car if they first put down a deposit. No one drives it without putting down that deposit. Because if you don't do this, you'll spend all your time giving free joy rides to a lot of people and you still have the car, not the cash.

When you are giving someone a ride, letting them drive the car, or take it off the market for a potential buyer, you may be passing up a true buyer who just passed by and didn't see your car. Ouch!

So don't try to be popular, or make everybody happy, or be a nice guy. You are involved in a serious business transaction here. And if they are serious about the business of giving you the full price agreed on, they shouldn't hesitate to give you a good deposit. Ask for it!

How To Answer the Question:
"How Did You Determine The Price
You're Asking For This Car? "

Some shrewd buyers will use this little trick to make you uneasy about the price you're asking and will try to get you softened up or rattled so they can get the price down to what they want to pay. If you're not careful you'll let them shake your confidence, you'll lower the price, and you'll end up losing a lot of money, and they'll end up laughing all the way to the bank!

So, whenever someone asks you, "How do you figure this car is worth this much?" Your response is simple and direct. You say:

"That's what I believe the car is worth to me."

It's that simple, and you owe them no other explanation. If they try to get you to justify the price, or compare your car to others, say, "That may be so, but this is what it's worth to me." And don't move from that answer. You win again!

How To Get Twice Or Even Three Times
What Your Car Is Worth Using
The "Trolling for Big Fish Method"

The best way to sell your car, if you really want to sell it, is to price it in a reasonable range of what similar cars are going for. However, if your heart is really not into letting it go because you're in love with the thing, you might want to try this little experiment that some artists have used for years -- and gotten rich doing it! They somehow grow attached to a painting they have done and really don't want to sell it. But since people keep asking if it's for sale, they put an outrageous price tag on it, knowing full well that it's not worth a fraction of that price.

Guess what happens? Some art-lover comes along, loves the painting, and after they get over the shock of the price tag, they start talking to themselves -- "Hmmm, this must be a special, really rare and one-of-a-kind work of art going for a price like this ... I could tell people how much it's worth and I am the proud owner." The ego is hooked and the sale is made.

Why not try the same thing with your car? You might be pleasantly surprised! Why ask why? ... Jack the price up high!

Let us give you one example. There's a guy in our area who has a really nice '60 Lincoln convertible, it's been in all the magazines, gotten loads of publicity, and it's probably worth about $35,000 right now. Does he have a $35,000 price tag on it? No way. If somebody wants to park that baby in his garage, it will set them back $60,000! Sure, a lot of people walk by and laugh when they see a price like that.   But just suppose a retired millionaire cruises by, sees it, it's love at first sight, and he just has to have it to impress his friends. What's sixty grand to him? Peanuts. Sold for $60,000! Our friend ends up with $35,000 that the car is worth, and an additional $25,000 for a room addition, or enough for two new nifty "toys" to play with at car shows. The extra $25,000 will help him get over the loss of his Lincoln, don't you think?

Now this strategy won't work for all cars. In fact, it probably works only for those high priced babies in the $25,000 range or higher. If you've got one of those cars and like gambling, try it. We're not recommending this for everyone, but for some risk- takers, it's a lot of fun!

How To Spot The Phony-Baloney
Idea-Collector vs. The Serious Buyer

Many times you will meet what seems to be an interested buyer, but when they get through with you, they have picked your brains, collected all kinds of good information, you have spent a lot of valuable time answering their questions, and they go off with loads of tips, and you end up with zip. These are the idea-collectors.

They approach you as if they are in the market for a car just like yours. In reality they already own a car just like yours, or very similar. But since your car is sharp and looking good, they decide to *use you* as an easy shortcut for getting their car in shape, giving it the edge.

Hey, there's nothing wrong with sharing tips and ideas with people who are into cars. We do it all the time. Telling them where you got your paint job done, who did the upholstery, what shop did the chrome work. That's great. But you don't want to be spending so much time with these idea-collectors and miss talking turkey with a real buyer.

So give him a few helpful hints, and then politely back away and wait for the real thing to come along. The real buyer will be interested in how hot your car looks, not where you got it done .

The Attitude That Works Best To Win Over The Buyer

The real key in selling your car is this: *Don't act like a car salesman!* You know the type -- they hover over the buyer, follow him around. Point out this and that feature. They try to talk up every single aspect of the car. Talk, talk, talk.

How do you feel when those salesmen pressure you like that? It makes you uncomfortable and you just want to get out of there, right? Sure it does, so don't do it to people looking at your car. They have eyes and can see what makes your car hot. Let them ask you questions if they have any. They will.

The best approach is to act a little independent. Get away from the car. Sit in your lawn chair or stand back a little distance from the car and wait until they approach you with comments or questions. You'll put them at ease when you do this, and a buyer at ease and comfortable is more likely to get emotionally into the car faster. And that means he or she is more likely to get their money out faster, too!

How To Answer The Question:
"Why Are You Coming Down On Your Price?"

Let's say you priced your car a bit too high and it's not selling, or you tried the Trolling for Big Fish Method and got no bites, but are ready to sell it and you need the cash. Some people who have seen it on the market for a while will notice that you are bringing the price way down all of a sudden. Some people may ask, "Why are you dropping the price so much ... is there something wrong with the car? We had this exact thing happen to a car we sold a few years ago. Here's how we answered them:

> "Well, we just had some kids get married, and we
> have some things we wanted to invest in."

Another response you might use could be this:

> "We've decided to come down on the price a little bit because
> the car has had a lot of exposure, we've had a good time with
> it, and we just want to pass that along to somebody else."

That's honest, basic, and straight.

Another good approach is to encourage them to talk to other people about your car. Just say something like, "You know what, most of the people here know my car, just walk up to anyone around here and say, 'do you know anything about that black Model A over there?' And listen to what they tell you." If you've got enough confidence to encourage them to do that, you will quickly build their trust that the car is worth what you're asking for it.

Use The Display Board To Grab
The Attention of the Serious Buyer

This is a large piece of white cardboard set on a three-legged easel that lists all the important selling features on your car. Using neat, bold lettering you outline everything about your car that makes it special in list form. Set the easel near the right front fender or grille. You can get real fancy, showing pictures of the car being built, along with the list of neat stuff, or just list the neat stuff without the pictures.

The important thing is that it can hook the attention and build the interest of a buyer who may have missed one or more of those important items. If your car can stimulate the interest and build the desire of a buyer, and get him excited just a tad more than a similar car at the same swap meet — you get the money. The display board just might help give you that slight edge. Try it.

The Thrill Of The Sell!

We bought our first '58 Impala for $1,800 and sold it for $3,000.

We paid $2,500 for our '57 Chevy Bel-Air and sold it for $13,800. Our third car was a '34 Coupe, we paid $6,800 for it, and sold it to a nice Japanese guy for $10,300. And we bought the '29 Model A for $12,000 and sold it for $19,200!

That's a lot of money on the profit side, to be sure. But even more fun is the thrill of making those sales for that kind of profit. And as we said in the beginning of this chapter: *How many sports do you know that will pay you for the fun of having fun?*

So, here's to you, and here's to both the fun and the profit of buying, showing, and selling classic, customs, rods and antique cars! You're into one of the most exciting and rewarding sports on planet earth. So enjoy — the cars, and the cash!

Chapter 8

How To Plan, Organize & Run
Your Own Car Show Or Cruise Nite

Simple, Step-By-Step Guidelines
& The Answers To All Your Questions

An Interview With Lee McCullough:
"Southern California's Top Cruise NIte Promoter"

Personal Notes & Ideas

CHAPTER EIGHT

How To Plan, Organize & Run
Your Own Car Show Or Cruise Nite

Simple, Step-by-Step Guidelines
& The Answers To All Your Questions

An Interview with Lee McCullough:
"Southern California's Top Cruise Nite Promoter"

L ee McCullough is, as far as we know, the only man in America whose full-time, 7-day-a-week, every-waking hour obsession is devoted to promoting rods, customs, classics and antique car events. He's not only involved in most of the biggest car shows and cruises in California, he's usually the brains behind their very existence — his ideas and enthusiasm draw the crowds.

In the west he's known as "Mr. Cruise Nite."

He's also affectionately known as "Mr. Harvey's Cruise-Nite" because that's where he started the well-known Harvey's Cruise-Nites at a Southern California '50s drive-in back in the mid 1980s. At that time business was slow at the diner, except on Wednesday nights. Wednesday was the night Lee put on his cruise nite at Harvey's. It started out with 42 cars and ended up going over 200 almost every week during the year. It got tremendously popular and people would come from miles around to share their cars, swap stories and do some serious "bench racing" for hours on end.

He has perfected the art of using flyers and ads to draw big crowds to all kinds of car events. Since Harvey's Cruise-Nites he has expanded his promotions activities to develop cruise-nites and car shows at numerous restaurants all over Southern California. On Tuesday, Wednesday, Thursday evenings, and every weekend, you'll find Lee greeting the people and doing crowd control at a local diner, drive-in, restaurant, fairground or some other hot spot where he's organized and promoted the car-lover's favorite sport.

In this chapter we want to ask the questions that you would ask if you could spend a few hours sitting down with Lee McCullough to pick his brains about everything you always wanted to know about putting on exciting cruise-nites. So, sit back and enjoy some nuts-&-bolts know-how you can use setting up your own cruise nite:

All About The Basics

QUESTION: Lee, what is the difference between a *cruise-nite* and a *car show?*

ANSWER: A *car show* is an event where cars are displayed for purposes of winning a trophy, an award, or a plaque. At a *cruise-nite* this is not the case; people are enjoying cars simply for the purpose of having a good time. Cruise-nites are simply for entertainment rather than for competition.

Another important difference is that cruise-nites are put on with the family in mind, rather than an emphasis on the cars of individuals (although families love car shows as well). Kids love cruise-nites, and after all, the kids are the future of the sport! Cruise-nites give the whole family something to do together, rather than everyone going their separate ways, and it's one of the few sports that is designed with the whole family in mind.

QUESTION: What does a family typically do at a cruise or cruise-nite?

ANSWER: It's a great place for the family to come together and enjoy the sights, the sounds, and meeting other cruisers. They'll go out and eat dinner and just get away from the normal pressures and problems of life. Their plumbing may be broken, but they'll go to a cruise-nite! And most people don't go to "*a* cruise- nite." They'll go to cruise-nites every month for six months straight and never miss.

QUESTION: What's the fascination about cruise-nites? Week after week and never missing for months -- people must get something special out of this sport?

ANSWER: That's absolutely right. Basically, you keep meeting new people all the time who are really special to you. My girlfriend, Jenni, and I have made a lot of super friends that are like a little family to us. We hang around together at different cruises and shows. We go to Vegas together, vacations, and a lot of different fun things that are not even car-related. But had it not been for the cruise-nites and car shows, we would never had met these people.

QUESTION: Can you say anything more about the difference between car shows and cruise-nites?

ANSWER: The cruise-nite is much more laid back. You don't feel the competitive atmosphere you sometimes feel at car shows.
Car shows are also put on to benefit certain things, like non-profit organizations and good causes, and that type of thing. Whereas cruise-nites are set up for fun and getting together. Not too long ago there was a gigantic car show put on by the California Highway Patrol for the benefit of needy families and kids in the community.   There were 1,050 cars there at this show! Tremendously successful. I worked with a few other people to help promote this show, which was called "CHIPS FOR KIDS" and put together the flyers to promote it. It was a lot of fun and raised a lot of money for the kids.

QUESTION: In a later section, I'd like to come back to fund raisers. You started at Harvey's Broiler, a '50s diner. What exactly is a "'50s diner" for those who may not remember those good old days, having Cokes and burgers at a diner?

ANSWER: A '50s diner is a place built to look as if it were right out of the 1950s. There are '40s diners, '50s diners, and '60s diners. But a '50s diner would definitely have an old jukebox in it, maybe smaller jukeboxes on the tables, a lot of neon signs, and old '50s record album covers and old 45s all over the walls. Some nicer diners even have the front end of a '57 Chevy sticking out of the wall. At one of the better places in southern California they even have the actual Gold Records from groups like Jan and Dean and other '50 rockers decorating the walls. They have the napkin holders that were popular back then on every table, the stainless steel counter tops, and the old squeeze mustard and ketchup bottles. They all use the muted 5 colors for the interior. Some have the stainless steel siding on the outside. And of course there's always good old '50s rock playing on the jukebox. The only thing that's different now is the prices!

Tips On How To Set Up Your Own Cruise-Nite

QUESTION: Now, suppose somebody wants to organize a cruise-nite to bring car buffs together to have some fun and meet people with similar interests. Suppose they don't know where to start and they have never done it before. Could you give them some step-by-step tips on how to set it up from scratch?

ANSWER: The first thing you have to do is to find a venue for it -- a restaurant that would want to get actively involved in a cruise-nite. The place has to have certain basic requirements, such as adequate outside lighting, a decent-sized parking lot big enough for 25 cars or more who could attend the cruise-nite, plus parking for the rest of their regular customers. You don't want a place where the cruise would harm the rest of their customer business.

The look of the place should be somewhat in the right style and mood of the time period. It ought to look kind of *'50's-ish*. You wouldn't want to do it at a Denny's or Burger King.

Location is a *must*. It should not be too far out in the boonies, but pretty close in to freeways. If it isn't freeway close, it should at least be close enough to a large base of people who live in the immediate area who are possible cruisers. People are going to want to come often, so you don't want them to have to drive for too long a distance to get there.

QUESTION: OK, now let's say you've found a perfect place to hold a cruise-nite. A place with good lighting, adequate parking, the whole atmosphere of the place has the '50s mood to it, and it's near a large population. What would you do to approach the owner of the restaurant to get him interested in putting on cruises at his restaurant?

ANSWER: There's one thing that the restaurant owner is interested in more than anything. That's improving his business. And that's what you tell him.

You go in and say something like this, "Hey, I'd like to do a cruise-nite for custom, classic and antique car people on Thursday nights; what's your Thursday night business like?" If his business is really busy and they have a steady clientele, he will probably not be interested. But he may very likely say, "Gee, I could sure use some more people on Thursday nights!" You've already got him interested because the bottom line for him is money. You are offering to bring in a steady, new clientele. He's doing you a favor providing a good place for people to get together, swap stories, have a meal, and enjoy themselves. But you are doing him an even bigger favor by increasing his business. Everybody wins with this deal.

QUESTION: How do you handle the financial aspects of the cruise-nite with the restaurant owner?

ANSWER: You've already sold him on the benefits to him. The next step is crunching the numbers. You spell out what you'll need, like flyers and advertising, for example.

Before you go, call and find out the name of the owner. Set up an appointment with him to talk. And don't forget this important step: Before you become a cruise-nite promoter, *become a customer!* Go sample the food and service. You don't want to be holding your cruise-nites at a place where you'll lose most of them because it's a ptomaine kitchen! You also don't want a place where prices are through the roof with $5 hamburgers and $2 cokes.

And by the way, in addition to sampling the food and the prices, be sure you check out the place *at night.* You don't want to pick a place in a gang-infested area of town. A place can have a whole different personality at night.

So go right to the owner, and don't be intimidated by the fact that they own this place and you have never done this kind of thing before. As a matter of fact, in offering to build his business you may even be bailing his business out! If his business is slow, the income generated each week from that cruise-nite may be enough to keep his doors open. At one place we did this, the business we brought in kept bringing in more business to this small diner. It got bigger and bigger and before long it turned into a really nice restaurant. From the cruise-nite income alone they updated the place, made it nicer, put in artifacts of the era, made more tables available, put up more neon signs, enlarged their parking lot, and generated customers that came in during other nights of the week. With the economy in the shape it's in, restaurant owners will love your ideas.

QUESTION: Good points. Getting back to the basics of how to handle the restaurant owner. Could you give us a sample of how your first meeting with him might sound?

ANSWER: I have made an appointment with him at the restaurant. When we sit down I tell him this: "How would you like to have an extra 30 or 40 customers each Thursday night?" He'll say, "How would you do that?" Then I'd say, "I can bring in a bunch of old cars and a great group of people and we can create a cruise-nite." Then he would likely say, "Well, what's that going to do for me?" And then you say, "Well, the people who come to the cruise-nite to enjoy old cars are not just going to congregate here; they have to eat and guess where they'll spend their money on food? Right here, and they'll be here, most of them, week after week at the cruise-nites, and at other times during the week as well."

You can suggest to the owner, also, that he offer "Cruise-Nite Specials" for those who attend. A deal like 10% off, or certain menu items on special only to the cruisers -- like a burger, fries and Coke, or a steak sandwich, or a chicken sandwich -- something different every week for the cruisers on that particular night. Other places offer free coffee or free Cokes to the cruisers.

I did this recently with one man in Walnut, California, and his cruise-nite has grown in three months from 30 cars a week to 80. And he loves to pay me for the privilege, believe me. He can't pay me quick enough every month for promoting his cruise-nites!

QUESTION: What exactly did you do for him to get such dramatic results, from 30 to 80 cars in 3 months?

ANSWER I brought in mass numbers every week. I consult with him over any problems he might be having in running the cruise-nite. I suggest to him that he gives away a trophy one night a month and see how that goes. That idea brought in 40 extra cars that week. I do his flyers for him and get them distributed to get the word out.

Then, after we got as many old-car buffs as possible interested in the cruise-nite, we did flyers for him to get as many people who don't own old cars interested. They started coming down from the nearby community and got involved -- spending their money at his restaurant as well. Without the cruise-nite being held there, these people may have never come to his place at all. So he was happy, and the people at the cruise-nite got to meet some nice, new friends.

How To Handle Money Issues

QUESTION: Let's get back to talking business with the owner. Continue the dialogue you'd have with him regarding money.

ANSWER: I just did this with a guy a week ago. I proposed that he pay me $1 per car per week for each car I bring in. He said, "Gee, it sounds like a lot of money, a dollar a car ... how can I afford it?" So I said to him, "Well, you're getting about 2 or 2 1/2 people per car on the average and they're going to spend their money in your restaurant. I'll give you the first week or two for free; I won't charge you a thing. All you have to do is let me do my thing -- I'll bring the customers in to you. And I'll do the cruise and after a couple of weeks, we'll sit down together, go over your books, and see if it makes an impact on your business. If you can see an increase in it, and can see your way to pay me, than wonderful. If not, then I'll go somewhere else."

And those are important points to remember. First, that his books will tell the story about how profitable it is for him. Secondly, the cruise you bring in is yours, not his, and if you leave, you take it with you. And put the whole deal in writing.

QUESTION: How do you determine how much to charge the restaurant owner?

ANSWER: You judge this by the prices on the menu. If it's a real high dollar place, you might charge more than a dollar a car. If the place has reasonable prices, a dollar might be just fine.

QUESTION: How do you know how many cars attend the event?

ANSWER: What I do is to give each car owner a free ticket for a drawing or raffle when they first arrive. This tells you how many cars actually showed up. It also is a good "hook" to use to get people to stick around longer at the cruise-nite. They don't want to leave early because they might win a free dinner or free gift later in the evening when the drawing is held. You hold off doing the drawing until about 8 o'clock. The D.J. you use (if you use one) will call the numbers and give away a record album or tape, a dinner for two at the restaurant, or maybe a copy of this book. We start the cruise at 6 o'clock and they stick around for at least two hours. A lot of money can be spent in his restaurant during those two hours, even if only for drinks alone. You point this out to the owner.

A free giveaway drawing or raffle is a proven thing. It draws more people and keeps them happily enjoying themselves for hours.

The 7 Rules For Running
A Successful Cruise-Nite

QUESTION: What are some of the rules for organizing and running a successful cruise-nite?

ANSWER: The rules for those who attend would include these:

1.   One of the rules I adhere to as a promoter is to always deal honestly, fairly and with the utmost integrity with everyone you meet, whether it's the restaurant owner or the cruisers themselves.

2.   I also make it my business to get to know the people who come to cruise-nites and to maintain a high visibility as the promoter.

3.   No loud radios.   You don't want someone coming with one of those boomboxes like the minitrucks have.   They make so much racket that people can't talk with each other.

4.   No burnouts.   No tire squealing because it's dangerous, it's obnoxious, and it's uncalled for.   It also upsets the neighbors.

5.   No alcohol.   *None.*   Even if the restaurant sells it, we don't allow it outside at the cruise.   If I see someone outside with a beer, I ask them either to leave or get rid of it.   This implies, of course, no drugs, either.

6. No pets.   You don't want to concern yourself about any damage being done to people's cars, and you don't want to have to watch out where you're stepping, either!

7.   No minitrucks.   Most cruises are set up for 1970 or older cars. The minitrucks came into being after this, and they are mostly owned by kids, and they have their own activities that are even more specialized for their needs.   So they would not be likely to mix well with an older, more mature crowd.

If you find people who consistently violate these rules, you politely ask them to leave when you see them at the next event, or you tell the person at the gate not to allow them in.   People will support you if you do this, and you have to enforce these rules so that everybody has a good time, and so that you don't make enemies of the people in the nearby neighborhood.

QUESTION: Now, let's say the first couple of weeks go by and the cruises are going great.   You have not charged the owner anything, he reaps the benefits of more business coming in.   Then what do you say to him?

ANSWER: Well, now you go and sit down with him and look at the books.   Ask him to tell you honestly whether he is making money, or not.   He looks at the figures and says that he has definitely brought in more money over the past two weeks.

Then I say, "OK, here's how it's going to work.   You pay me $1 per car.   We can count the cars ourselves, you and me, or someone you deem qualified to go and count the cars for you with me, so you know I'm not cheating you.   When we have the count, you give me the money and I give you a receipt that night."

You also might tell him that flyers cost money, so if he could set you up each week with money to buy 3,000 or 4,000 flyers this would really help bring more people in.   You hand out flyers at car show, car clubs, car swap meets, car races, parts stores, and other events.   And we're only talking about $100 or so for him to sponsor your flyers.   That $100 is money well spent for him, because it's good advertising for his restaurant, and it's tax deductible, too.

And since gasoline is so expensive anymore, try to find restaurants near your home where you'll promote cruise-nites.

And another thing you should ask from the owner is free dinners for yourself.   You simply tell him that since you're investing your time and effort into the thing, if you have to give him back some of your money for meals, that's not too smart on your part.   So you expect that he will give you free dinners and drinks during each cruise-nite.   They have no problem with this.

QUESTION: Regarding the promoting of the cruise-nite: Do you handle all this yourself and the owner of the restaurant has nothing to do with this end of it?

ANSWER   That's right. Number one, I want to be sure to keep control of that end of the event so that the cruise is my thing, not his. This gives you the ability to move the cruise should you have a falling out with the owner down the line.

Number two, I doubt that the owner would know how to handle the promotions end of it, other than handing out some of the flyers you make up. So, you make him depend on you to keep it going successfully.

Where *Not* To Put On A Car Event

QUESTION: What about putting on a cruise-nite at a local bar?

ANSWER: The answer to that question is this: *Alcohol and gasoline don't mix!* Ten or fifteen years ago drinking and things to do with cars were quite acceptable. But not any more. And people will tell you that they disapprove of holding the cruise-nite at the bar and they'll tell you by not showing up.

We tried it years ago at a really nice bar, but it just didn't work. It seemed to split up the family because the kids couldn't go in. People got rowdy and obnoxious. And before long people quit coming altogether.

Alcohol and gasoline don't mix!
Alcohol and car events don't mix!

Where To Set Up A Successful Car Event

QUESTION: If someone wants to set up a cruise in their area, how can they be sure there are enough car lovers in that location?

ANSWER: You've got to pass out massive numbers of flyers. The flyer is *your most important marketing tool.* Attend every car event you can and pass out flyers to everybody you meet, and in a friendly manner invite them to attend. Visit the cruise-nites that a lot of the different organizations hold each month. Give them flyers and talk to them about what and when and where. Ask people at the local body shops, paint shops, auto parts stores and so forth, ask them to take a stack of your flyers and offer them to their customers. They'll be glad to do it. You can also pin them up on bulletin boards all over town.

A 16-Step Mini-Course On Creating A Good Flyer For Your Car Event To Bring In Big Crowds

QUESTION: Obviously Lee, the flyer is your most important way of effectively reaching people to get them to come to your event. Can you give us a step-by-step mini-course on how to create a good flyer that will draw crowds?

ANSWER: The first thing to do is to make your flyer as attractive as possible. Don't use a dull, white paper. Use color that is attractive to the eye. There is everything from gray paper, pink, blue, yellow, green, all the way to the wild eye-catching astrobright colors. The neon colors cost about twice as much, but are worth it.

Then you should use one color ink only. Don't let some printer talk you into using four colors on your flyer -- it really drives the cost sky high. Use only one color. There is one exception to this: If you have a backer or sponsor who wants their four-color logo on the flyer, and he's willing to pay for it, fine. Otherwise, go with one color ink.

Be sure your paper is not so dark that it's hard to read the words. If people have to work too hard to read your flyer, they won't. A light colored paper is best with dark, black or brown ink.

There are certain "musts" that you need to have on every flyer:

1. In bold, large type tell the reader what the event is called. For example, "SUPER CRUISE '93!"

2. Who is sponsoring the event? Use bold, but a bit smaller type to mention this right under the title.

3. If the event is a fund-raiser to support a worthy cause, put this in somewhat smaller type under the name of the event, like, "Proceeds For The Neighborhood Boys' Club."

4. If you are offering games for the kids, food, a raffle or drawing, and entertainment, go ahead and mention it.

5. If the show is for pre-'70 cars, say so.

6. If you're giving awards, say so. For example, "Dash Plaques for All Show Cars ... Club Participation Trophy & Class Plaques."

7. If there is a charge to get in or enter, give the prices.

8. Let them know what they might win at the raffle or drawing!

9. Tell them when the event will be held, the day and date, the starting and ending times, and where the event will be held.

10. Give a easy-to-read map directing them to the event.

11. If kids get in free, say so!

12. Present a simple list of Cruisin' Rules in a border. For example:
 • No Alcohol
 • No burnouts
 • No pets
 • No Mini's
 • Open to all rods, classics & customs, pre-1969

13. Put a picture of a car or two to illustrate the typical kind of car that will be featured at the event.

14. If the restaurant is offering a special deal on food and beverages for cruisers, say so. For example: "SPECIAL CRUISIN' COMBO!"

15. Display the logo of the restaurant holding the event.

16. Give a daytime and evening phone number where people can call for more information.

Where To Go To Get Quality Help For Your Event

QUESTION: If you want to have special dash plaques and awards made for your event, where's a good place to get this done?

ANSWER: The person I recommend does a terrific job on plaques and awards. Here's his name and address:

> Stuart Tritt
> American Automobile Awards
> 1720 Broadway
> Scottsbluff, Nebraska 69361
> *1-(800)-336-9667*

You make up a sample copy of how you want the dash plaque to look, or do a camera-ready layout to send to Stuart. An artist or printer can help you with this. They will do it on gold or silver or black or white background. He can even do silk screening for you. The plaques usually measure about 2 x 2 1/4 or 3 x 3 inches square. I prefer the larger ones because people tend to notice them more easily.

It's a good idea to use the same look for everything you put out for the event, the dash plaques, T-shirts and flyers all having the same title and logo, for instance.

QUESTION: Suppose you want to sell or give away T-shirts at your show or cruise. Who would you recommend using for this work?

ANSWER: There's one name that comes to mind right away, and that's Ed "Big Daddy" Roth. He's somewhat of a legend in car circles and his "Rat Fink" T-shirts are classics! Here's how to get in touch with him:

> Ed "Big Daddy" Roth
> 296 E. 400 South
> Manti, Utah 84642
> *1-(801)-835-0835*

Ed is a wild man -- he even built a car out of cement just recently -- and he's been in the business about 35 years. He's a real genius when it comes to promotions of car events and art work. He is important in our field and is the forerunner of a lot of what you see happening. If Ed Roth does the art work for your cruise or show, you'll have a first-rate, great-looking job, and people will love it.

More Tips On Getting People Excited About Your Events

QUESTION: Now, for the person who has never experienced the fun of a cruise-nite, would you describe exactly what happens from start to finish?

ANSWER: The cruise begins promptly at 6 o'clock. You and whomever you have out there helping you need to be in the parking lot before 6 to help people park their cars properly. You want to be sure that the cars do not take up more than one space. You try to park them side by side so that other customers can find spaces for parking when they arrive.

As Rod and Sherry encourage people to do, you should have people put their car windows half-way down. This allows people to see in easily without opening doors, and there's another benefit -- it allows people to slip their flyers inside on the seat, so they don't have to stick them on the windshield, which looks tacky. People hand out a lot of flyers at cruises and shows to keep everybody aware of upcoming events of interest. When you are putting on a cruise-nite or car show, take hundreds of flyers to every car get-together you attend and hand them out to everyone personally, and put them in the cars. People enjoy getting them because they look forward to the new things going on. Also be sure to leave them in body shops, paint shops, diners, speed shops, upholstery shops, and wherever you have a lot of walk-in traffic of car buffs. All you have to do is go up to the owner of the establishment and say, "Hey, I've got a flyer here for an upcoming event, it's a non-profit group that we're doing a cruise for (or car show), and would you mind if we put a stack of flyers on your counter?" They will usually say, "Be my guest!" I then leave a hundred or so next to the cash register. A lot of these places will talk up the event for you, in addition to handing out your flyers.

And don't forget to send your flyers to the president of car clubs. Send a little note with the flyer saying something like, "Would you be kind enough to put this in your newsletter for the month of _____ (or for these months)?" You'd be amazed that 99% of the time they will announce your cruise or show for no charge.

And send your flyer to car magazines. Many times they will run your news in their calendar of events. Sometimes these are for free, sometimes they are for pay. You're doing them a favor helping them inform their subscribers of what's coming up. One good magazine to send your flyer to would be *Miss Information*. This informs people of upcoming car happenings, and it's nation-wide and no charge to you. Send it to:

> *Miss Information*
> c/o Bobbie-Dine Rodda
> 1232 Highland Avenue
> Glendale, California   91202

At *Miss Information* you'll find nice people and the magazine is packed with good stuff to keep you current on what's happening, when it's happening, and where it's happening.

What About Using Swap Meets To Promote
Your Own Successful Car Events?

QUESTION: We haven't said much about car swap meets. Is this another good place to get the word out using your flyers for an upcoming cruise or show someone might be putting on?

ANSWER: Absolutely. When you talk about swap meets, you are talking about the heartland of cruisin'! These are serious car people. For example, if someone wants a car part for a 1950 Ford, if they want an original part; they're not going to go to one of the chain auto parts stores for it. This is especially true for the customs, the lowering kits, or hot rod parts. These guys are quite receptive to anything to do with cars, and that includes your flyer.*

As a matter of fact I just talked to a man from Oregon today who I met at a swap meet last Sunday. He called me about the Winternationals Car Show coming up that I did the flyer for. He said he noticed it and wanted to come back. It was because of our flyers that he was here this year, last year, and he'll be back next year. *Those flyers work!**

---

* If you need help creating effective flyers for your own car events, call **1-800-410-7766**. Personal marketing assistance can help you or your group design custom, ready-to-use flyers for drawing big crowds to your events. Or use the sample flyers at the end of the book to create your own.

QUESTION: How do you get people to fill out a name and address card so you can put a good mailing list together and mail them your flyers?

ANSWER: When people come to a cruise, you can just give them a little name and address card and ask them when they arrive to fill it out. At a car show they are going to come up and register for the show, so then they have to fill it out anyway.

But the best way is to link it to your raffle. Any time you're giving away something free, people will do almost anything! They won't mind taking the time to fill out the card as part of entering the raffle. And you've got your mailing list.

How To Use Direct Mail Marketing To Attract
The Crowds To Your Car Events

QUESTION: Do people on this kind of mailing list tend to come to your events?

ANSWER: You bet!   When people attend car shows, cruise-nites and swap meets, these are people who are proven car lovers, most likely. If they are interested in an event today, it's highly likely they will be tomorrow.

Let's say you get 200 cars at one of your car shows or cruises. You have everybody fill out a name and address card at the event. *Get these name cards at every single event you do.* Then, if you have some non-profit organization sponsoring you, you can get them to pop for the postage -- and that isn't cheap these days, and it's about to go up again! Then, send your flyers to the whole list.

And don't try saving a few bucks sending your flyers out by anything other than first class mail. You can lose a lot of valuable information doing it. If you send them out first class, and mark on the envelope under your return address these words: *Forwarding and address correction requested.* The post office will inform you of any change in their address, and they will forward the flyer to them at their new address. This gets your message to them, and it keeps your mailing list up to date with their most recent addresses.

And try this little trick: If you have a friend who wants to get the word out about their event or product or service or store, get them to do a piggy-back mailing. They put their flyer in the same envelope with yours and share the postage with you.

And if someone gets your flyer in the mail, and they get one at a car event, and they see the same flyer in an auto parts store -- great! There's nothing like repetition to motivate people. As a matter of fact, the man who was responsible for most of the promotions for the Highway Patrol car show for kids, the show that drew 1,050 cars ... he got those cars there by using all of these methods, including the mail. He got those flyers handed out from San Diego to Santa Barbara to Riverside. Get those flyers out!

How To Successfully Use TV, Radio & Newspaper Advertising

QUESTION: What about using other types of advertising in addition to the flyers? Have you had any success using radio and TV ads to promote your events?

ANSWER: Sure. Last year we did the Winternationals Car Show in January and used a local cable TV station to promote it. It ran on ESPN. Cable advertising is a lot cheaper than network stations. The people at the cable companies will give you all the help you need putting together the TV ad. They'll help you create ads that use still pictures, or videos or a combination of both. They'll do the voice-overs and announcing and whatever you need.

Ours was a 30 second commercial, and it cost about $2,000. You reach a lot of people with ads like this, but there's one problem. You never know what kind of people you are reaching. Most of them watching the commercial may not care much about cars. You could be wasting your $2,000. But if you've got the money to spend, go ahead and experiment.

Radio is the same thing. It's cheaper, but you still will be reaching a lot of non-car people, which could waste a lot of money.

QUESTION: What about getting exposure for your event in newspapers? How do you go about doing that?

ANSWER: This is a good way to go. Most newspapers will give you quite a bit of free publicity for your event if you are being sponsored by a non-profit organization. If it's an important, well-known group backing you, you can get an awful lot of ink out of it that will save you thousands of dollars you don't have to spend on advertising. You can have someone who knows how to write good news releases write up the story about your event and how the proceeds will be used and you can then send it to the paper, along with a good photo showing a similar event. The paper might edit it a bit, but most of the time, if you write it like the paper writes, they'll run it free of charge. Send it to all the papers in your area.

Sometimes if you call the editor of the paper and tell him or her about the upcoming event and what group is sponsoring it, they will assign a reporter to do the story for you. But that's work for them and a little less likely to get you the free publicity you need. Try doing it both ways.

And if you're wondering about taking out a paid ad in a local paper to promote your event, *don't waste your money.* You don't know if any cruisers even read that paper. Save your money.

QUESTION: So, of all the methods open to you for getting the word out about your cruise-nite or car show, you prefer the flyer?

ANSWER: That's right. Radio, TV, or newspaper advertising or publicity is really a crap shoot. You never really know when you use those methods if you are reaching serious car people.

But with the flyers you know for sure. You hand them out at places where cruisers and car people hang out. It's your most direct way of getting to the people that really matter.

Putting On Your Own Fund-Raisers

QUESTION: When you get a non-profit organization or worthy cause to back your event, how important is it to be a big believer in that cause or organization?

ANSWER: There are a bazillion different organizations out there that would love to have you help them raise money for their work. But if you don't believe in what they stand for, you can't promote it. You have to really believe in what you're doing. You get a great deal of satisfaction for what you are doing for them, and it makes you believable when you promote the event.

QUESTION: Suppose you want to do a car event for a special cause that has nothing to do with any non-profit organization or other group, is there any difference in how you would go about it?

ANSWER: Not really. You can contact the needy person or family and say, "We are aware of your need and here's what we would like to do for you by holding a special fund-raiser car event." You organize the event the same way, put out flyers that show what the proceeds of the event will be used for. You hold a raffle and periodically throughout the event you mention the need or cause to get people interested.

You can either collect all monies and turn them over to the particular person, or you can go to a bank and have a special trust fund set up for the cause that all the monies collected are deposited into for proper handling of the funds.

A perfect example of this was the car show fund-raiser put on by Rod and Sherry Reprogle for the young boy who broke his neck playing high school football. This event raised more than $4,000 for this needy boy and his family. (see the flyer used for this successful fund-raiser on the next page).

When the Persian Gulf War broke out a member of a local car club was sent to Saudi Arabia, leaving behind his girlfriend. This left her without any means of support whatever. So, the car club got together and held a fund-raiser car show for her and raised a couple thousand dollars. Car people are special people, and fund-raisers are great ways to enjoy cars and help people.

QUESTION: Do fund-raisers draw as many people as car events that do not promote some special cause?

ANSWER: Many times fund-raisers draw more people. People will see the announcement and say, "Hey, that's a good cause; I'd like to be a part of that." They may not have gone just for the sake of the event, but they want to do something worthwhile, and enjoy cars at the same time.

Super Cruise '90

Presented by *CRUISIN' FIFTIES*

on

MAY 26th, 1990

KIDS TWELVE & UNDER FREE

KIDS TWELVE & UNDER FREE

LONG BEACH POLICE ACADEMY
11:00 - 8:00
7390 E. Carson Street

(West of 605 Freeway - South Side of Carson Street)

Proceeds For JASON KNIGHT Trust Fund

Games for the kids - Food - Raffle

Pre-'70's Car Show

Dash Plaques For All Show Cars-

Club Participation Trophy & Class Plaques-

$5.00 per carload -- Walk-in $2.00

Buy a Raffle Ticket for $1.00
for a chance to
WIN THIS CAR

Call 325-1972 for Ticket
& Cruise Information

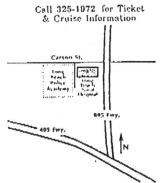

The JASON KNIGHT Story

I have a life-size story that needs to be told. It involves
Jason Knight, a local community youth who used to play football for
the 1989 Sophomore Football Team at Torrance High School. Jason no
longer plays because his neck was broken while making a tackle
during a football game in September 1989. He has endured several
operations not only attempting to correct a crushed cervical vertebra
but to ensure his survival.

Currently, Jason is undergoing rehabilitation at Rancho Los
Amigos Hospital in Downey. Due to the trauma to his spinal cord,
he is paralyzed but has shown signs of limited arm movement. His
road back to recovery will take time and will require a great deal
of both spiritual and financial support.

A trust fund for Jason has been initiated at Torrance National
Bank in Torrance. The proceeds from the Super Cruise and Raffle
will be donated to the fund to assist Jason with current and future
needs and to improve the quality of his life.

A lot of good comes out of car events. And car people tend to be givers. They give their time, their money, their knowledge, and themselves. You don't find a group of people quite like car people in any other sport. That's why I devote all of my time to it.

How To Get A Non-Profit Group
To Back Your Events

QUESTION: It sounds like linking your event with a good cause can help get you a lot of community interest. How do you go about getting a non-profit organization to agree to back you?

ANSWER: There are so many non-profit organizations out there that they are dying for anybody to come out and help them. They are overjoyed when you approach them with a car show, let's say, and are happy to lend their name to it.

You find out who's in charge of the organization, contact them and say, "Hey, here's what we plan to do, here's how many cars we think we can get, here's how much you'll get of the gate (if any), and here's how much you'll get out of the raffle. And the raffle is important. You give them all of whatever you get from the raffle, less your expenses for flyers, dash plaques, trophies, and any other money you've had to shell out of your own pocket. Giving them part of the gate and all of the raffle can bring in a lot of money for them and they love it.

You try to have them send someone out to handle the raffle -- sell the tickets and collect the money, do the raffle, and hand out the raffle prizes. And these are free bodies that can help you do the event for free; help that you don't have to pay for.

How To Get A Local Radio Station To Back You
(And Provide The D.J. Free)

Sometimes you can contact a local radio station that plays the '50s and '60s stuff and work a deal with them to lend their name to the event, in addition to the special cause you are raising funds for. This way you get the services of their D.J. at the event and you don't have to hire one out of your own pocket. A good D.J. can run you about $100 to $200 a night! And on a good weekend, sometimes as much as $250 to $300! If the station manager likes the cause, and if you buy a certain number of ads on their station, they might do it. But many stations will be so glad to get the exposure for their station that they will do it for nothing. And they'll promote the event for weeks on the air for you *at no charge.*

How To Conduct An Exciting Raffle

During the event the D.J. promotes the raffle ticket sale. They are usually a buck a piece and you give away about 15 prizes -- like waxes, car polish, gas cans, jumper cables, sets of tires, wheels, shifters, gift certificates, T-shirts, hats, free meals, or copies of this book. The raffle is held a few hours into the event. Ten to fifteen gifts is a good idea for a cruise up to about 50 cars. With more cars, you want to give away more prizes.

Then, as the numbers are called you let people who win come up and pick their own prize. Then at the end you have a large grand prize that's pretty special, like a deal on a paint job, or body work, or a nice set of tires or wheels. Only one person gets this. I usually let the previous winner pick the next ticket. This gets everybody involved.

And be sure to lay all your prizes out real nice on a big table. This will get people interested and will sell a lot of raffle tickets.

And people want their raffle ticket at the top of the barrel, so you will sell a lot of tickets just before the raffle starts! It's human nature!

Sometimes you hold part of the raffle, give out a couple of prizes, wait a while, and space it out throughout the evening. But the grand prize is always saved for last to make a big deal out of it.

Now another good idea is to give out a special award each week at your cruise-nite. Right before the raffle starts, you pick one car (and you never pick the same car twice), and you interview the guy or gal who owns the car. He tells you a little about the car, where he's from, how long he's owned it, what kind of car, motor, and so on. It makes him feel good and makes the crowd knowledgeable about that particular vehicle. The people also feel like you really care about them and what you're doing -- and you do.

And remember that if you're doing the raffle for a worthy cause, be sure to have the D.J. mention it a lot, "Remember that the money from the raffle is going to be donated to the County Burn Association" and hype it up throughout the evening. Give the cause you're sponsoring a boost and encourage people to pick up their brochures and talk to representatives of the organization.

What To Do When The Party's Over

And once your raffle is over, your event is pretty well over, too. You try to maintain some semblance of order, make sure cars aren't doing burnouts or racing. You make sure everything is picked up and cleared away in the lot, so that you leave it much like you found it, nice and neat.

Promoting and running car events is great fun and does a lot of good for a lot of people. Now you have all the tools you need to put on and promote your own events — So go ahead, there are a lot of car people out there just waiting to get your flyer!

A Great Sport For Great People

When you promote your own car events, you're into the sport with the greatest people you'll find anywhere. You are one of those people, and I look forward to the opportunity of meeting you — and admiring *your* car — at some car event real soon!

Chapter 9

The Step-By-Step Ingredients For Putting On A Successful Fund Raiser

A Question-&-Answer Interview
With Bob French — The "Magic Man" Who Will
Show You All the Tricks To Make Your Event A Big Hit

CHAPTER NINE

The Step-By-Step Ingredients For
Putting On A Successful Fund Raiser

A Question-&-Answer Interview
With Bob French — The "Magic Man" Who Will
Show You All The Tricks To Make Your Event A Big Hit

A lthough Bob French dreams up, organizes, promotes and runs over 15 major car shows and fund raisers every year, he says that he's "not in the car show promoting business." Why? Because Bob is a professional entertainer who does magic shows for comedy clubs, civic and business organizations, conventions, parties, and cruise lines. He has performed as a magician all over the world.

But some of his greatest "magic" takes place throughout the year at Southern California's largest and most popular automotive events.

He got into promoting car shows and fund raisers by accident. While sitting at the head table waiting to perform his magic show for a local business organization, Bob overheard some of the local business leaders complaining about what the miserable turnout local merchants had at their annual sidewalk sale. Since Bob was into showing his own classic car and had attended many car shows as a participant, he turned to the city manager and mayor sitting next to him and said, "You guys ought to have a car show."

As Bob explained how car shows work, the city leaders got excited and asked him to run one for them. Bob agreed. A few weeks later they closed down the main street; four-hundred cars went on display; and *over 20,000 people came out to the show and*

179

"absolutely buried the town." They couldn't get any more bodies in the place! It turned out to be such a big success that they asked him back year after year. The popularity of this show spread far and wide and other groups and charities began asking him to do shows for them. In addition to shows for business organizations he runs fund raisers for local police causes, associations for retarded citizens, drug abuse resistance programs, local school projects, church groups, and special environmental causes. His reputation for putting on successful quality car shows has become so well known that he is forced to turn down over 100 requests each year for his services.

Bob is an unusual guy, accepting no money at all for his time and talents. His philosophy?—"I want to do car shows to benefit as many people as possible. I'm not doing it for Bob French, but for the car show participants, the car cruiser, the people with classic cars, to enable them to have a nice place to come to show off or enjoy cars, bring their families, and at the same time help some worthy organization." He says, "If it wasn't for somebody like me putting on these car shows, there wouldn't be a place for the people with the cars to go to show them; and if it wasn't for the people with the cars, there'd be no need for a guy like me!." A real win-win situation for everybody.

So, if you want to plan and run your own fund raiser or car show, sharpen your pencil and get out your notebook because Bob French is about to give you everything you'll need, step-by-step, to make it a tremendous success!

The Magnetic Power of Car Events

QUESTION: What is it that seems to attract so many people to car events week after week, month after month?

ANSWER: It's an event of high interest. It's an event that people find exciting. There's a lot of camaraderie. It's much like a bunch of fisherman sitting around talking about the fish they caught! People love to reminisce and every car has a story—"I had a car like that when I was a kid...My next-door neighbor has one of those...Gee, I saw one of those sitting in a barn...My grandfather had a car like this and I remember riding in the rumble seat...Where did you get a car like this?"—there are a million stories and every one of those car people out there love telling them, hours on end. People love to talk about their cars and to answer questions about their cars. My car alone is a whole hour's story and I could tell you interesting things about that car you wouldn't believe, and you'd never hear that story about another car. So car shows are fascinating and festive events. It's a great family event and people love it.

QUESTION: What makes a car show a good fund raiser and why is showing classic and vintage cars a good way for groups and organizations to raise money?

ANSWER: Well, generally speaking, I would say that most people are interested in automobiles — especially automobiles that are out of "print" and those that are unusual and ones you typically never see. How often do you see on the street a 1932 Ford Roadster, or some of the cars your dad used to drive? You don't see them any more. These examples of automotive art and rolling sculptures of yesterday are really something to see.

Cars are things that people like to go out and reminisce about. For example, the other day at a car show I saw a car that was exactly like the one my dad had; a '47 Chevy, 2-door. As I stood there and looked inside the car and remembered back when I was a little boy, sitting on the same pinstripe upholstery, the same dashboard and all the things about the car—it brought me back to those days.

Attending car shows can also remove you from all the stresses of the work week and it's just plain fun where people can go with their family in a safe, enjoyable place.

I just did a car show yesterday in downtown Long Beach in which we closed off 4 city blocks in the main business district and about 10,000 spectators came out to see 200 cars. This was a special show called "Chevys versus Fords" with Fords on one side of the street and Chevy's on the other and it was an absolutely blockbuster day with everything from 1903 Fords all the way up to 1957 Chevys and everything in between.

These events show you things you'd normally never get to see. It's like opening up a treasure chest of some of the best automobiles in the world!

How To Make Your Events Attract More People

QUESTION: The "Chevy vs. Ford" theme is a great idea. What other unusual shows have you put on that have been big hits?

ANSWER: I did a car show one time that was called "The Silver Dollar We-Pay-You Car Show." This was done for a charitable organization and we didn't charge anybody to display their car at the show—a free pre-registration. But when you showed up with your car on the day of the show, you not only received your commemorative dash plaque, but you were also paid a silver dollar. Well, we absolutely buried the place!

It was for a local private school that needed funds for new facilities and they made real good money off this show.

I did this show again the next year and called it "The We-Pay-You A $2 Bill Car Show" and everybody who entered their car at the show got a two-dollar bill. This was also a huge success!

QUESTION: Using the idea of "We-Pay-You" in a fund raiser, how would an organization or group make any money if they have to pay people to display their cars?

ANSWER: It's obvious that the charity doesn't have the money to be able to give a silver dollar or $2 to everyone who enters their car—that's why they're putting on a car show. And obviously I, Bob French, don't have the money. But the key is to *arrange for sponsorships* for these shows.

You need to arrange for various people, businesses, groups or companies to help out by buying the trophies, pay for flyers, pay for an ad in the newspapers, or donate some money so we can give people a silver dollar or a two-dollar bill when they enter their cars.

Another way to raise money is through venders—people who want to sell their products at the events. They pay a small fee to display their wares at the show. We have vendors who sell polishing wax, polishing rags, snow cones, food, drinks, and so forth. The venders pay anywhere from $10 up to $150 to set up their displays.

Now in some shows we let vendors come in for free. But in exchange for displaying their wares, they donate some of their products that we can use in the door-prize drawings that raise money when raffle tickets are sold. So instead of charging the venders, we get an equal amount in their products. Many times a local automotive store will donate a couple cases of oil, some jumper cables, or gift certificates for products and services. Restaurants will give you dinners for two, or local amusements will give two admissions, or local hotels will give a stay with dinner for two, etc.

What's in it for the venders or the sponsors? They get good exposure at the show, and they are mentioned in any newspaper ads or articles about the show.

QUESTION: What is your most popular car show, and describe a typical turnout?

ANSWER: Every year I put on the Belmont Shore Car Show. It's the largest one-day car show on the west coast. It starts at 10 and ends at 4. It brings out 1,000 cars, and attracts over 100,000 spectators in six hours! It's sponsored by a non-profit organization of local merchants. The cost to put it on is $10,000—for permits, police, barricades, city services, street sweeping, insurance, etc., etc. But although it costs that much, I was told that this show brings in an estimated half-million dollars spent by spectators in that town in those six hours! There are over 200 businesses in that district that runs for 15 blocks. All of the local fast-foods and restaurants and retail stores are jammed with customers during the show.

Finding A Sponsor For Your Car Show

QUESTION: Can you give an example of how you approached a typical sponsor or vendor to solicit their involvement in the event?

ANSWER: Let's take the "Chevy vs. Ford" show I mentioned earlier. Two of the sponsors were a local Chevy and a local Ford dealer. I simply went into their showrooms and talked to the owners. All I do is say, "How would you like to be a sponsor of one of the most unusual shows that's ever been put on for cars, Chevy vs. Ford?" They were both very interested, of course, but the first words out of their mouth was, "How much?" I said, "No charge, I don't want any money, but what I want is some cooperation and some perks." And the perks were that "we want you to come out, set up your display at our show, and for the owner or general manager of your dealership here to go out and select one Chevy (in the case of the Chevy dealer) or one Ford (for the Ford dealer)—the car that you think is the best car at the show. Then, we want you to invite that car to be displayed on your showroom floor. And if that person elects to display their car on your showroom floor, while their car is on display, you will give them a new Chevy or a new Ford to drive for the same length of time. And, since you are not a charity, we won't charge anyone to come to the show, we need to do something for these people that are nice enough to bring out their cars and spend the day at the event, so I want you to give each driver a hamburger, french fries and a coke for them and their family."

They loved it, said yes, and got tremendous exposure. The people who got the trophies and awards got an extra-special perk.

With most people you approach to sponsor a show, you say something like this: "Look, I'm a guy who has a circus at the edge of town—I have the animals, the tents, the jugglers, the trapeze artists, and the clowns, everything at the edge of town. What I want to do is to bring my circus to your town. All you have to provide me with is a spot to put my circus. I'll put on the circus, but it's up to you to fill the bleachers. My car show will be the same whether one person comes to see it, or a thousand, so it behooves you to go out and let the town know that the circus is here because every person that walks through the gate to see the circus is money in *your* pocket, because every person pays to see the show."

At one show I did for a local shopping center there was a big turnout, they all spent money with the center's merchants on the day of the event, and they came back later to shop the stores.

Step-By-Step Basics For Organizing Your Car Events

QUESTIONS: What is the most important first step in setting up a good fund raiser car show?

ANSWER: 1. Three words say it all: Location. Location.
Location. Location is everything when it comes to making your
event a success. You try to hold your show in the most pleasant
location possible. Try to hold it on a grassy area, not at "Joe's Gas
Station" on hot asphalt. Hold it where there are shade trees, if
possible. Something with a view. For example, I'm getting ready to
do a show in a few weeks that is probably the prettiest location in the
state of California for a car show. It's behind a beautiful hotel
overlooking the bay, the Queen Mary, and the city skyline. The
hotel is sponsoring the event to increase interest in the hotel.
Parking is free. Spectator admission is free. And the hotel is
providing a 2-for-1, buy 1 get 1 free brunch for those bringing in
their cars; including a nice dash plaque. Another hotel sponsored my
"Go Topless" car show for convertibles only. We buried the place
with cars and drew a big crowd.

I recently did a big car show for Travel Land U.S.A., the largest
R.V. shopping center in the world. The show was held in the middle
of the property where there's a beautiful park with grass and trees
and waterfalls and ponds and lakes and ducks, with good restroom
facilities. It's a beautiful location. This is the kind of place you're
looking for to make your show a success.

Now if you put your show on in an area where there are no
restroom facilities, you have to bring them in, and this can get costly.
So try to set it up where there are good restroom and food facilities.

One fund raiser I did for a local school was held in their own
grassy field area. The way they made money was to charge a small
fee for those showing their cars, say $10. At this show we had 100
cars entered.

2.   Then you need a date that will not necessarily conflict with
any other car shows in your immediate area. Most areas have
automotive calendars of events. Certain magazines list the upcoming
events; for example, Bobbie 'dine Rodda's *Automotive Calendar* of
events, *Hotline News, Street Rodder Magazine, Custom Rodder*

Magazine, Drive Magazine, Auto Trader and other good publications, both national and local to your area, list future events that you don't want to compete with. You can also learn about planned events by going to car shows, cruise nites and swapmeets and collecting flyers that are passed out and placed in cars. You don't want to make enemies or step on anybody's toes, so plan your date carefully.

Most car shows and fund raisers are set up on a Saturday or Sunday. And try to avoid scheduling it during other events, not just car shows; such as a local or county fair, or marathon, or other event. Try to set your event way ahead. I schedule mine a year in advance.

QUESTION: What about awards and dash plaques for those entering their cars. Where is the best place to purchase these items?

ANSWER: Generally speaking, a trophy shop in your area can supply these things. But I deal with a place through mail order where it's hard to beat their price or their quality. It's called:

American Auto Awards.
Randy and Deanna Ludwig, Owners
107 South Main Street,
Canton, South Dakota 57013
Phone: 1-800-366-9667.

You can call them for information or suggestions on how to design plaques, or order their free catalog containing all kinds of automotive awards.

But I don't recommend giving awards and trophies any more. This is because there are often so many cars that you cannot realistically or intelligently or accurately pick out 20 cars from a field of 500. So I give the all cars an extra-nice dash plaque and special perks that outweigh sitting around wondering if you're going to win a trophy. The problem with trophies, in my opinion, is that if you have a show with 500 cars in it and you give away 100 trophies, *you've got 400 people mad at you!* So forget it.

Now in some shows you almost have to have some kind of awards. The "Chevy vs. Ford" show I did was one such show. We gave "Top 10 Chevy" and "Top 10 Ford" in the form of a nice trophy. At this show one guy came up to me after the show and was unhappy his car didn't win. I pointed out to him that we had 300 cars competing, only 20 trophies, and unfortunately the judges didn't pick his car, even though it was a beautiful truck. I pointed out to him that even in the Miss America pageant, you've got all these beautiful women to choose from, all dazzling knockouts, which one do you pick? But they all can't win,, can they?

QUESTION: How do you select judges for a car show?

ANSWER: The way we did it at the "Chevy vs. Ford" show was that we invited some of the representatives of each dealership to judge for us. Or, for example, a show we did at a Catholic school used 3 or 4 of the priests to act as judges. At other times we ask a group of knowledgeable people together—people with no conflict of interests—and they will do the judging.

And when we do the judging we do what we call a visual overall judging. When people look at cars they generally see a car with the doors, the trunk, and the hood closed. However, opening up the doors, trunk and hood is done in some events to show off the chrome and other things. In my opinion, when showing cars a general overview is best.

QUESTION: When you do fund raisers and shows in the downtown section of various cities, how do you go about getting permits and street closures from the city?

ANSWER: This can be a real can of worms! The first thing to do is for the person in your organization who is responsible for the car show to go to the special events or special services section of the city where you plan to locate the show. They will give you a long list of things that must be done to qualify for the permit. For one show I did, the city gave me a 6-page list of things that had to be adhered to, to the letter! If you plan to put the show on in a local park, you contact the parks and recreation department of that city and pull a permit to use the park. In most cases you will also have to pay the city a fee for the permit.

Also keep in mind that it's sometimes who you know that helps make the whole project flow a lot easier. If someone in your group or organization knows someone with influence in the city, ask them to help smooth the way for your permits with the city. Having the right people pulling the strings makes all the difference!

QUESTION: Let's assume that a group wants to do a car show to raise money for a good charity, but no one in the group knows anything about cars and no one has a car to enter. How do you go about attracting people who have really nice cars and getting them excited about displaying their cars at the upcoming event?

ANSWER: People with nice cars have a lot of shows to choose from. There are over 5,000 car shows every year in the state of California alone. But in my opinion, there are only a handful of shows that do a good job of publicizing their shows. So you have to let them know about your show and what's special about it.

The first thing you need to do is print up an attractive flyer that's 8 1/2 x 11." The flyer explains what the shows's all about, and includes all the details someone would need to enter their car, what's in it for them, what's the charity, how the money will be used, and so on. (You'll find some actual examples of good flyers in the back of this book. You can use these as models to create your own, or contact a printer for assistance in designing professional-looking flyers ready to use).

We probably put out a couple of thousand flyers a week announcing upcoming shows. You need to find a printer who will give you good service and good prices. Prices to print flyers varies dramatically, so take plenty of bids, or have people in your organization talk to printers they know. Don't be afraid to ask people to help out with the printing. Let's say you were a good friend of mine and I come to you and say, "Hey, we're going to put on a car show to help crippled children; we need some flyers printed and wonder if you could help us by donating some printing?" He'll very likely say yes and print out a few thousand flyers as his contribution. Then at the bottom of the flyer we put, "This flyer printed and donated by . . ." to promote his business.

I estimate that it takes about 20,000 flyers to bring out about 200 cars. You have to pass out flyers till the cows come home! Keep reminding and reminding people about your show. These 20,000 flyers may not go to 20,000 different people—I may put the same flyers in the same person's car 20 times over the course of a year. This is because most of these people attend many car shows, and you've gotta keep on reminding them to build their interest.

QUESTION: What is the best way to distribute the flyers announcing your upcoming events?

ANSWER: One of the best ways to reach people who have good cars to enter in car shows is to place your flyer inside the cars is an accepted practice at all shows. You can simply set your flyer on the front seat of the car, or, if the owner is sitting at a table next to his or her car, walk up and give them your flyer. They will appreciate it. Also, attend other car show events in your area, like cruise nites and swapmeets and hand out your flyers to everyone who has a car on display. This way you reach serious car people.

QUESTION: What kind of perks do you offer people to get them to want to enter their car in your show?

ANSWER: You must do something that will make a person want to clean up his or her expensive car, bring it out to your show, and sit around all day at your car show rather than doing something else with their time. What's the incentive for them to do this? A very nice, safe location, suitable for the family to attend, sometimes a free lunch, dash plaques, live entertainment, music and good facilities, all at an entry fee that gives them much more than their money's worth. You have to let them know that "the customer is the most important person in the world" and they are the customer. Because without them there would be no show.

Money Matters

QUESTION: How do you go about raising money for your fund raiser other than the amount charged to those participants entering their car in the show?

ANSWER: First of all, anybody who wants to put on a car show to make all kinds of grandiose money off the car show participants better forget the whole idea. There is no way you can make any real money by charging $10 to people showing their cars. That money will barely be enough to put on the show.

Here's the secret to making your car show financially successful: You make your real money from the venders, sponsorships, and people who want to help you put on the show. For example, I did a car show for a local private school. There must be about 100 teachers and administrators at this school, and all of them have husbands, wives, and other family members that belong to various organizations, clubs and various business connections. So you encourage the group or organization putting on your show to talk to these people and see if they can get their contacts to contribute in some way to your show. Let's say one of the teachers knows the owner of a tire store. The teacher would ask the owner to donate a set of tires for a raffle? Or someone else might own a garage and might donate a gift certificate for a lube job. Or someone else might own a restaurant and could offer free dinners. Someone else might own a print shop and could offer free printing for your flyers. You also take donations of products and services from venders who display their wares at the show.

Then, if you put your show on in a controlled area where people have to pass through a gate, you can charge a small fee for admission; say $1 or $2 (not much more than that),and kids under 12 free. Now, at the school I just mentioned, it's a big school and has about 1,000 kids attending; most of those kids have parents, grandparents, neighbors, etc. And most of them will want to go and support the school, so if 5,000 people come to the show, the school makes $5,000! Not to mention those from the public who are invited by ads in newspapers. Incidentally, many times if someone has a connection in a local newspaper, you can get a free ad or a big story about the show. You may also be able to appear on local talk shows on radio or cable TV and gets loads of free publicity. Call these shows and let them know about your event, and many times you can get thousands of dollars of free exposure for your show, and you'll reach tons of people. If you're a non-profit organization or a charitable group, you can always get free public service announcements about your upcoming show. And remember to notify the media that have calendar of events. All you have to do is ask—it's free!

QUESTION: You mentioned that a raffle is a good way to raise money at your fund raiser. Could you describe how a raffle or drawing is handled?

ANSWER: First of all, you get as many prizes donated as you can possibly get. Don't turn anything down. You go to the bicycle shop in your area, for example, and say, "Would you like to donate a bike to us for our fund raiser? Of if you can't donate it, could you let us have it at a really good price?" I did one show for a local police department's drug abuse education program and got bikes, microwaves, TVs, and all kinds of things donated. What they can't get donated, they get donations of money from local businesses and then go and buy their prizes.

Then during your drawing all the prizes are displayed on a big table. You have volunteers sitting there selling the tickets. The tickets are sold for $1 a piece, 6 for $5, 15 for $10, 35 for $20, and 100 for $50. Most people will typically buy $5 or $10 worth of tickets; a lot buy $20 worth; and some car clubs will get together, pool their money and buy 100 tickets for $50. The numbered tickets are put into a big tumbler for drawings at the end of the day.

Occasionally you might have what is called a 50/50 drawing, if it's legal in your area. You do the same thing, selling different color tickets for the same price. Then a separate drawing is taken for the general raffle, and another for this 50/50 raffle. Let's say the 50/50 raffle takes in $500. The organization or charity putting on the show keeps $250, and the other $250 goes to the person holding the lucky ticket.

The important thing about the raffles is that it is all pure profit. And incidentally, the word "raffle" is not a good word to use.

This is because in many places a "raffle" is considered a form of gambling. So it is better to call it a "doorprize drawing." (Remember that gambling is only illegal when the federal, state and local governments aren't getting their cuts!). These doorprize drawings are a great way to make money.

With regard to the prizes: *You're better off having 10 great prizes than you are having 100 mediocre prizes.*

Now let's talk about how the raffle is run: There are a couple of ways to do it. (1) You can say, "OK, this next ticket that will be drawn is for a bicycle..." and name each prize. Start with the lesser-value prizes and work up to the bigger ones. This is the best method to use if you don't have many prizes to give away. (2) If you have a lot of mediocre prizes (I mean prizes that are all about the same worth or value), you can say, "OK, the winner of this ticket can come up and pick whatever prize he or she wants on the table."

When you run a raffle some people will be roaming around the show and may not hear their ticket called. In this case you can pin their number up on a board so they can periodically come over and check on their number. But for the most part, do the raffle and awards ceremony at the end of the show. Let's say the show is over at 4 o'clock; you should start the raffle and awards at 3 o'clock. It usually takes a half-hour to 45 minutes to raffle off everything, and then about 15 minutes to give the car show awards away.

QUESTION: When setting up your raffle or drawing, what is the best place to set it up when planning the layout of your show?

ANSWER: Position is very important. You have to set up the raffle so it's out in front of God and everybody! Depending on the show, figure out where the "crossroads" are—the place where everybody will have to walk by as they walk through the show. Sometimes you can position the raffle nearby the food concession.

In one show we did we put the raffle right outside Johnny Rockets, a '50s diner and hamburger place that provided 2-for-the-price-of-1 burgers and cokes. So everybody who was there went into Johnny Rockets, and many of them bought raffle tickets as they went in and out. So put your raffle in the center of the action and you'll sell more tickets and raise more money.

QUESTION: You mentioned that venders are a good way to raise money for the event. Can you describe specifically how this is handled?

ANSWER: Sometimes the venders are charged anywhere from $10, $25, $50, or $150 or more—it really depends on the size and worth of the show. If you're doing a show for a small school, let's say, the vendor is not going to make as much as he or she would at a larger event.

Many times the venders are allowed to set up for no charge at all. In this case they are asked to donate their products. For example, a guy comes in and he's selling wax. I'll say, "Look, it would normally be $50 to be a vendor here. Give us $50-worth of your wax products that we can use a doorprize. He's more than happy to do this, especially since the wax only cost him about $20. He gets good exposure for his products and we get to offer great prizes that sell a lot of raffle tickets! Another win-win situation.

QUESTION: Let's say you've collected money from entry fees, collected at the gate, and collected money at the raffle; how do you handle all this money safely?

ANSWER: An example: We did a show for the Association for Retarded Citizens. At the gate where monies are collected we had 2 or 3 people there working together to make it safe enough. We also had a "money pick up" about every 20 minutes in which a couple of people would go around who were members of the event committee and collect the money, leaving, of course, some money for change. This prevents a pile-up of money at the gates. Then someone on the committee had a motor home and the monies were kept safe and counted there by a few people who stayed there with the funds at all times. It is important to plan for this kind of safety.

What Car Shows Mean To Business Organizations

QUESTION: What impact have your car shows had on drawing attention and new business to various stores or business groups?

ANSWER: I'll give you a perfect example. The other day we did a car show in downtown Long Beach. If there hadn't been a car show there yesterday, on a Sunday, the place would have been a ghost town! A ghost town! We had 10,000 people down there between 10 a.m. and 4 o'clock in the afternoon. All the shops were open and the people stopped in and made purchases. Then, 20 minutes after I said "Thank you for coming" and closed up the show, it was a ghost town because those 10,000 people left and went home. The place would have been deader than yesterday's news without that show. But during the time the event is going on, it is big-time.

Another example: The car show we did at a local hotel in a grassy area overlooking the bay behind the hotel; all that grass doesn't do a thing to attract people to the hotel or its restaurant for Sunday brunch. But when the people who attend the show are there, they might say, "Gee, this is a beautiful place—I never knew it was here" and they just might come back for brunch, or to use the facilities for a wedding, anniversary party or some other special event.

One more example. Belmont Shore, a beautiful little city in southern California, was one of the best-kept secrets around before we started putting on our annual car show there in September. The locals knew about it, but nobody else did. On a regular Sunday afternoon this town might draw about 30,000 to 40,000 people throughout the day. Our car show draws over 100,000 to the local merchants as well as to our show. That show is like wall-to-wall people, like a New York subway. It is estimated that each person who attends this show spends an average of $5 at local businesses; that's over a half million dollars spent! This year we are expecting over 150,000 people.

So the car show is like a magic magnet that draws people in to make them aware and get them involved with whatever you are trying to offer them.

Handling Potential Problems

QUESTION: What happens if you have invested all this time and effort organizing and promoting a car show on an upcoming weekend and it rains or some other bad weather sets in?

ANSWER: Two words: Tough luck. People just will not come out for anything when it's pouring down rain. So when you set up an event you take your chances. But you don't look for trouble—you don't want to hold a car show during times when bad weather is likely. For instance, out here in California we try to avoid setting up shows in March, our rainy season. But even here, it's not likely it will rain in August or September, but it's always possible.

The first show I did this year we were rained out. When that happens, you have a "rain date," which means we held the show the following week. But when you do this, it never seems to be as strong a showing. For instance, for that show I had 100 cars signed up to display. It rained and we did the show a week later. Only 50 cars showed for that event. People had already made other plans for that day. Now when we do this there are no refunds for those who have entered their cars. The only time you refund the money completely is when you cancel the show and don't give them anything.

QUESTION: What do you do if you're putting on a car show and you need insurance in case someone attending the show slips and falls or somehow hurts themselves? Lawsuits are not fun!

ANSWER: It's absolutely critical that you are covered by insurance at your events. If someone trips and falls and breaks a leg while attending your show, they can, and usually will, sue somebody. And you don't want that somebody to be you! You can arrange for extra liability insurance through the local city or through the establishment sponsoring the show. You can get a one-day liability policy that will give you a million-dollar-per-incident coverage for $500 or so for the day.

The Key Do's & Don'ts For Putting On
A Really Successful Car Event

QUESTION: Could you   give us a list of practical "Do's and Don'ts" — important things to do and things to avoid doing at car shows and fund raisers that will make them run smoothly and produce positive results?

ANSWER: 1.   Select a good location for your event in a good, safe neighborhood.
   2. You don't want to plan your event during a time when bad weather is likely, or when you anticipate temperature extremes (like one show I did where it was so hot I saw a dog chasing a cat *and*

they were both walking!)

3.   If you do hold your event during periods of hot weather, try to plan it in a place where there is plenty of shade, if possible.

4.   Don't charge people who enter their cars too much for the show. The *magic number* is $10. You could go to $12 or $15, but ten dollars brings in the most cars.

5.   Do charge a small fee for each car entered. It has been my experience that people do not value things if they don't pay something for. Many times they won't even show up if there is not some small entrance fee.

6.   Don't run car shows for more than one day.

7.   No alcohol. No drugs. You would be amazed at the problems that are alleviated when you ban alcohol at your events.

8.   Don't allow your show to be promoted by anything that is not a worthy cause. For example, I have had top-level executives from beer and cigarette companies ask to sponsor some of our car shows and I decline.

9.   No pets.

10.   Hold your event from about 10 a.m. till about 4 p.m., letting the vendors set up between 7 and 8 o'clock, and the cars set up between 8 and 10 a.m.

QUESTION: If you had one word of advice for those who want to put on their own fund raiser using classic and vintage cars as the special attraction, what would it be?

ANSWER: Putting on car events is not a matter of getting rich or just getting money. But what it's all about is people. The bottom line and the most important thing is this:

Take care of the people!

---

*   To contact Bob French for magic show bookings you can call him at (310) 869-4977 or write to P. O. Box 622, Downey, CA 90241.

What's In The Trunk?

(Also Called *The Appendix*)

Car Club Finder
Sample Promotional Flyers
Directory of Top Car Publications
Classic Slogans I.Q. Test
Gift & Raffle Copies Order Forms

Car Club Finder

National & International Organizations

Car Clubs — State-By-State
Car Clubs — Make-By-Make
Other Special Interest Organizations

Personal Notes & Ideas

Car Club Finder

A *State* of the Art, Make-by-Make Directory

Y ou've heard the old saying, "Birds of a feather flock together." That's true for birds, and it's true for car buffs, too. Birds prefer to "flock" together to admire one another's feathers. Car lovers, on the other hand, would rather get together and admire each others' nifty oldies than sit alone in their garages polishing chrome.

In almost every city in America, and extending to countries around the world, you will find clubs and associations forming to celebrate the excitement and the memories of a specific class or make of car.

In the "Car Club Finder" directory you will find hundreds of organizations for every taste, fancy and car-mania under the sun. There are clubs for vintage antiques, street rods, classics, collectables, customs and more. You'll enjoy the creative names of some of these clubs; for example: Asphalt Draggins', Airheads (for convertible owners!), Old Boys Toys, Hi-Way Rodders, Blood Sweat & Gears, Rust To Riches, Counts of The Cobblestone, and even *Classy Women With Classic Cars!* We've separated the directory of national and international clubs into 3 sections to make it easier for you to find the club that best fits your needs:

(1) *State-By-State Listings*
(2) *Make-By-Make Listings*
(3) *Other Special Interest Organizations*

Most of these organizations not only hold local car shows, cruises, runs and other get-togethers, but they also publish monthly or quarterly newsletters and magazines. You might want to join these clubs and check out what others are doing, thinking and talking about; and find out about dates and times of club events. They'll be happy to send you complete club info and maybe a sample copy of their newsletter if you drop them a letter.

When car clubs change officers they often change addresses. So when you write to a certain club, add this under your name and return address on the left-hand side of the envelope: *"FORWARDING AND ADDRESS CORRECTION REQUESTED."* This way the post office should notify you of the club's most current address.

And if you are aware of a newly formed car organization, or one we missed, send us the information for the next edition of the "Car Club Finder" and we'll include it. Happy hunting!

National and International Organizations
State-By-State Club Finder

ALABAMA

CRIMSON CRUISERS
Box 71224
Tuscaloosa AL 35407

DIXIE CLASSICS, LTD.
25 W. Oxmoor Rd. #3-B
Birmingham AL 35209

ALASKA

MIDNIGHT SUN STREET
ROD ASSN.
Box 92061
Anchorage AK 99509

ARIZONA

ARIZONA AUTOMOBILE
HOBBYISTS COUNCIL
Box 1945
Phoenix AZ 85001

ARIZONA BOWTIE CLASSIC
CHEVYS
Box 1956
Glendale AZ 85311

ARIZONA STREET ROD ASSN.
1516 W. Main St.
Mesa AZ 85201

CABALLEROS DE YUMA, INC.
Box 5987
Yuma AZ 85366

RELICS & RODS OF
LAKE HAVASU
Box 1516
Lake Havasu City AZ 86405

REMEMBER WHEN CRUISE
ASSOCIATION
2930 W. Clarendon Ave.
Phoenix AZ 85017

RIVER CRUIZERS
Box 1301
Bullhead City AZ 86430

SIERRA VISTA CAR CLUB
Box 3304
Sierra Vista AZ 85636

THE PACK
Box 9300
Scottsdale AZ 85252-9300

ARKANSAS

ARKANSAS STREET ROD ASSN.
Box 4, Harver Hills
Malvern AR 72104

HILLBILLY WHEELS
HC 33, Box 30
Harrison AR 72601

OUACHITA RODDERS
Box 843
Waldron AR 72958

RIVER VALLEY RODDERS
1012 N.W. 2nd St.
Atkins AR 72823

ROLLIN' RELICS
Rt. 3, Box 6100
Garfield AR 72732

CALIFORNIA

BAY CITY RODDERS —
SEAL BEACH
Box 2538
Seal Beach CA 90740

BEACH STREET REVIVAL
557 Hacienda Dr.
Scotts Valley CA 95066

BENT AXLES STREET ROD CLUB
956 E. Moonlite Dr.
Santa Maria CA 93455

CALIFORNIA ROADSTERS
1500 Birch St., #200
Newport Beach CA 92660

CALIFORNIA RODDERS
1022 Vista Brisa
San Luis Obispo CA 93405

CENTRAL CALIFORNIA
CLASSIC CHEVY CLUB
1041 Springfield Wy.
Modesto CA 95355

CENTRAL VALLEY RODS, INC.
1909 Larkin Dr.
Roseville CA 95661

CHRISTIAN RODS & CUSTOMS
Box 1323
Bonsall CA 92003

CLASSIC CHEVYS OF
SOUTHERN CALIFORNIA
Box 7047
Van Nuys CA 91409

COASTSIDE CRUISERS
87 Kathleen Ct.
Pacifica CA 94044

CORNERSTONE CRUISERS
CHRISTIAN CAR CLUB
16919 Ardmore Ave.
Bellflower CA 90706

CRUISIN' 50s SOUTH BAY
Box 5119
Torrance CA 90510

DIABLO VINTAGE STREET RODS
Box 5898
Concord CA 94524

EARLY FORD V-8 CLUB
OF AMERICA
1511 Van Bibber
Orange CA 92666

EARLY IRON OF UKIAH, INC.
Box 107
Ukiah CA 95482

EARLY TIMES CAR CLUB
OF SOUTHERN CALIFORNIA
Box 7194
Long Beach CA 90807

FOREVER CLASSICS CAR CLUB
Box 184
Upland CA 91785

FORTIES LTD. OF ORANGE
COUNTY
Box 222
Buena Park CA 90621

FOR EVER FOUR CYLINDER
CLUB
4606 Beatty Dr.
Riverside CA 92506-2305

FRANKLIN SYNDICATE
AUTO CLUB, INC.
Box 109
Stockton CA 95201

FRESNO AREA CLASSIC
CHEVY CLUB
Box 1141
Clovis CA 93613

GOLD COUNTRY STREET RODS
Box 1170
Marysville CA 95901

GOLDEN STATE CLASSICS
Box 939
Paso Robles CA 93447

HIGH DESERT VINTAGE TIN
Box 1041
Victorville CA 92392

HOT ANTIOCH NIGHTS
2938 Delta Fair Blvd., #211
Antioch CA 94509

KERNVILLE STREET RODS
Box 725
Kernville CA 93238

KINGS STREET RODDERS
18990 Hanford/Armona Rd.
Lemoore CA 93245

LAKEPORT REVIVAL
290 S. Main
Lakeport CA 95453

L.A. CLASSIC CHEVY CLUB
Box 91413
Los Angeles CA 90009-1413

L.A. ROADSTERS
Box 3056
Hollywood CA 90078

LOWRDS
Box 1566
Clovis CA 93613

NIFTY 50s CAR CLUB
OF CALIFORNIA
2928 Moss Point Dr.
San Jose CA 95127

NORTHERN CALIFORNIA
CRUISERS
Box 20503
El Sobrante CA 94802

NORTHERN CALIFORNIA
PACKARD CLUB
Box 7763
Fremont CA 94537

ORANGE COUNTY CRUISIN'
ASSOCIATION
9242 Walker St. #C
Cypress CA 90630

OVER THE HILL GANG
(SAN BERNARDINO CHAPTER)
9473 Emerald St.
Fontana CA 92335

ROAM'N RELICS CAR CLUB
Box 1173
Simi Valley CA 93062

SAN DIEGO PROWLERS
8631 Cuyamaca St.
Santee CA 92071

SANTA BARBARA CLASSIC
CHEVROLET CLUB
Box 6540
Santa Barbara CA 93111

SIERRA-CASCADE STREET
RODDERS
Box 4077
Quincy CA 95971

STREET RODS UNLIMITED
Box 2082
Montclair CA 91763

SULTANS CAR CLUB
9556 Flower St.
Bellflower CA 90706

TOURIN' TIN STREET RODS
1307 Garrett St.
Anaheim CA 92804-4817

TRAVLIN' T'S
5112 Coke St.
Lakewood CA 90712

VACA VALLEY VINTAGE
STREET RODS, INC.
Box 504
Fairfield CA 94533

COLORADO

COLORADO ROLLIN' RODS
Box 284
East Lake CO 80614

COLORODANS OF LONGMONT
209 Kimbark St.
Longmont CO 80501

GOOD TIMES CAR CLUB
4741 Pawnee Dr.
Greeley CO 80634

ROAD KNIGHTS, INC.
Box 5275
Loveland CO 80539

ROCKY MOUNTAIN
PACKARD CLUB
Box 343
Wheatridge CO 80033

CONNECTICUT

CLASSIC NIGHTS CAR CLUB
1136 Capitol Ave.
Bridgeport CT 06606

CONNECTICUT CRUISERS
280 E. Main St. #18
Branford CT 06405

CONNECTICUT STREET
ROD ASSOCIATION
Box 72
Wethersfield CT 06109

DREAM MACHINE CLASSICS
57 Woodchuck Hill Rd.
Canterbury CT 06331

FAIRFIELD COUNTY
STREET RODS
2 Powder Horn Ridge
Danbury CT 06811

GOOD TIMES MOTORING CLUB
Box 852
Colchester CT 06415

GOLDEN RODS
Box 565
Norwich CT 06360

SUMMER KNIGHTS
222 Robbins Ave.
Newington CT 06111

TY—RODS AUTO CLUB
Box 3133
Talcottville CT 06066

US 1 MOTORING CLUB
Box 222
Waterford CT 06385

WATERTOWN CUSTOMS
12 Butternut Lane
Watertown CT 06795

DELAWARE

SOUTHERN DELAWARE
STREET ROD ASSN.
516 Sussex Ave.
Seaford DE 19973

FLORIDA

CARS & RODS OF SARASOTA
Box 10335
Sarasota FL 34278

CENTRAL FLORIDA
STREET ROD ASSN.
Box 910
Haines City FL 33845

EARLY IRONS OF ORLANDO
Box 580924
Orlando FL 32858-0924

FLORIDA GOLD
COAST CLASSICS
6202 S.W. 55 Ct.
Davie FL 33314

FLORIDA STREET RODS, INC.
Box 3653
West Hollywood FL 33083

OSCEOLA RODDERS
Box 421981
Kissimmee FL 34731

PENSACOLA ROD-TIQUES
Box 10293
Pensacola FL 32524

SPACE COAST STREET RODS
Box 101
Rockledge FL 32955

SPIRIT OF THE 50s
3606 23rd St. E.
Alva FL 339200-1314

TAMPA KNIGHTS
Box 290464
Tampa FL 33687

GEORGIA

PO BOYS CAR CLUB (ATLANTA)
Box 788
Woodstock GA 30188

IDAHO

CRUISIN' CLASSICS CAR CLUB
Box 758
Nampa ID 83653

EASTERN IDAHO EARLY
IRON ORGANIZATION
114 12th St.
Idaho Falls ID 83404

MAGIC VALLEY EARLY IRON
Box 931
Twin Falls ID 83301-0931

R.I.O.
820 E. Commercial
Weiser ID 83672

UNITED STREET RODS
OF IDAHO
2165 Bruneau Dr.
Boise ID 83709

VINTAGE GEMS OF IDAHO
11034 W. Edge Hell Dr.
Boise ID 83709

ILLINOIS

ANTIQUE TOWN RODS
Box 50
Galena IL 61036

GATEWAY STREET RODS
3463 Harris Lane
Bethalto IL 62010

GREATER CHICAGO
CLASSIC CHEVY CLUB
111 Dato Ct.
Streamwood IL 60107

JACKSONVILLE STREET RODS
114 Havendale Dr.
S. Jacksonville IL 62650

LAKERS CAR CLUB
2039 5th St.
Madison IL 62060-1540

LIMITED RODS
1168 Maple Ave.
Galesburg IL 61401

MID-CENTURY MERCURY CLUB
1816 E. Elmwood Dr.
Lindenhurst IL 60046

MIDWEST STREET ROD
ASSN. OF ILLINOIS
617 Bryn Mawr
Bartlett IL 60103

NORTH SHORE RODS
SOUTHSIDE
Box 277
Oak Lawn IL 60454

OLD STYLE RODS
Box 32
Mt. Prospect IL 60056

RIVER VALLEY DRIFTERS
Box 28
Mackinaw IL 61755

POSEN CRUISERS CAR CLUB
Box 272
Posen IL 60469

POVERTY RODS
Box 244
Milford IL 60953

SLOWPOKES OF PEORIA
Box 29
Mossville IL 61552

STRAIGHT AXLE CORVETTE
ENTHUSIASTS
Rt. 1, Box 106
Chapin IL 62628

STREET SWEEPERS CUSTOM
CAR CLUB
2607 30th St.
Rock Island IL 61201

VINTAGE RODS OF DANVILLE
Box 6022
Tilton IL 61833

WESTERN ILLINOIS ANTIQUE
AUTO CLUB
86 Phillips St.
Galesburg IL 61401

WHITE SQUIRREL CRUISERS
CAR CLUB
Box 181
Olney IL 62450

INDIANA

CENTRAL INDIANA OLD
CAR CLUB
7208 E. CR 350N
Muncie IN 47303

CIRCLE CITY VINTAGE
Box 44616
Indianapolis IN 46244-0616

CLASSIC RODS
Box 4306
South Bend IN 46634

ELKHART VINTAGE WHEELS
58142 C.R. 115
Goshen IN 46526

E'VILLE IRON STREET RODS
Box 3011
Evansville IN 47730

FWSRA-MRR
Box 11561
Ft. Wayne IN 46859

GREAT LAKERS AUTO CLUB
4777 N. 1100 West
Michigan City IN 46360

HOOSIER MODEL CAR ASSN.
5925 N. Rosslyn
Indianapolis IN 46220

INDIANA STREET ROD ASSN.
RR #1, Box 165
Tipton IN 46072

LIME CITY CRUISERS
Box 334
Huntington IN 46750

MICHIANA CLASSIC
CHEVY CLUB
Box 713
Ellkhart IN 46515

MODERN ANTIQUES
Box 4
Anderson IN 46015

OUTLAWS CAR CLUB
4828 S. Co. Rd. 150W
Connersville IN 47331

RIVER CITY CLASSICS
OF EVANSVILLE
4100 Clement St.
Evansville IN 47720

ROAD EARLS II
716 W. Christian St.
Princeton IN 47670-2367

ROSE CITY RODS & MACHINES
4656 W. US 36
Middletown IN 47356

20TH CENTURY CHEVY, INC.
Box 371
Washington IN 47501

VINTAGE WHEELS CAR CLUB
2200 Hawkins Rd., Box 1950
Richmond IN 47375

IOWA

CAPITOL CITY STREET RODS
1520 S. W. Payton
Des Moines IA 50315

CENTRAL IOWA TRI-5
CUSTOM CAR CLUB
Box 484
Des Moines IA 50302

CLASSICS CAR CLUB, INC.
720 Iowa Ave., Box 418
Onawa IA 51040

MOPARS UNLIMITED, INC.
325 N.W. Aurora Ave.
Des Moines IA 50313

RAMBLIN RODDERS
403 McArthur
Muscatine IA 52761

RESURRECTED TIN
211 E. Third
Pella IA

VINTAGE COACHES
2102 Boies St.
Sioux City IA 51109

KANSAS

ARKANSAS CITY
TUMBLEWEEDS
Box 368
Arkansas City KS 65005

CENTRAL KANSAS
STREET RODS
1220 Van Buren
Great Bend KS 67530

EARLY IRON OF WESTERN KS.
Box 213
Goodland KS 67735

EMPROIA FLATHEAD CRUISERS
101 S. Chesnut
Emproia KS 66801

GOLDEN OLDIES CLASSIC
CAR CLUB
Box 911
Olathe KS 66061

LAKE GARNETT CRUISERS
306 N. Oak St.
Garnett KS 66032

MCPHERSON HOT ROD ASSN.
536 S. Park Ave.
McPherson KS 67460

OLD CAR NUTS
718 Lane St.
Clay Center KS 67432

TRI-VALLEY STREET ROD ASSN.
RR 4, Box 102-A
Fredonia KS 66736

WESTERN KANSAS
MUSTANG CLUB
Box 1511
Hays KS 67601

YARD ART CLASSICS
2012 Magnolia
Manhattan KS 66502

KENTUCKY

DALE HOLLOW STREET
RODDERS
Rt. 1, Box 252
Albany KY 42602

DIXIE STREET RODS, INC.
7507 Mallard Dr.
Pleasure Ridge Park KY 40258

RIVER CITY CLASSICS OF KY.
3711 Rouge Way
Louisville KY 40218

RIVER TIN STREET RODS
Box 9422
Paducah KY 42002

LOUISIANA

CALCASIEU STREET RODDERS
2343 Jeff Allen Rd.
Vinton LA 70668

KAJUN KRUIZERS
STREET ROD ASSN., INC.
700 Oak Lane
Thibodaux LA 70301

RAMBLIN' OLDIES OF
DENHAM SPRINGS, INC.
Box 61
Denham Springs LA 70727

RED RIVER STREET ROD ASSN.
Box 2074
Shreveport LA 71166

TWIN CITIES CLASSIC CHEVY
Box 7573
Monroe LA 71211

MAINE

STREET RODDERS OF MAINE
315 Old County Rd.
Rockland ME 04841

MARYLAND

CHESAPEAKE CLASSIC
CAR CLUB
Box 2233
Easton MD 21601

CRUZIN UNLIMITED, INC.
Box 28489
Parkville MD 21234

EARLY EDITIONS
STREET RODDERS
Box 131
Cumberland MD 21502

LIBERTY STREET RODS
7110 Ridge Rd.
Marriottsville MD 21104-1114

MARYLAND AUTOMOTIVE
MODELERS ASSN.
317 Roosevelt Ave. S.W.
Glen Burnie MD 21061

MASON DIXON STREET RODS
Box 1502
Cumberland MD 21502

SOUTHERN MARYLAND
STREET RODS
2020 Ann Cl.
Mechanicsville MD 20659

WESTERN MARYLAND
STREET ROD ASSN.
Box 904
Cumberland MD 21502

MASSACHUSETTS

BOSTON AREA ROADSTERS
55 Middlesex Ave.
Natick MA 01760

BRISTOL COUNTY STREET
ROD ASSOCIATION
Box 194
Chartley MA 02712

FLYWHEELS AUTO CLUB
Box 134
Holbrook MA 02343

MASSCAR MODEL CLUB
Box 274
Westwood MA 02090

MASSACHUSETTS CRUISERS
AUTO CLUB
51 School St.
Plainville MA 02762

MOSCOFFIAN'S
Box 269
Oxford MA 01540

SOUTH SHORE STREET RODS
Box 406
Holbrook MA 02343

THE STROKERS
4 Betsy Way
Danvers MA 01923

MICHIGAN

CEREAL CITY STREET ROD
ASSOCIAITON
215 N. Main St., Box 55
Ceresco MI 49033

COWTOWN CRUISERS
215 S. LaFayette
South Lyon MI 48178

EASY RODDERS OF MICHIGAN
Box 5044
Warren MI 48090

MID-MICHIGAN STREET ROD
ASSOCIAITON
Box 565
DeWitt MI 48820

MIDNIGHT CRUISERS
8195 Belleville Rd.
Belleville MI 48111

MILL WINDERS CAR CLUB
36575 Fierz Pl.
Mt. Clemens MI 48043

MODEL-A RESTORERS CLUB
24800 Michigan Ave.
Dearborn MI 48124

MOTOR STATE STREET RODS
Box 2471
Dearborn MI 48123

OLD BOYS TOYS CAR CLUB
Box 826
Niles MI 49120

ROD BENDERS OF WEST MI.
2908 Berry St.
Kalamazoo MI 49001

SOUTHERN MICHIGAN
STREET ROD ASSN.
4424 "D" Dr. S.
Battle Creek MI 49017

STONE CITY STREET RODDERS
5667 Greenwood Rd.
Petoskey MI 49770

SUNSET OUTLAWS CAR CLUB
Box 844
Petoskey MI 49770

WEST MI. MUSTANG CLUB
14474 State St.
Marne MI 49435

WOLF-PACK AUTO CLUB
26811 Van Buren St.
Dearborn Hts. MI 48127-1016

WONDERLAND CUSTOMS
Box 1106
Grand Rapids MI 49501

MINNESOTA

MID-AMERICA WILLYS CLUB
18819 Valley Dr.
Minnetonka MN 55345

MINN. STREET ROD ASSN.
1550 148th Lane N.E.
Ham Lake MN 55304-6209

MINI BIRDS OF MINN.
6842 Olympia St.
Minneapolis MN 55427

NORTHERN KNIGHTS
Box 611
Park Rapids MN 56470

NORTHERN LIGHTS CAR CLUB
21860 Iden Ave. N.
Forest Lake MN 55025

ST. CLOUD ANTIQUE
AUTO CLUB
Box 704
St. Cloud MN 56302-0704

210   /   The Mother of All Car Books   Car Club Finder

TWIN CITIES ROADSTERS
Minneapolis MN 55422

TWIN CITY F-100 CLUB
4709 Beachside Rd.
Mound MN 55364

MISSISSIPPI

MISS. STREET ROD ASSN.
Box 6600
Jackson MS 39282-6600

SINGING RIVER STREET ROD
ASSOCIATION
5139 Eden Pl.
Biloxi MS 39532

VICKSBURG CRUISERS
CAR CLUB
1015 National St.
Vicksburg MS 39180

MISSOURI

CAVE STATE CRUISERS
Box 457
Waynesville MO 65583

CLASSIC CHEVY CLUB
OF SPRINGFIELD
Box 10111 GS
Springfield MO 65808

CLASSIE CHASSIS CAR CLUB
Box 2095
Hillsboro MO 63050

DAM CAR CLUB
Box 842
Osage Beach MO 65065

HI-WAY RODDERS
Rte. 7, Box 304
Perryville MO 63775

HIWAY RODDERS
Box 100
Uniontown MO 63783

K.C. KUSTOMS
Box 1613
Independence MO 64055

MID-MISSOURI STREET RODS
Box 1094
Sedalia MO 65302-1094

RESTORODS OF MISSOURI
Rt. 1, Box 1638
Ste. Genevieve MO 63670

RIVER CITY RODDERS
Box 171
Jackson MO 63755

SHADETREE CLASSICS
CAR CLUB
Box 381
Marshall MO 65340

SHOW-ME F-100 CLUB
Rt. 2, Box 288
Purdy MO 65734

SHOW-ME-RODS
Box 346
Independence MO 64051

VINTAGE RODS
Box 592
Carthage MO 64836

WEST PLAINS CAR CLUB
Box 991
West Plains MO 65775

MONTANA

GLACIER STREET ROD ASSN.
Box 1362
Kalispell MT 59901

HELENA STREET RODDERS
Box 5562
Helena MT 59604

NEBRASKA

FREMONT ANTIQUE CAR CLUB
300 E. 12th St.
Fremont NE 68025-4238

NEBRASKA STREET MACHINE
ASSOCIATION
2270 26th Ave.
Columbus NE

NEVADA

GOLDEN MEMORIES CAR CLUB
4302 Kinobe Ave.
Las Vegas NV 89120

KARSON KRUZERS
Box 3004
Carson City NV 89702

RUBY MOUNTAIN
MORRODDERS
181-2 W. Bullion Rd.
Elko NV 89801

SAGEBRUSH STUDEBAKERS
1029 Litch Ct. #1
Reno NV 89509

SOUTHERN NEVADA CLASSIC
CHEVY CLUB
Box 28391
Las Vegas NV 89126

WESTERN VEHICLE ASSN./
PACIFIC CUSTOMS
2756 N. Green Valley Pkwy.
Suite 100
Henderson NV 89014

NEW HAMPSHIRE

GRANITE STATE STREET
RODDERS
Box 1403
Rochester NH 03867

NEW JERSEY

BERGEN COUNTY CRUISERS
170 Preston St.
Ridgefield Park NJ

EAST COAST ROD & CUSTOM
ASSOCIATION
313 Washington St.
Saddle Brook NJ 07662

JERSEY LATE GREAT GREATS
58-64 CHEVYS
Box 1294
Hightstown NJ 08520

MILD TO WILD AUTO CLUB
Box 63
Lambertville NJ 08530

NORTH JERSEY STREET
ROD ASSN.
Box 376
Hibernia NJ 07842

NORTH SHORE ANTIQUE
AUTOMOBILE CLUB OF N.J.
230 Pension Rd.
Englishtown NJ 07726

NEW MEXICO

NORTHERN NEW MEXICO
STREET RODDRS
Box 651
Flora Vista NM 88415

RATON CRUISERS
1031 Cottonwood
Raton NM 87740

ROUTE 66 RODDERS
Box 53121
Albuquerque NM 87153

SAN JUAN VALLEY
CLASSIC CHEVY CLUB
Box 682
Farmington NM 87499

ZIA RODDERS
Box 456
Hobbs NM 88420

NEW YORK

BUTTERNUT VALLEY
STREET RODS
Box 124
Morris NY 13808

CENTRAL N.Y. STREET RODS
Box 151
Mattydale NY 13211

KENT CRUISERS
Box 1063
Carmel NY 10512

LAKER'S ROD & CUSTOM
1603 Ingram Rd.
Penn Yan NY 14527

PHANTOMS CUSTOM CLUB
44 Malibu Hill
Renss NY 12144

ROCHESTER STREET RODS
Box 15526
Rochester NY 14615

RODS & CUSTOMS OF BUFFALO
Box 1132
Amherst NY 14226

STREET CLASSICS
5309 Ramblewood Dr.
Cuba NY 14727

STREET MACHINES OF
ROCHESTER
409 Bennington Dr.
Rochester NY 14616

TRI-STATE MAJESTIC CRUISERS
Box 174
White Plains NY 10603

VENTURES CUSTOM
CAR CLUB
46 Treehaven Rd.
West Seneca NY 14224

NORTH CAROLINA

CHATHAM STREET ROD ASSN.
Box 244
Siler City NC 27344

HEART OF CAROLINA
STREET RODDERS
1433-B Jonestown Rd.
Winston Salem NC 27103

LINCOLN COUNTY
STREET ROD ASSN.
109 Benfield St.
Lincolnton NC 28092

QUEEN CITY STREET
RODDERS
Box 23542
Charlotte NC 28227

NORTH DAKOTA

CLASSTIQUES CAR CLUB
Box 459
Bismark ND 58502

GREATER DAKOTA CLASSICS
Box 314
Devils Lake ND 58301

NORTH DAKOTA STREET
ROD ASSOCIATION
Box 459
Bismark ND 58502

PRAIRIE CRUISERS
Rt. 2, Box 26
Dickinson ND 58601

OHIO

BROWN COUNTY CRUISERS
Box 113
Georgetown OH 45121

4 DEUCES CAR CLUB
10107-A State Rt. 15
Ottawa OH 45875

BUCKEYE RAMBLIN' RODS
960 Curtwood Ave.
Wooster OH 44691

BUCKEYE ROD BUILDERS
562 E. Torrence Rd.
Columbus OH 43214

CENTRAL OHIO STREET
ROD ASSOCIATION
6700 Borror Rd., Rt. 2
Orient OH 43146

CHRYSLER CLASSIC CAR CLUB
5851 Jackman Rd.
Toledo OH 43613

CLINTON COUNTY ANTIQUE
& CLASSIC CAR CLUB
662 W. Locust
Wilmington OH 45177

COACHMEN STREET ROD ASSN.
2749 New Milford Rd.
Atwater OH 44201

CRUISING THE 50s
CLASSIC CAR CLUB
4875 Lower Elkton Rd.
Leetonia OH 44431

FORT'S STREET CAR CLASSICS
Box 285
Ft. Recovery OH 45846

GEM CITY CLASSICS
Box 659, Wright Bros. Station
Dayton OH 45409

INDEPENDENT CRUISERS
OF OHIO
Box 13849
Whitewall OH 43213

INDEPENDENT KUSTOMS
3315 Bristol Dr.
Springfield OH 45503

LAKE ERIE CLASSICS
6570 Nicoll Dr.
N. Ridgeville OH 44039

MID-OHIO BUNCH
4368 Hansen Dr.
Hilliard OH 43026

PLACERS CAR CLUB
3425 149th St.
Toledo OH 43611

ROAD KNIGHTS, INC.
234 W. Woodland Ave.
Youngstown OH 44501

STARK COUNTY STREET RODS
Box 8593
Canton OH 44711

STREET ROD ASSOCIATES
9248 Peters Pike
Vandalia OH 45377

TOLEDO METRO CLASSIC
CHEVY CLUB
1434 Appomattox
Maumee OH 43537

WARREN COUNTY KUSTOMS
909 Victoria
Franklin OH 45005

Y-CITY CUSTOM CAR ASSN.
2090 Shady Lane
Zanesville OH 43701

OKLAHOMA

BLOOD, SWEAT & GEARS
Box 582161
Tulsa OK 74158

C.C. RIDERS OF CENTRAL OK.
400 Cactus Rd.
Yukon OK 73099

CENTRAL OKLAHOMA CLASSIC
CHEVY CLUB
Box 676
Wheatland OK 73097-0676

CLASSIC CHEVY CLUB
OF OKLAHOMA, LTD.
Box 35747
Tulsa OK 74135

CREEK CAPITOL STREET RODS
2720 N. 54th St.
Muskogee OK 74401

KIAMICHI STREET RODS
Rt. 2, Box 759
Broken Bow OK 74728

OKIE BUGGIES CAR CLUB
Box 26541
Oklahoma City OK 73126

OLDIES & GOODIES CAR CLUB
Box 732
Bartlesville OK 74005

OVER THE HILL GANG — OKC
Box 26541
Oklahoma City OK 73126

RUST TO RICHES CAR CLUB
911 W. Gentry
Checotah OK 74426

STREETERS CAR CLUB
Box 1031
Blackwell OK 74631

TWISTERS CAR CLUB
Box 45
Enid OK 73702

VINTAGE ROAD RUNNERS
OF TULSA, INC.
Box 323
Jenks OK 74037

OREGON

ALBANY STREET RODS
Box 1783
Albany OR 97321

BURNOUTS
215 S.E. First
Newport OR 97365

CENTRAL OREGON CLASSIC
CHEVY CLUB
Box 6343
Bend OR 97708

EMERALD VALLEY
CLASSIC CHEVYS
Box 2202
Eugene OR 97402

KLAMATH KRUISERS
Box 7363
Klamath Falls OR 97602

LAKE COUNTY
DESERT CRUISERS, INC.
Box 749
Lakeview OR 97630

REFLECTIONS STREET RODS
Box 1003
Springfield OR 97478

ROGUE VALLEY
CLASSIC CHEVYS
Box 5055
Central Point OR 97502

PENNSYLVANIA

ANTIQUE AUTOMOBILE
CLUB OF AMERICA —
SUSQUEHANNA VALLEY
RR 3, Box 3047
Berwick PA 18603-9418

BLUE MOON CRUISERS
ROD & CUSTOM
717 Market St. Ste. 400
Lemoyne PA 17043

CRUISIN' RODS-N-KUSTOMS
Box 3133
Erie PA 16508

CUMBERLAND VALLEY
ROD & CUSTOM CLUB, INC.
Box 781
Waynesboro PA 17268

FAR NORTHEAST CRUISERS
1519 Marcy Pl. #B
Philadelphia PA 19115

GOLDEN TRIANGLE STREET
RODDERS OF PITTSBURGH
730 Euclid Rd.
West Sunbury PA 16061

MOD-TIQUES OF EASTERN PA.
Box 342
Hatboro PA 19040

OVER THE HILL GANG OF PA.
2599 Eberhart Rd.
Whitehall PA 18052

POCONO MOUNTAIN
STREET ROD ASSN.
304 York Ave.
West Pittston PA 18643

POTTSTOWN CLASSIC CHEVYS
Box 1144
Pottstown PA 19464

PRETZEL CITY ROD & CUSTOM
110 Spook Lane
Reading PA 19606

STEEL CITY CLASSICS
701 Prestly Ave.
Carnegie PA 15106

UPPER BUCKS STREET
ROD ASSOCIATION
2295 Silver Creek Rd.
Hellertown PA 18055

VINTAGE TIN OF WESTERN PA.
Box 442C, Rd. 1
Trafford PA 15085

WHEELS OF TIME
STREET ROD ASSN.
4950 Buckeye Rd.
Emmaus PA 18049-1003

RHODE ISLAND

HEAVEN ON WHEELS
Box 273
Ashaway RI 02804-0003

OCEAN STATE OLDIES
CAR CLUB
Box 985
Coventry RI 02816

RHODE ISLAND SINNERS
CAR CLUB
12 Holyoke Ave.
Warwick RI 02889

RHODE ISLAND STREET
RODDING ASSOCIATION
54 Thelma Irene Dr.
N. Kingstown RI 02852

RHODE ISLAND VINTAGE
WHEELS
Box 722
Hope Valley RI 02832

SOUTH CAROLINA

WINYAH CRUISERS
Box 1574
Georgetown SC 29442

SOUTH DAKOTA

NATIONAL IMPALA ASSN.
Box 968, 830 3rd St.
Spearfish SD 57783

COUNTS OF THE
COBBLESTONE
Box 488
Rapid City SD 57709

TRI-STATE CLASSIC CHEVYS
RR 2, Box 114
Hartford SD 57033

VINTIQUES CAR CLUB, INC.
Box 135
Watertown SD 57201

TENNESSEE

BUICK STREET ROD ASSN.
824 Kay Cl.
Chattanooga TN 37421

CLEVELAND CRUISERS
Rt. 1, Box 143
Ocoee TN 37361

HARD TIMES STREET RODS
529 Crawley Dr.
Newport TN 37821

MIDNIGHT RODDERS
115 Jacksonian Dr.
Hermitage TN 37076

SHADE TREE STREET RODS
Box 22008
Nashville TN 37202

SHADES OF THE PAST
STREET ROD ASSN.
3114 Old Niles Ferry Rd.
Maryville TN 37801

SHILOH AREA STREET RODS
Rt. 2, Box 522
Selmer TN 38375

STARR MOUNTAIN
STREET RODDERS
2987 High. 39W
Athens TN 37303

STROLLERS CAR CLUB
824 Kay Cl.
Chattanooga TN 37421

TEXAS

287 CAR CLUB
1704 Lewis
Dumas TX 79029

ABILENE MODEL A CLUB
Box 2962
Abilene TX 79604

AMARILLO ANTIQUE CAR CLUB
2521 12th Ave.
Amarillo TX 79015

BAYOU CITY CRUISERS
1812 Oakwood Dr. E.
Pearland TX 77581

BAYOU CITY CRUISERS
8562 Forum
Houston TX 77055

CARRIZO SPRINGS
STREET RODS
Box 872
Carrizo Springs TX 78834

CENTRAL TEXAS CLASSIC
CHEVY CLUB
5209 Fort Mason Dr.
Austin TX 78745-2314

CLASS ACT MOTOR CLUB
Box 1123
Killeen TX 76540

CLASSIC ROLLERS UNLIMITED
604 Arnold Pl.
Amarillo TX 79107

CONCHO CLASSIC CHEVY CLUB
1200 South Oaks
San Angelo TX 76905

DALLAS AREA CLASSIC CHEVYS
Box 810364
Dallas TX 75381

DALLAS AREA STREET RODS
Box 1025
Cedar Hill TX 75104

DEEP CREEK CRUIZERS
1300 25th St.
Snyder TX 79549

DEUCES LIMITED
159 Cook Court
Willow Park TX 76087

EARLY FORD V-8 CLUB
OF AMARILLO
5143 Kirk
Amarillo TX 79110

HANSFORD SHOW TIME
CAR CLUB
303 Barkley
Spearman TX 79081

HART OF TEXAS CLASSIC
CHEVY CLUB
Box 1392
Waco TX 76703

HEART OF TEXAS
STREET MACHINES
Box 2044
Hewitt TX 76643

HIGH PLAINS DRIFTERS
STREET RODS
1500 E. Bonita
Amarillo TX 79108

HUB CITY CRUZERS
Box 53281
Lubbock TX 79453

KRANKERS KAR KLUB
100 Invernoss
Borger TX 79007

LONE STAR CHRYSLER
300 CLUB
27 Gay Dr.
Kerrville TX 78028

LONGHORN RODS & CUSTOMS
17803 Comoro Lane
Spring TX 77379

MAC'S PACK
306 Whitestone Cl.
Cedar Park TX 78613

MCCLEAN ROAD RUNNERS
CAR CLUB
Box 304
McClean TX 79057

MODEL A FORD
CABRIOLET CLUB
Box 515
Porter TX 77511

MOPAR MUSCLE CARS
OF AUSTIN
Box 49829
4300 Speedway
Austin TX 78765

NORTHEAST TEXAS
TRAVELERS
Rt. 3, Box 1600
Mt. Pleasant TX 75455

NORTH HOUSTON
STREET RODS
8562 Forum
Houston TX 77055

OVER THE HILL GANG —
MESQUITE
1906 Lucille
Mesquite TX 75149

PANHANDLE COUNCIL
OF CAR CLUBS
7000 Chelsea
Amarillo TX 79109

PANHANDLE RODS
4401 S. Georgia
Amarillo TX 79110

SAN ANTONIO GEAR GRINDERS
6220 Culebra
San Antonio TX 78228

SLO-POKES ROD & CUSTOM
CAR CLUB
2310 Judy St.
Amarillo TX 79106

SNYDER WHEELS
Box 795
Snyder TX 79549

SOUTHEAST TEXAS MUSTANGS
Box 8848
Lumberton TX 77711

SOUTHERN STREETERS
Box 1031
Azle TX 76020

SOUTHWEST STREET
MACHINES OF HOUSTON
8515 Concho
Houston TX 77036

STREET ELITE
7401 Bluestem St.
Dallas TX 75249

TARRANT COUNTY
STREET ROD ASSN.
5801 Graham
Ft. Worth TX 76114

TEXAS PANHANDLE
MUSTANG CLUB
5107 W. 53rd.
Amarillo TX 79109

TEXAS PANHANDLE
MODEL A CLUB
8713 Blubonnett
Amarillo TX 79108

TEXAS PLAINS CHAPTER OF
2-CYLINDER CLUB
4009 Terrace
Amarillo TX 79109

TOP OF TEXAS CLASSIC
CHEVY CLUB
5209 While-A-Way
Amarillo TX 79108

TOP TIN STREET RODS
OF DENTON
Box 476
Krum TX 76249

WEST TEXAS STREET
ROD ASSOCIATION
1311 E. 43rd St.
Odessa TX 79762

UTAH

BONNEVILLE CLASSIC
CHEVY — OGDEN CHAPTER
1145 N. Main
Farmington UT 84025

FUGARWE CAR CLUB
Box 61
Millville UT 84326

INTERMOUNTAIN'S FINEST
TRUCK CLUB
276 N. Harrison Blvd.
Ogden UT 84404-4153

STAGS CAR CLUB
Box 217
Roy UT 84067

UINTAH BASIN ROD & CUSTOM
Star Route, Box 155
LaPoint UT 84039

VERMONT

RUTLAND AREA VEHICLE
ENTHUSIASTS
Box 519
West Rutland VT 05777

VERMONT STREET RODDERS
1011 Williston Rd.
Williston VT 05495

VIRGINIA

CUSTOM CRUISERS OF
NORTHERN VIRGINIA
Rt. 1, Box 271
Leesburg VA 22075

NORTHERN VIRGINIA
STREET MACHINES
6372 Torrence St.
Burke VA 22015

TRI-CITY CRUISERS
6058 Mill Creek Dr.
Prince George VA 23875

VALLEY CRUISERS OF
WINCHESTER
Box 2465
Winchester VA 22604

VIRGINIA STREET RODS
Box 35237
Richmond VA 23235-0257

WASHINGTON

CUSTOMS NORTHWEST
14116 419th St., CT.E.
Eatonville WA 98328

EASTSIDE STREET ROD ASSN.
Box 158
Redmond WA 98052

HENRY'S HAULERS
FORD F-100 TRUCK CLUB
1315 Hollis Tr.
Bremerton WA 98310

MIDNIGHT RIDERS
STREET ROD ASSN.
Box 73551
Puyallup WA 98373

MODEL A FORD CLUB,
EVERGREEN CHAPTER
Box 15133
Wedgewood Station
Seattle WA 98115-0133

NILE SHRINE CAR CLUB
6803 Greenwood Ave., N.
Seattle WA 98103

NORTH CASCADE STREET
ROD ASSOCIATION
Box 864
Mt. Vernon WA 98273

PIPERS CAR CLUB
1207 N.W. 73rd
Seattle WA 98117

SEATTLE ROD-TIQUES
Box 27076
Seattle WA 98125

SLO POKS
2700 N.W. 289th St.
Ridgefield WA 98642

STREET TIN AUTO CLUB
N. 8216 General Lee Way
Spokane WA 99208

TRI-CITIES RODS & ROADSTERS
Box 2101
Tri-Cities WA 99302

WENATCHEE VALLEY
STREET RODS
Box 7053
E. Wenatchee WA 98802

WEST VIRGINIA

DREAM MACHINE CAR CLUB
Box 3194
Saberton WV 26503

EAST RIVER STREET ROD ASSN.
Box 454
Bluefield WV 24701

ROLLIN' OLDIES CAR CLUB
1710 Grand Central Ave.
Vienna WV 26105

TRI-STATE STREET RODS
3414 Waverly Rd.
Huntington WV 25704

WISCONSIN

BLUE RIBBON CLASSIC CHEVY
1150 Inman Pkwy.
Beloit WI 53511

BREWTOWN CRUISERS
MERCURY CAR CLUB
N21 W22139 Glenwood Ln.
Waukesha WI 53186

EARLY IRON ROD AND
CUSTOM CLUB
Box 182
Appleton WI 54912

FOX VALLEY STREET ROD
ASSOCIATION
Box 2612
Appleton WI 54913

R&D MOTOR CLUB LTD.
Box 54
South Milwaukee WI 53172

RIVERSIDE CRUISERS
CAR CLUB
Box 230E
Merrillan WI 54754-0230

RIVER CITY STREET RODS
Box 400
Spring Valley WI 54767

WISCONSIN STREET
ROD ASSN.
W140 N6717 Lilly Rd.
Menomonee Falls WI 53051

WYOMING

CHEYENNE RODS & CUSTOMS
Box 253
Cheyenne WY 82003

CLASSIC CHEVYS OF
CHEYENNE
Box 6703
Cheyenne WY 82003

KARZ CLUB
2254 Papago Dr.
Sheridan WY 82801

RAGTOPS & RELICS
1415 Citadel
Green River WY 82935

ROCKY MOUNTAIN
ROAD AGENTS
2601 Ina Ave.
Cody WY 82414

SCOTTSBLUFF VALLEY
STREET RODS
Box 381
Torrington WY 82240

International Club Finder

AUSTRALIA

PHANTOMS ROD CLUB
C/-P. O. Box 143, Dimboola, 3414
Victroria, Australia

ARGENTINA

ARGENTINE HOT ROD ASSN.
C/O Luis Ciccone
Martin Miguel Guernez 1267
Hurlingham
Buenos Aires, Argentina

BELGIUM

BSCA STREETCRUISERS, INTL.
Scherpstuklei 27
2820 Bonheiden
Belgium

BRAZIL

CLASSIC CHEVY CLUB
OF BRAZIL
Rua Dr. Zuquin 126
Sao Paulo 02035
Brazil

RACE DODGE V8
Rua Tagua 317
Parque Joao Ramalho
Santo Andre, Sao Paulo 09290
Brazil

CANADA

EDMONTON STREET ROD ASSN.
Box 6237 Station "C"
Edmonton, Alberta T5B 4K6
Canada

EDSEL OWNERS CLUB —
PRAIRIE CHAPTER
97-53050 Range Rd. 211
Ardrossan, Alberta T0B 0E0
Canada

FOOTHILLS STREET RODS
136 Woodford Cl. SW
Calgary, Alberta T2W 6E2
Canada

LEBARONS CAR CLUB
3130 2nd Ave. N.
Lethbridge, Alberta T1H 0C6
Canada

MAINSTREET CRUISERS
Box 32107, Millwoods Post Office
Edmonton, Alberta T6K 4C2
Canada

PISTON POPPERS STREET
ROD CLUB
Box 192
Ponoka, Alberta T0C 2H0
Canada

RODHOPPERS CAR CLUB
2317-138A Ave.
Edmonton, Alberta T5Y 1B9
Canada

TOURING TIN CAR CLUB
17904 80A Ave.
Edmonton, Alberta T5T 0S4
Canada

KINGS MEN CAR CLUB
Box 1534
Sakatoon, Saskatchewan, S7K 3R3
Canada

STAMPEDE CITY MODEL A
FORD CLUB
Box 412, Station J
Calgary, Alberta T2A 4X7
Canada

STREET WHEELERS CAR CLUB
Box 261
Lethbridge, Alberta
Canada

THREE HILLS STREET
FREAKS AUTO CLUB
Box 1302 Three Hills
Calgary, Alberta T0M 2A0
Canada

UNIQUELY STREET CAR CLUB
1203-544 Blackthorn Rd. NE
Calgary, Alberta T2K 5J5
Canada

WESTLOCK WHEELS OF CLASS
Box 2705
Westlock, Alberta T0G 2L0
Canada

CAR JAMMERS CAR CLUB
Box 592
Vernon, B.C. V1T 6M4
Canada

COLUMBIA VALLEY
CLASSICS AUTO CLUB
Box 247
Radium Hot Springs, B.C. V0A 1M0
Canada

COWICHAN VALLEY ROD
& CUSTOM
6234 Parkside Pl.
Duncan, B.C. V4L 4T1
Canada

P.I.S.R.A.
15280 - 101st Ave., Unit 119
Box 55535
Surrey, B.C. V3R 8X7
Canada

TOTEM MODEL A & T CLUB
Box 82181
North Burnaby, B.C. V5C 5P7
Canada

VAN ISLE CLASSIC CHEVYS
Box 6001, Station C
Victoria, B.C. V8P 5LR
Canada

VINTAGE CAR CLUB OF CANADA
Box 32
Sardis, B.C. V0X 1Y0
Canada

MANITOBA STREET ROD ASSN.
Box 2195
Winnipeg, Manitoba R3C 3R5
Canada

CLASSIC CHEVY CLUB
OF NOVA SCOTIA
Box 8513, Station A
Halifax, Nova Scotia B3K 5M2
Canada

CANADIAN CLASSIC CHEVYS
19 Casablanca Blvd.
Grimsby, Ontario L3M 3Y9
Canada

CANADIAN STREET ROD ASSN.
Box 308, Station U
Toronto, Ontario M8Z 5P7
Canada

FOREST CITY STREET RODS
19 Metcalfe Crescent
London, Ontario N6E 1H8
Canada

OTTAWA STREET ROD ASSN.
Box 3142, Station C
Ottawa, Ontario K1Y 4J4
Canada

RADICAL RIDES TRUCKLUB
105 Meadowbrook Dr. #133
London, Ontario N6L 1G4
Canada

ROAD ANGELS OF BELLEVILLE
RR-5, Trenton, Ontario K8V 5P8
Canada

ROAD RUNNERS CAR CLUB
OF HAMILTON
Box 6365, Station F
Hamilton, Ontario L9C 6L9
Canada

ROCK & ROLL CLASSICS
CAR CLUB OF ONTARIO
312 Montreal St.
Kingston, Ontario K7K 3H3
Canada

SOUTHERN ONTARIO
CLASSIC PICKUPS
886 Meadowhill Ct.
Oshawa, Ontario L1K 5X5
Canada

SOO STREET ROD ASSN.
Box 1393, Sault Ste. Marie
Ontario P6A 6N2
Canada

TORONTO CLASSIC CHEVYS
9 Camperdown Ave.
Toronto, Ontario M9R 3T3
Canada

PRINCE EDWARD ISLAND
STREET ROD ASSN.
Cardigan, RR #6
P.E.I. C0A 1G0
Canada

DRAGGINS ROD
& CUSTOM CLUB
Box 1682
Saskatoon, Saskatchewan
S7K 3R8, Canada

DUSTY WHEELS AUTO CLUB
Box 1813, Rosetown
Saskatchewan, S0L 2V0
Canada

MAJESTICS CAR CLUB
Box 881, Regina
Saskatchewan, S4P 3B1
Canada

OTTAWA STREET ROD ASSN.
Merivale Postal Outlet, Box 65072
Nepean, Ontario K2G 5Y3
Canada

ENGLAND

ELIMINATORS
17 Greenbank Rd., May Bank
Newcastle, Staffordshire, ST5 0RU
England

NATIONAL ASSN. OF
STREET CLUBS
18 Francis Rd., Wollaston,
Stourbridge
West Midlands, DY8 3LT
England

NATIONAL STREET ROD ASSN.
(U.K.)
63 Chadacre Rd., Stoneleigh,
Epsom, Surrey KT17 2HD
England

SOUTHERN ROADSTERS
202 Ringwood Dr.
North Baddesley,
Southampton S052 9HP
England

SURREY STREET RODDERS
Guildford, Essex, England

BSCA STREETCRUISERS
98 Arundel Dr., Fareham
Hants. 1P6 N7V
England

FINLAND

CLASSIC CHEVY CLUB
OF FINLAND
Porvoonkatu 15 AF 162
00510 Helsinki
Finland

FRANCE

FRANCE STREET ROD ASSN.
8, Square du Doyen-Yves-Milon,
atelier #13
35000 Rennes,
France

ROAD RUNNERS
15, rue Leon-Ricotier
35000 Rennes
France

BSCA STREETCRUISERS
R.D. Freres Dheret 10
78700 Conflans St. Honorin
France

GERMANY

BSCA STREETCRUISERS
Burgsdorferstr. 4
1000 Berlin 65
Germany

THE MAN'S VAN ROD & CUSTOM
Postfach 10 36 64
69026 Heidelberg,
Germany

NETHERLANDS

BSCA STREETCRUISERS
Overweertstr. 15
6004 XS Weert
Netherlands

NEW ZEALAND

HERETAUNGA ROD
& CUSTOM CLUB
Hawkes Bay
New Zealand

KIWI KLASSICS
Box 15-539
Henderson, Auckland
New Zealand

NORWAY

BSCA STREETCRUISERS
Kr. Sonjusvei 34
3600 Konigsberg
Norway

NORSK STREET ROD REGISTER
Valeur GT 3A
3181 Horten
Norway

SOUTH AFRICA

DIAMOND CITY STREET
ROD CLUB
18 Hermes St.
Kimborley, 8301
South Africa

SWEDEN

CLUB OF THE AMERICAN FORD
Gyllenborgsgaten 5
112 43 Stockholm
Sweden

CUSTOM KEMPS OF SWEDEN
Box 52
S-740 30 Bjorklinge
Sweden

SWEDISH STREET ROD ASSN.
c/o Pandraggers, Box 110
S-776 00 Hedemora,
Sweden

SWITZERLAND

BSCA STREETCRUISERS
Groserstr. 27A
5015 Niedererlinsbach 01
Switzerland

Make-By-Make
Club Finder

ABARTH

ABARTH OWNERS INT'L.
P. O. Box 1917
Thousand Oaks CA 91360

AHRENS-FOX

AHRENS-FOX FIRE BUFFS ASSN.
365 Neiffer Rd.
Schwenksville PA 19473

ALFA ROMEO

ALFA ROMEO OWNERS CLUB
2468 Gum Tree Ln.
Fallbrook CA 92028

ALLARD

ALLARD REGISTER
1100 Pebble Creek Rd.
Ft. Worth TX 76107

ALVIS

ALVIS 12/50 REGISTER
Wanborough Manor, Nr.
Guildford, Surrey GU3 SJR
Great Britain

NORTH AMERICAN ALVIS
OWNER CLUB
104 Eagle Ln.
Doylestown PA 18901

AMC

AMC RAMBLER CLUB
2645 Ashton Rd.
Cleveland Hts. OH 44118

AMC WORLD CLUBS, INC.
7963 Depew St.
Arvada CO 80003-2527

AMERICAN MOTORS OWNERS
ASSOCIATION, INC.
6756 Cornell St.
Portage MI 49002-3412

CLASSIC AMX REGISTRY
21 Creek Rd.
Dauphin PA 17018

NATIONAL AMERICAN MOTORS
DRIVERS & RACERS ASSN.
Box 987
Twin Lakes WI 53181-0987

ASTON MARTIN

ASTON MARTIN OWNERS
CLUB, EAST
204 Penn View Dr.
Pennington NJ 08534

AUBURN, CORD, DUESENBERG

AUBURN-CORD-DUESENBERG
CLUB
Box 18
Ringoes NJ 08551

AUSTIN

AMERICAN AUSTIN/BANTAM
CLUB
351 Wilson Rd. W.
Rt. 1, Box 137
Willshire OH 45898-9551

AUSTIN-HEALEY

AUSTIN-HEALEY CLUB
OF AMERICA
603 E. Euclid Ave.
Arlington Hts. IL 60004-5707

AUSTIN-HEALEY SPORTS
& TOURING CLUB
Box 3539
York PA 17402

NORTH TEXAS
AUSTIN-HEALEY CLUB
Box 45332
Dallas TX 75245

AVANTI

AVANTI OWNERS ASSN. INT'L.
Box 28788
Dallas TX 75228-0788

BENTLEY

BENTLEY EXCHANGE
46 Elm St.
N. Andover MA 01845

BMW

BMW CAR CLUB OF AMERICA
345 Harvard St.
Cambridge MA 02138

BMW VINTAGE CLUB OF AMER.
Box "S"
San Rafael CA 94913

BORGWARD

BORGWARD OWNERS CLUB
77 New Hampshire Ave.
Long Island NY 11706

BRICKLIN

BRICKLIN INT'L. OWNERS CLUB
213 Southwoods Dr.
Fredericksburg TX 78624

BRUSH

BRUSH OWNERS ASSN.
1222 N. 168th St.
Omaha NE 68118

BUGATTI

AMERICAN BUGATTI CLUB
44844 Howe Hill Rd.
Camden ME 04843

BUICK

BUICK CLUB OF AMERICA
Box 401927
Hesperia CA 92340-1927

BUICK GS CLUB OF AMERICA
1213 Gornto Rd.
Valdosta GA 31602

50 BUICK REGISTRY
54 Madison St.
Pequannock NV 07440

1932 BUICK REGISTRY
3000 Warren Rd.
Indiana PA 15701

1937-1938 BUICK CLUB
1005 Rilma Ln.
Los Altos CA 94022

RIVIERA OWNERS ASSN.
Box 26344
Lakewood CO 80226

CADILLAC

CADILLAC CONVERTIBLE
OWNERS OF AMERICA
Box 269
Ossining NY 10562

CADILLAC DRIVERS CLUB
5825 Vista Ave.
Sacramento CA 95824-1428

CADILLAC LASALLE CLUB, INC.
223 S. Fairfield Rd.
Devon PA 19333

CHECKER

CHECKER CAR CLUB OF AMER.
469 Tremaine Ave.
Kenmore NY 14217

CHEVY

BOWTIE CHEVY ASSN.
Box 608108
Orlando FL 32860

CHEVROLET NOMAD ASSN.
8653 W. Hwy. 2
Cairo NE 68824

CHEVY ASSN.
Box 172
Elwood IL 60421

CHEVY PERFORMANCE
CLUB OF AMERICA
Box 4306
South Bend IN 46634

CLASSIC CHEVY INT'L.
Box 607188
Orlando FL 32860

CORVAIR SOCIETY OF AMERICA
Box 607
Lemont IL 60439-0607

COSWORTH VEGA
OWNERS ASSN.
Box 2039
Bloomington IN 47402

GOLDEN CHEVY ASSN.
25621 Helena Ave.
New Prague MN 56071

INT'L CAMARO CLUB
2001 Pittston Ave.
Scranton PA 18505-3233

LATE GREAT CHEVYS
Box 607824
Orlando FL 32860

NAT'L ASSN. OF CHEVROLET
OWNERS
Box 9879
Bowling Green KY 42102-9879

NAT'L CHEVELLE OWNERS
ASSOCIATION
7343-J W. Friendly Ave.
Greensboro NC 27410

NAT'L CHEVY ASSN.
947 Arcade
St. Paul MN 55106

NAT'L CHEVY/GMC TRUCK ASSN
Box 607458
Orlando FL 32860

NAT'L IMPALA ASSN.
Box 968
Spearfish SD 57783

NAT'L MONTE CARLO
OWNERS ASSN.
Box 187
Independence KY 41051

NAT'L NOSTALGIC NOVA
Box 2344
York PA 17405

1965-1966 FULL SIZE
CHEVROLET CLUB
15614 St. Rd. 23
Granger IN 46530

U.S. CAMARO CLUB
Box 608167
Orlando FL 32860

VINTAGE CHEVROLET
CLUB OF AMERICA
Box 5387
Orange CA 92613-5387

CHRYSLER

AIRFLOW CLUB OF AMERICA
796 Santree Cl.
Las Vegas NV 89110

CALIFORNIA CHRYSLER
PRODUCTS CLUB
Box 2660
Castro Valley CA 94546

CHRYSLER 300 CLUB
Box 274
Bloomington IL 61702

CHRYSLER 300 CLUB, INC.
Box 566
Riverton UT 84065

CHRYSLER 300 CLUB INT'L., INC.
4900 Jonesville Rd.
Jonesville MI 49250

CHRYSLER PRODUCT
OWNERS CLUB
806 Winhall Wy.
Silver Spring MD 20904

CHRYSLER TOWN & COUNTRY
OWNERS REGISTRY
406 W. 34th St.
Kansas City MO 64111

HURST 300 REGISTRY
5844 W. Eddy St.
Chicago IL 60634

IMPERIAL CLUB OF AMERICA
Box 1471
Boca Raton FL 33419-1471

IMPERIAL OWNERS CLUB INT'L.
Box 991
Scranton PA 18503

INT'L. MOPAR CLUB
Box 991
Scranton PA 18503

NAT"L. CHRYSLER
PRODUCTS CLUB
313 S. Jackson St.
Strasburg PA 17579

NAT'L. HEMI OWNERS ASSN.
1693 S. Reese Rd.
Reese MI 48757

NORTHEAST HEMI
OWNERS ASSN.
681 Black Rd.
Bryn Mawr PA 19010

RAPID TRANSIT SYSTEM
MOPAR AUTO CLUB
8827 Strathmoor
Detroit MI 48228

SLANT 6 CLUB OF AMERICA
Box 4414
Salem OR 97302

WALTER P. CHRYSLER CLUB
Box 3504
Kalamazoo MI 49003-3504

CITROEN

CITROEN CAR CLUB
Box 743
Hollywood CA 90028

CITROEN CAR CLUB
8180 Miramar Rd.
San Diego CA 92126

CITROEN QUARTERLY
Hanover St., Sta. Box 30
Boston MA 02113

COLE

COLE MOTOR CAR CLUB
OF AMERICA
4716 Northeastern Ave.
Indianapolis IN 46239

CORVETTE

CORVETTE CLUB OF AMERICA
Box 9879
Bowling Green KY 42102-9879

CORVETTES LTD.
11 Liberty Ridge Trail
Totowa NJ 07512

LT-1 CORVETTE REGISTRY
25 Lido Blvd.
Lido Beach NY 11561

NAT'L. CORVETTE
OWNERS ASSN.
900 S. Washington St.
Falls Church VA 22046

NAT'L. CORVETTE
RESTORERS SOCIETY
6291 Day Rd.
Cincinnati OH 45252-1334

NAT'L. COUNCIL OF
CORVETTE CLUBS, INC.
Box 813
Adams Basin NY 14410-0813

WESTERN STATES
CORVETTE CONCIL
2321 Falling Water Ct.
Santa Clara CA 95054

CROSLEY

CROSLEY AUTOMOBILE CLUB
217 N. Gilbert
Iowa City IA 52245

DELOREAN

DELOREAN OWNERS ASSN.
879 Randolph Rd.
Santa Barbara CA 93111

DESOTO

DESOTO CLUB OF AMERICA
403 S. Thornton St.
Richmond MO 64085

NAT'L. DESOTO CLUB
1521 Van Cleave Rd. N.W.
Albuquerque NM 87107

DE TOMASO

PANTERA INT'L. CAR CLUB
18586 Main St., Ste. 100
Huntington Beach CA 92648-1720

PANTERA OWNERS CLUB
OF AMERICA
3935 Sky Crest Dr.
Pasadena CA 91103

DODGE

DODGE BROTHERS CLUB
Deveau Rd.
North Salem NY 10560

DURANT

DURANT FAMILY REGISTRY
2700 Timber Ln.
Green Bay WI 54303

EDSEL

EDSEL OWNERS CLUB
Rt. 1, Box 206
Jacksonville TX 75766

EDSEL OWNERS CLUB, INC.
1234 Bayview
Los Osos CA 93402-4406

INT'L. EDSEL CLUB
Box 371
Sully IA 50251-0371

FERRARI

DINO REGISTER
6305 Monero Dr.
Rancho Palos Verdes CA 90274

FERRARI OWNERS CLUB
1708 Seabright Ave.
Long Beach CA 90813

FIAT

FIAT CLUB OF AMERICA, INC.
11 Linden Cl.
Somerville MA 02143

FORD

CAPRI CAR CLUB LTD.
Box 111221
Aurora CO 80042-1221

CLASSIC THUNDERBIRD
CLUB INT'L.
Box 4148
Santa Fe Springs CA 90670-1148

COUGAR CLUB OF AMERICA
O-4211 N. 120th Ave.
Holland MI 49424

CROWN VICTORIA ASSN.
Box 6
Bryan OH 43506

EARLY FORD V-8 CLUB
OF AMERICA
Box 2122
San Leandro CA 94577

FABULOUS FIFTIES FORD
CLUB OF AMERICA
Box 286
Riverside CA 92502

FAIRLANE CLUB OF AMERICA
2116 Manville Rd.
Muncie IN 47302-4854

FALCON CLUB OF AMERICA
Box 113
Jacksonville AR 72078-0113

1954 FORD CLUB OF AMERICA
1517 N. Wilmot #144
Tucson AR 85712

FORD GALAXIE CLUB OF AMER.
Box 360
Salkum WA 98581

INT'L. FORD RETRACTABLE
CLUB, INC.
Box 92
Jerseyville IL 62052

MUSTANG OWNERS CLUB, INT'L.
2720 Tennessee NE
Albuquerque NM 87110

ROCKY MOUNTAIN
THUNDERBIRD CLUB
Box 27581
Lakewood CO 80227

SANTA CLARA VALLEY
THUNDERBIRDS
6371 Firefly Dr.
San Jose CA 95120

THUNDERBIRDS OF AMERICA
Box 2766
Cedar Rapids IA 52406

VINTAGE MUSTANG OWNERS
ASSOCIATION
6371 Firefly Dr.
San Jose CA 95120

VINTAGE THUNDERBIRD CLUB
INT'L.
Box 2250
Dearborn MI 48123-2250

FRANKLIN

H.H. FRANKLIN CLUB
Cazenovia College
Cazenovia NY 13035

GRAHAM

GRAHAM OWNERS CLUB
2909 13th St.
Wausau WI 54401

HUDSON

HUDSON-ESSEX-TERRAPLANE
CLUB
100 E. Cross
Ypsilanti MI 48198

HUPMOBILE

HUPMOBILE CLUB
158 Pond Rd.
North Franklin CT 06254

JAGUAR

CLASSIC JAGUAR ASSN.
2860 W. Victoria Dr.
Alpine CA 91901

JAGUAR CLUBS OF NORTH
AMERICA
2323 N. Champlain St.
Arlington Hts. IL 60004

ROCKY MOUNTAIN
JAGUAR CLUB
6562 E. Asbury Ave.
Denver CO 80224

JENSEN

ASSN. OF JENSEN OWNERS
800 Maywood Ave.
Maywood NJ 07607-1653

KAISER/FRAZER

KAISER/FRAZER OWNERS
CLUB INT'L.
Box 1251
Wellsville NY 14895

LAMBORGHINI

LAMBORGHINI OWNERS CLUB
Box 7214
St. Petersburg FL 33734

LANCIA

AMERICA LANCIA CLUB
2100 E. Ohio St.
Pittsburgh PA 15212

LINCOLN

CONTINENTAL MARK II
OWNERS ASSN.
26676 Holiday Ranch Rd.
Apple Valley CA 92307

LINCOLN & CONTINENTAL
OWNERS CLUB
Box 157
Boring OR 97009

LINCOLN OWNERS CLUB
Box 1434
Minocqua WI 54548

LINCOLN-ZEPHYR OWNERS
CLUB
Box 165835
Miami FL 33116

ROAD RACE LINCOLN
REGISTER
461 Woodland Dr.
Wisconsin Rapids WI 54494

MASERATI

CHRYSLER MASERATI
TC REGISTRY
Box 66813
Chicago IL 60666-0813

MASERATI CLUB INT'L.
Box 772
Mercer Island WA 98040

MASERATI CLUB OF AMERICA
945 Middle Country Rd.
Selden NY 11784

MAXWELL

MAXWELL REGISTRY
Rd. 4, Box 8
Ligonier PA 15658

MERCEDES-BENZ

GULLWING GROUP INT'L.
15875 Oak Glen Ave.
Morgan Hill CA 95037

INT'L. 190 SL GROUP
3 Westpark Ct.
Ferndale MD 21061

MERCEDES-BENZ CLUB
OF AMERICA
1907 Lelaray St.
Colorado Springs CO 80909

MERCURY

ACC-USA
Rt. 4, Box 116
Alexandria IN 46001

CLASSIC COMET CLUB
OF AMERICA
419 N. Fulton St.
Allentown PA 18102

COMET ENTHUSIASTS GROUP
4878 Hobe Ln.
White Bear Lake MN 55110

EAST COAST COMETS
10023 Martin Ave.
Lake City PA 16423

INT'L. MERCURY OWNERS ASSN
6445 W. Grand Ave.
Chicago IL 60635-3410

MID-CENTURY MERCURY
CAR CLUB
1816 E. Elmwood Dr.
Lindenhurst IL 60046

MESSERSCHMITT

MESSERSCHMITT OWNERS
CLUB
39 Sylvan Wy.
West Caldwell NJ 07006

METZ

METZ REGISTER
721 E. State St.
Millsboro DE 19966

MG

AMERICAN MGB ASSN.
Box 11401
Chicago IL 60611-0401

CALIFORNIA MG-T REGISTER
4911 Winnetka Ave.
Woodland Hills CA 91364

NEW ENGLAND MG-T REGISTER
Drawer 220
Oneonta NY 13820

NORTH AMERICAN MGB REG.
Box MGB
Akin IL 62805

NORTH AMERICAN MMM REG.
Box 510-394
Melbourne Beach FL 32951

MORGAN

MORGAN THREE-WHEELER
CLUB
3708 California Ave.
Long Beach CA 90807

MORRIS

MORRIS MINOR REGISTRY
OF NORTH AMERICA
318 Hampton Pk.
Westerville OH 43081-5723

MORRIS OWNERS ASSN.
OF CALIFORNIA
211 Dimmick Ave.
Venice CA 90291

NASH/METROPOLITAN

METROPOLITAN OWNERS CLUB
OF NORTH AMERICA
5009 Barton Rd.
Madison WI 53711

NASH CAR CLUB OF AMERICA
4151 220th St.
Clinton IA 52732-8943

OLDSMOBILE

CURVED DASH OLDSMOBILE
CLUB
3455 Florida Ave. North
Minniapolis MN 55427

HURST/OLDS CLUB OF AMER.
1600 Knight Rd.
Ann Arbor MI 48103-9371

OLDSMOBILE CLUB OF AMER.
Box 16216
Lansing MI 48901

OPEL

NORTH AMERICAN OPEL GT
15 Valewood Rd.
West Chicago IL 60185

OPEL MOTORSPORT CLUB
A.G. Dept. B, 1101 Cerritos Dr.
Fullerton CA 92635

OPEL USA
Box 2462
Vernon CT 06066

PACKARD

EASTERN PACKARD CLUB, INC.
Box 5112
Hamden CT 06518

MOTOR CITY PACKARDS
4601 Rattle Run Dr.
St. Clair MI 48079

OLD DOMINION
PACKARD CLUB
426 First St.
West Point VA 23181

PACKARD AUTOMOBILE
CLASSICS
420 South Ludlow St.
Dayton OH 45401

PACKARD CLUB
Box 28788
Dallas TX 75228-0788

PACKARDS INT'L. MOTOR
CAR CLUB
302 French St.
Santa Ana CA 92701

PIERCE-ARROW

PIERCE-ARROW SOCIETY
135 Edgerton St.
Rochester NY 14607-2945

PLYMOUTH

BARRACUDA/'CUDA
OWNERS CLUB
4825 Indian Trail Rd.
Northamptom PA 18067

PLYMOUTH OWNERS CLUB, INC.
Box 416
Cavalier ND 58220

PONTIAC

FIERO CLUB OWNERS CLUB
OF AMERICA
2165 S. Dupont Dr., Unit 1
Anaheim CA 92807

STUDEBAKER

STUDEBAKER DRIVERS CLUB
Box 28788
Dallas TX 75228-0788

STUTZ

STUTZ CLUB
7400 Lantern Rd.
Indianapolis IN 46256-2120

SUNBEAM

CALIFORNIA ASSN. OF
TIGER OWNERS
5165 Slauson Ave.
Culver City CA 90230

SUNBEAM ALPINE CLUB
1752 Oswald Pl.
Santa Clara CA 95051

SUNBEAM CAR CLUB
43 Terrace Ave.
Ossining NY 10562

TIGERS EAST/ALPINES EAST
Box 1260
Kulpsville PA 19443

TRIUMPH

6-PACK, THE TRIUMPH TR6
OWNERS CLUB
1012 West 9th Ave.
Oshkosh WI 54901

TR8 CAR CLUB OF AMERICA
266 LInden St.
Rochester NY 14620

TRIUMPH REGISTER OF AMER.
1641 N. Memorial Dr. Ste. TR3
Lancaster OH 43130

VINTAGE TRIUMPH REGISTER
15218 West Warren Ave.
Dearborn MI 48126

TUCKER

TUCKER AUTOMOBILE CLUB
OF AMERICA
311 W. 18th St.
Tifton GA 31794-3446

TVR

TVR CAR CLUB
4450 South Park Ave. #1609
Chevy Chase MD 20815

VOLKSWAGEN

VINTAGE VOLKSWAGEN
CLUB OF AMERICA
5705 Gordon Dr.
Harrisburg PA 17112

VOLKSWAGEN CLUB OF AMER.
Box 154
North Aurora IL 60542-0154

VOLVO

VOLVO CLUB OF AMERICA
Box 16
Afton NY 13730-0016

VOLVO SPORTS AMERICA 1800
1203 W. Cheltenham Ave.
Melrose Park PA 19126

WHIPPET

MODEL 96 WHIPPET NEWSLTR.
RR. 3, Box 28-A
Parsons KS 67357

WHITE

WHITE OWNERS REGISTER
1624 Perkins Dr.
Arcadia CA 91006-1841

WILLYS

WILLYS AERO SURVIVAL COUNT
952 Ashbury Hts. Ct.
Decatur GA 30030-4177

WILLYS OVERLAND
JEEPSTER CLUB
Box 12042, Coronado Stn.
El Paso TX 79913

WILLYS-OVERLAND-KNIGHT
REGISTRY
1440 Woodacre Dr.
Mc Lean VA 22101-2535

Other Special Interest Organizations

AMERICAN NOSTALGIA
RACING ASSN.
10922 Chestnut Ave.
Stanton CA 90680

AMERICAN TRUCK HISTORICAL
SOCIETY
Box 531168
Birmingham AL 35253

ANGLIA OBSOLETE/ENFO
NEWSLETTER
1311 York Dr.
Vista CA 92084

ANTIQUE AUTO RACING ASSN.
Box 486
Fairview NC 28730

ANTIQUE AUTOMOBILE
CLUB OF AMERICA
Box 412
Hershey PA 17033

ANTIQUE MOTORCYCLE
CLUB OF AMERICA, INC.
Box 333
Sweetzer IN 46987

ANTIQUE TRUCK CLUB
OF AMERICA
Box 291
Hershey PA 17033

ASPHALT DRAGGINS'
RACING ASSN.
Box 1890
St. Paul MN 55101

ATLANTIC COAST OLD
TIMERS AUTO RACING CLUB
4 Elm Dr.
Newtown CT 06470

CLASSIC CAR CLUB OF AMER.
2300 E. Devon Ave. Ste. 126
Des Plaines IL 60018

CLASSIC CARS AGAINST
CANCER
Box 69
Lewiston MN 55952

CLASSY WOMEN WITH
CLASSIC CARS
170 Belvedere Ave.
Fanwood NJ 07023

ELECTRIC CAR OWNERS CLUB
167 Concord St.
Brooklyn Hts. NY 11201

FABULOUS FIFTIES FORD
CLUB OF AMERICA
Box 286
Riverside CA 92502

GOODGUYS ROD &
CUSTOM ASSN.
Box 424
Alamo CA 94507

GREAT AUTOS OF YESTERYEAR
Box 4
Yorba LInda CA 92686

HISTORICAL AUTOMOBILE ASSN
Box 10313
Ft. Wayne IN 46851-0313

HORSELESS CARRIAGE
CLUB OF AMERICA
128 S. Cypress St.
Orange CA 92666-1314

INT'L. SOCIETY FOR
VEHICLE PRESERVATION
Box 50046
Tucson AZ 85703-1046

INT'L. SPECIALTY CAR ASSN.
Rt. 3, #2 Star Kustom Ave.
Afton OK 74331

ITALIAN CAR REGISTRY
3305 Valey Vista Rd.
Walnut Creek CA 94598-3943

KUSTOM KEMPS OF AMERICA
Rt. 1, Box 152A Bill Hailey Dr.
Cassville MO 65625-9724

KUSTOMS OF AMERICA
9678 B E. Arapahoe Rd. #186
Englewood CO 80112

LOST HIGHWAYS TRAILER
ARCHIVES
Box 43737
Philadelphia PA 19106

MICROCAR & MINICAR CLUB
Box 43137
Upper Montclair NJ 07043

MID-AMERICA OLD TIME
AUTO ASSN.
Rt. 3, Box 306 Petit Jean Mtn.
Morrilton AR 72110

MILESTONE CAR SOCIETY
Box 24612
Speedway IN 46224

NAT'L. MOTORISTS ASSN.
6678 Pertzbom Rd.
Dame WI 53529

NAT'L. STREET ROD ASSN.
4030 Park Ave.
Memphis TN 38111

NAT'L. WOODIE CLUB
29 Burley St.
Wenham MA 01984

NOSTALGIA DRAG
RACING ASSN.
Box 9438
Anaheim CA 92812

PARALYZED WHEELS FOUNDN.
4703 S. Division
Wayland MI 49348

PIONEER AUTO ASSN./
ST. JOSEPH VALLEY
922 E. Jefferson
Misawaka IN 46544

PIONEER AUTO CLUB, INC.
10550 C.R.C. Rt. 3
Leipsie OH 45856

PIONEER AUTO TOURING CLUB
374 Harvard Ave.
Palmerton PA 18071

PROFESSIONAL CAR SOCIETY
Box 09636
Columbus OH 43209

SOCIETY OF AUTOMOTIVE
HISTORIANS
Box 339
Matamoras PA 18336

SOUTHERN CALIFORNIA
AIRHEADS (CONVERTIBLES)
Box 10818
Marina Del Rey CA 90292

SPECIALTY EQUIPMENT
MARKETING ASSN.
1575 S. Valey Vista Dr.
Box 4910
Diamond Bar CA 91765-0910

STEAM AUTOMOBILE
CLUB OF AMERICA
1680 Dartmouth Ln.
Deerfield IL 60015

STEPPIN' BACK NOSTALGIA
ASSOCIATION
Box 94
Glendale AZ 85311

STREET ROD MARKETING
ALLIANCE
1575 S. Valley Vista Dr. Box 4910
Diamond Bar CA 91765-0910

UTAH SALT FLATS RACING
ASSOCIATION
536 E. 200 S.
Kaysville UT 84037

VETERAN MOTOR CAR CLUB
OF AMERICA
Box 360788
Strongsville OH 44136

VINTAGE AUTO RACING ASSN.
3416 N. Knoll Dr.
Los Angeles CA 90068

VINTAGE SPORTS CAR
CLUB OF AMERICA
170 Wethreill Rd.
Garden City NY 11530

WEST COAST KUSTOMS
Box 8028
Moreno Valley CA 92552

Sample Promotional Flyers
For Attracting Big Crowds

Create Your Own Flyers
Using These As Good Models

Created By Bob French & Lee McCullough
Who Used These Flyers To Draw Thousands
Of People To Their Popular Car Events

CHEVY - VS - FORD
F A C E to F A C E

CAR SHOW

LIMIT 125 CHEVYS   **LIMIT 125 FORDS**

ANY MODEL PRE '75 QUALITY CHEVY OR FORD ONLY

SUNDAY, AUGUST 28
10 A.M. to 4 P.M.

PINE SQUARE
DOWNTOWN LONG BEACH

- $20 Pre Reg. (See form below)
  - Includes Drivers Only Commemorative Dash Plaque)
  - Drivers only receive a special buy 1 get 1 FREE COUPON
  - for a hamburger, fries & med. drink at Johnny Rockets!
- No Day of Event Registration
- Reserved Street Parking
- D. J. plus Live Entertainment
- Food & Refreshments Available
- Event T-Shirts Available
- No Alcohol • No Refunds

DOWNTOWN LONG BEACH PINE SQUARE
MAIN SHOPPING DISTRICT, WILL BE
CLOSED TO TRAFFIC FOR (4) CITY
BLOCKS - BETWEEN 1st & 3rd and PACIFIC & THE PROMENADE. CHEVYS & FORDS
ONLY WILL BE DISPLAYED FACE TO FACE - ALONG BOTH SIDES OF THE STREETS.
THIS SPECIAL ONE OF A KIND CAR SHOW WILL SELL OUT FAST! IF YOU HAVE A
PRE '75 QUALITY CHEVY OR FORD, SEND YOUR PRE-REG. IN THE MAIL TODAY!

T R O P H I E S
2 Classes - Chevy & Ford (No Categories)
20 Trophies will be awarded
Top 10 Chevys + Top 10 Fords
Plus 2 Best of Show Trophies
1 for Chevy - 1 for Ford
Each winner will also receive an extra
special award T.B.A.!

VENDOR SPACES AVAILABLE,
CAR RELATED ITEMS ONLY
CORPORATE SPONSORSHIPS AVAILABLE
FOR CHEVY OR FORD
CALL BOB FRENCH FOR DETAILS
(310) 869-4977

F R E E   S P E C T A T O R   A D M I S S I O N

REGISTRATION INFORMATION: Open to all pre-'75 Chevy & Ford quality show cars only, any model. Complete form
below and mail to: BOB FRENCH, Box 622, Downey, CA 90241. Make check payable to Bob French. Be sure to
include a SELF ADDRESSED, STAMPED ENVELOPE to receive confirmation, map and entry pass.

• PRE-REG. DEADLINE AUGUST 21, 1994
- CLIP & MAIL -
Register my vehicle in the CHEVY vs. FORD CAR SHOW!

Name _____

Address _____ City _____ Zip _____

Phone (Day) (_____)_____ (Night) (_____)_____

Vehicle (year, make, model) _____

In consideration of inclusion as a participant in the Chevy vs. Ford Car Show, the participant agrees to indemnify and
hold harmless Downtown Long Beach Business Association, the City of Long Beach, its members, agents, employees,
Bob French, and other volunteers, from and against all liability of loss that the participant and/or participant's guests,
including family and relatives, may sustain or incur as a result of claims, demands, costs or judgments arising from
participant's involvement in the Chevy vs. Ford Car Show.

Participant's Signature _____ Date _____
BE SURE TO ENCLOSE REGISTRATION AND A SELF-ADDRESSED, STAMPED ENVELOPE!

Official Sponsors

Massey
Chevrolet • Geo

GO TOPLESS
8th Annual Convertibles ONLY Car Show
(Includes Retractables and Conversions)

ANY YEAR ■ ANY MAKE ■ ANY MODEL

Saturday, August 13
10 A.M. to 4 P.M.
TRAVELAND U.S.A.

SANTA ANA (I-5) FWY. AT SAND CANYON EXIT, IRVINE, CA

TOP 20
TROPHIES
PLUS SPECIAL
TROPHIES

FREE
SPECTATOR
ADMISSION &
PARKING

For information, call Bob at (310) 869–4977

**ALL SHOW CARS WILL BE DISPLAYED ON
GRASS IN THE BEAUTIFUL TRAVELAND PARK
OVERLOOKING THE LAKES, GARDENS &
WATERFALLS, PLUS LOTS OF SHADE TREES!**

ALL CONVERTIBLES
TO BE DISPLAYED
WITH TOPS DOWN

FOOD &
REFRESHMENTS
AVAILABLE
DJ
DASH PLAQUE
(Pre-Reg Only)

**LIMITED VENDOR SPACE AVAILABLE
Call Bob (310) 869–4977 for details!**

- -(CLIP & MAIL)- -
YES!!! I WOULD LIKE TO GO TOPLESS - SAVE ME A SPACE

$10 PRE-REGISTRATION (must be received by August 8, 1994)

OWNER'S NAME_____

ADDRESS_____CITY_____STATE_____ZIP_____

PHONE (____)_____ PHONE(____)_____

YEAR AND MAKE OF CONVERTIBLE_____

_____   _____
SIGNATURE OF PARTICIPANT   DATE
SEND PRE-RIGISTRATION AND A <u>SELF-ADDRESSED, STAMPED ENVELOPE</u> TO RECEIVE CONFIRMATION
AND ENTRY PASS.
MAKE $10 CHECK PAYABLE TO BOB FRENCH.   **MAIL TO: BOB FRENCH, P.O. BOX 622, DOWNEY, CA 90241**

ANNUAL

☆ CASTAIC ☆
LAKE

CAR SHOW
SATURDAY • SEPT. 24th
10 A.M. to 4 P.M.

CASTAIC LAKE RECREATION AREA
INTERSTATE 5 AT LAKE HUGHES RD. - EXIT, CASTAIC CA.
(JUST A FEW MILES NORTH OF MAGIC MT.)

CHECK THIS OUT!	*ALL SHOW CARS WILL BE DISPLAYED LAKESIDE ON GRASS SURROUNDED BY GREEN HILLS OVERLOOKING THE BEAUTIFUL BLUE CASTAIC LAKE LAGOON WITH LOTS OF SHADE TREES! THIS CAR SHOW EVENT WILL FILL UP FAST, DON'T MISS YOUR CHANCE TO SPEND A DAY AT THE LAKE WITH YOUR FAMILY AND FRIENDS! SEND YOUR PRE-REG. IN THE MAIL TODAY ! ! !*

$10 Pre-Reg. (Form Below)

INCLUDES: Admission to Park for Car, Driver & Family • (Drivers Only) will reveive a Special Commemortive Dash Plaque • Reserved Grass Parking Lakeside • 2 for 1 Lunch Coupon • 2 for 1 Event T-Shirt Coupon • $6.00 OFF Coupon for Magic Mt. •1 Free Drivers only Drawing Ticket for a chance to win Dinner for 2 at the World Famous Magic Castle In Hollywood, courtesy of your host Bob French!

- DJ + Live Entertainment
- All Food & Refreshments provided by Frisco's
- Giant Door Prize Drawing
- No Alcohol • No Refunds

OPEN TO ALL PRE '75 SHOW QUALITY CARS

ANTIQUE • CLASSIC • COMMERCIAL • CUSTOM
CONVERTIBLE • EXOTIC/HANDCRAFTED • FOREIGN
MUSCLE CAR • SPECIAL INTEREST • SPORTS CAR
STREET ROD • STOCK/ORGINAL • ROADSTER/HOT ROD
T-BUCKET

NO JUDGING • NO DISAPPOINTMENTS • JUST FUN!

VENDOR SPACE AVAILABLE
(Car Related Items/Arts & Crafts)
CONTACT BOB FRENCH FOR DETAILS: (310) 869-4977

FREE SPECTATOR ADMISSION TO CAR SHOW!
(CASTAIC LAKE PARKING $6 PER CAR)

REGISTRATION INFORMATION: Complete form below and mail to: BOB FRENCH, Box 622, Downey, CA 90241. Make check payable to Bob French. Be sure to include a SELF ADDRESSED, STAMPED ENVELOPE to receive confirmation, map and entry pass.
FOR MORE INFO. CALL BOB FRENCH AT (310) 869-4977

 HURRY, PRE-REG. DEADLINE Sept. 20, 1994! NO DAY OF EVENT REGISTRATION!
- CLIP & MAIL -
Register my vehicle in the CASTAIC LAKE CAR SHOW !

Name_____
Address_____City_____Zip_____
Phone (Day)__(____)_____(Night) (____)_____
Vehicle (year, make, model)_____

In consideration of inclusion as a participant in the Castaic Lake Car Show, the participant agrees to indemnity and hold harmless County of Los Angeles Dept of Parks & Recreation, City of Castaic, its members, agents, employees, Bob French, and other volunteers, from and against all liability of loss that the participant and/or participant's guests, including family and relatives, may sustain or incur as a result of claims, demands, costs or judgments arising from participant's involvement in the Castaic Lake Car Show

Participant's Signature_____Date_____

☞ *BE SURE TO ENCLOSE REGISTRATION AND A SELF-ADDRESSED, STAMPED ENVELOPE!!*

Street Rod
HI PERFORMANCE
COLLECTOR CAR
OPEN AIR MARKET
& CAR SHOW

No Dogs ● No Firearms or Food For Sale

★ RAIN OR SHINE ★

JANUARY 13

★ *24 Hour Information: (213) 726-0350* ★

LONG BEACH VETERANS STADIUM

SELLERS $20/Space	PREFERRED PARKING $5	ADMISSION $3
Gates Open 6 A.M.	Show or Sell	Free Parking-Open 6:30 A.M.
Reservations 1-800-762-9785 (Tom)	Gates Open 6:30 A.M.	Childern Under 12 *Free*

FUTURE DATES ★ 1/13 ★ 2/10 ★ 3/10 ★ 4/14 ★
★ 5/12 ★ 6/9 ★ 7/16 ★ 8/11 ★ 9/8 ★ 10/13 ★
★ SECOND SUNDAY EACH MONTH ★

LARGEST ONE DAY CAR SHOW
ON THE WEST COAST!

5th Annual

Belmont Shore
CAR SHOW

SUNDAY, SEPTEMBER 18
10 a.m. - 3:30 p.m.

- Preregistration required (form below)
- $15 Preregistration fee
- No day of event registration
- Special dash plaque
- 3 DJ's plus live entertainment
- Reserved street parking
- Absolutely NO alcohol
- Food & Refreshments available
- Event T-Shirts available
- No refunds

SIDEWALK SALE

EXPLORE THE SHORE!
FREE SPECTATOR ADMISSION

OPEN TO ALL PRE-'75 SHOW QUALITY CARS

• *ANTIQUE*	• *SPECIAL INTREST*
• *CLASSIC*	• *SPORTS CAR*
• *COMMERCIAL*	• *STOCK/ORIGINAL*
• *CONVERTIBLE*	• *STREET ROD*
• *CUSTOM*	• *HANDCRAFTED/EXOTIC*
• *FOREIGN*	• *ROADSTER/HOT ROD*
• *MUSCLE CAR*	• *T-BUCKET*

• *NO JUDGING* • *NO DISAPPOINTMENTS* •

JUST FUN!

All Pre-Reg. Owners will receive a
Special Commemorative
Dash Plaque

VENDOR SPACES AVAILABLE, PLUS
CORPORATE SPONSORSHIPS,
CALL BOB FRENCH AT (310) 869-4977

Belmont Shore's 2nd Street will be closed to thru traffic for 15 blocks. Show cars will line both sides of 2nd Street. For additional information, call Bob French at (310) 869-4977. This block-buster show will be an early sell-out-don't miss your chance to have a great time!!

PRE-REG. INFO. - Complete the registration form and mail to: Bob French, P.O. Box 622, Downey, CA 90241. Make check payable to Bob French, and include a SELF ADDRESSED, STAMPED ENVELOPE to receive confirmation and entry pass.

Pre-Registration deadline: Sept. 12, 1994. No exceptions!
NO DAY OF EVENT REGISTRATION!!!

- Clip & Mail -

Register my vehicle in the BELMONT SHORE CAR SHOW!

Day Phone # (_____)_____

Name_____ Night Phone # (_____)_____

Address_____ City_____Zip_____

Vehicle (year, make, model)_____

In consideration of inclusion as a participant in the Belmont Shore Car Show, the participant agrees to indemnify and hold harmless Belmont Shore, Belmont Shore Business Association, city of Long Beach, its members, agents, employees volunteers, Bob French, and other volunteers, from and against all liability of loss that the participant and/or participant's guests, including family and relatives, may sustain or incur as a result of claims, demands, costs or judgements arising from participant's involvement in the Belmont Shore Car Show.

Participant's Signature _____ Date _____

BE SURE TO ENCLOSE REGISTRATION FEE AND A SELF-ADDRESSED, STAMPED ENVELOPE!!

5TH ANNUAL

Signal Hill

CAR SHOW

at **SIGNAL HILL PARK**
Cherry Ave. & Hill St.
(1 mile south of the 405 Fwy.)

SUNDAY
JULY 16
10 AM to 3:30 PM

- *$10 preregistration fee*
- *Preregistration required*
- *NO! Day of Event Registration*
- *GIANT RAFFLE • 50/50 TICKETS*
- *D.J. • Event T-Shirts Available*
- *Grass parking*
- *No Alcohol/No Refunds*

FREE SPECTATOR
FOOD & REFRESHMENTS AVAILABLE

**OPEN TO ALL PRE-'75
QUALITY SHOW CARS!**

- ANTIQUE
- CLASSIC
- COMMERCIAL
- CONVERTIBLE
- CUSTOM
- FOREIGN
- MUSCLE CAR
- SPORTS CAR
- STOCK/ORIGINAL
- STREET ROD
- HANDCRAFTED/EXOTIC
- ROADSTER/HOT ROD
- T-BUCKET
- SPECIAL INTEREST

• No Judging • No Disappointments •
JUST FUN!!

VENDOR SPACE AVAILABLE
(Car Related Items / Arts & Crafts)
CONTACT BOB FRENCH AT:
(310) 869-4977

Registration Information: Open to all Pre-'75 quality show cars. Complete the registration form and mail to: **Bob French, Box 622, Downey, CA 90241.** Make check payable to Bob French, and include a **SELF ADDRESSED, STAMPED ENVELOPE** to receive confirmation, map & entry pass.

• PRE-REG. DEADLINE JUNE 10, 1995. NO EXCEPTIONS!
NO DAY OF EVENT REGISTRATION

- CLIP & MAIL -
Register my vehicle in the SIGNAL HILL CAR SHOW!

Name_____

Address_____ City_____ Zip_____

Phone (Day)__(____)_____ (Night)_(____)_____

Vehicle_(year, make, model)_____
In consideration of inclusion as a participant in the Signal Hill Car Show, the participant agrees to indemnify and hold harmless City of Signal Hill, Signal Hill Chamber of Commerce, Sigma Phi Gamma International, Theta Phi Chapter, D.A.R.E., all committees, members, agents, employees, Bob French, and other volunteers, from and against all liability of loss that the participant and/or participant's guests, including family and relatives, may sustain or incur as a result of claims, demands, costs or judgments arising from participant's involvement in the Signal Hill Car Show.

Participant's Signature_____ Date_____
BE SURE TO ENCLOSE REGISTRATION AND A SELF-ADDRESSED, STAMPED ENVELOPE!!

RANCHO HOSPITAL WHEEL SHOW
JULY 29

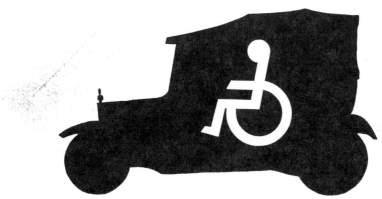

PUBLIC WELCOME!
COME LOOK,
TALK & RELAX

CARS • TRUCKS • SEMIS • BIKES • BOATS ★ DASH PLAQUES • HAT PINS • SNACK BAR
BARBECUED HOT DOGS & HAMBURGERS —
PROCEEDS GO TO RANCHO RECREATIONAL THERAPY DEPARTMENT
A Show for the Patients at
RANCHO LOS AMIGOS HOSPITAL
10:00 A.M. to 2:00 P.M.
7601 E. IMPERIAL HWY., DOWNEY, CALIFORNIA

OLD RIVERSCHOOL RD.
PARKING LOT

For information call: (818) 882-0432
or write: L.A. ROADSTERS
P.O. BOX 3056
HOLLYWOOD, CA. 90078

Orange High Happy Daze
CAR SHOW
Sunday July 22

Hundreds of:
All-American Hot Rods • Customs • Classics
Street Machines • Mini Trucks , too!
Specialty Cars of All Years,
Makes and Models Welcome!

ADMISSION FREE!
Show Car Entry - $15
(For Sale signs permitted)

Great Entertainment - Nostalgia Rock and Roll!
DOOR PRIZES! AWARDS! 50-50 RAFFLE!

CRUISE IT!

Orange High School
525 North Shaffer
Orange, CA 92667
(714) 750-9369
(714) 937-0761
(714) 634-8087

	Walnut	⊗		
		S h a f f e r	T u s t i n	55
5	Chapman 22			

Gates open Sunday at 8 a.m.

Sponsored by Orange High Football Boosters and Orange County Mustang

TOURIN' TIN

Est. 1973
ORANGE COUNTY

So. *Cal.*

TURKEY TROT 17
CHARITY RUN AND CAR SHOW
8699 Holder - Buena Park

NOVEMBER 11 — 7 A.M. TO 4 P.M.

BENEFIT FOR CYSTIC FIBROSIS AND SPEECH & LANGUAGE DEVELOPMENT CENTER

OPEN TO ALL VEHICLES

PRE-REGISTRATION $10 Donation (Deadline Oct. 20) INCLUDES PIN AND SPECIAL DRAWING
GATE REGISTRATION :$12 Donation (Does not Include Pin or Special Drawing)

PANCAKE BREAKFAST By HUBERT'S of Buena Park
7 a.m. to 9 a.m. or first 400 people (whichever comes first)
$2.50 Per Person - Pancakes, Bacon & Eggs

* DASH PLAQUES
* T-SHIRTS
  by Midnight Impressions
* KIDS' MAGIC SHOW
* HUGE RAFFLE

* 50'S MUSIC
* GAMES
* FOOD
* BINGO
* 50/50 DRAWING

* MODEL CAR CONTEST
  Open To All Ages
  Info: Doc 714/523-1059
* CLUB PARTICIPATION
  For All Clubs With 5 Or
  More Cars At Run

SUPER RAFFLE PRIZE
BRAND NEW!
BUSHTEC LUGGAGE TRAILER

INFO: Doc: 714/523-1059
Joe: 213/947-3914
Rob: 714/898-3698

NO
BOOZE!
NO LOUD MUSIC!

....

▲DETACH HERE

6th ANNUAL

Good Time Dance and Car Show

FRIDAY AUGUST 24TH

At the Long Beach Police Academy
7:00 pm to 12:00 am

**$10.00
Per Person**

Music provided by a Disc Jockey
and the Group WEST COAST

PARTY HOSTED BY STEVE LANIER

(213) 425-8454

PLEASE: 18 YRS AND OLDER
Hot Dogs and Pepsi available at 50's prices

TROPHIES AWARDED FOR...
- Best Hair • Best Dress
- Best Dance
- Hula-Hoop • Lip Sinc
- Pre-65 Cars
Multiple Categories

Judging starts at 8:30 pm

HONORING A SPECIAL (NHRA) DRIVER

Hollywood Park Race Track

1st Annual Rod & Custom CAR SHOW

Sunday, October 23

From 10 a.m. to 5 p.m.

PRE-REGISTRATION $20
(Includes Dash Plaque and Souvenir T-Shirt)

ADMISSION: **ADULTS $6** • CHILDREN UNDER 12 **FREE!**

Trophies for Show Winners!

VEHICLE CLASSES
- *Antique Stock - pre 1930*
- *Classic - Best of 1940*
- *Classic - Best of 1950*
- *Classic - Best of 1960*
- *Custom - Mild & Wild*
- *T-Bucket*
- *Stock Muscle - pre 1970*
- *Sports Car*
- *Pure Race*
- *Pure Stock - 1930-74*
- *Stock Modified*
- *Street Rod Sedan Coupe*
- *Special Interest*
- *Van / Panel*
- *Foreign / Exotic*
- *Truck - pre 1969*
- *Truck - post 1970*
- *Street Rod Roadster Open*

Space for 500+ Vehicles!

Vehicles will be judged Concourse Style by Automotive Industry Experts

Selected Winners will be in (NHRA) Winston Select Finals Parade, Sunday Oct. 30th.

RAFFLE BENEFITTING ⚡ FOR LA CADA

Win Prizes like: (NHRA) Winston Select Finals Tickets,
Set of Wheels, Waxes, Oil Gift Certificates & Much More!

Video Arcade and Playground

**Oldie DJ Music ◆ Food & Refreshments
Many Sponsor, Vendor and Specialty Displays
Cars of the Stars**

Casino & Satellite Horse Racing

Hollywood Park Race Track - 405 Fwy. East on Century

For More Show & Vender Space Info: Call

STAGEFRIGHT STAGING
(310) 441-9390 or
RAMCO PROMOTIONS
(310) 698-4846

Pre-registration Deadline,
October 7, 1994
- NO REFUNDS, ALCOHOL
or BURNOUTS
(Move in 7 a.m.)

"Hollywood Park Race Track Charity Car Show" Entry Form

Name _____ T-SHIRT SIZE L XL XXL

Address _____City_____ _____St. ____Zip _____

Phone (_____) _____Vehicle Class_____

Vehicle (Year, Make & Model _____

In conderation of inclusion as a participant in the Hollywood Park Race Track Charity Car Show, the participant agrees to indemnify and hold harmless Stagefright Staging, Ramco Promotions, the City of Inglewood, Hollywood Park Operating Co., plus all show associated sponsors, affiliates, committees, agents, employees, volunteers, from and against all liability of loss that the participant and / or the participant's guest, including family and relatives, may sustain or incur as a result of claims, demands, costs or judgements arising from participant's involvement in the Hollywood Park Race Track Charity Car Show.

Participant's Signature _____ Date _____

Mail check / money order for $20 payable to Stagefright Staging, with self addressed stamped envelope to 2265 Westwood Blvd #21, Los Angeles, CA 90064

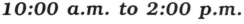 **Winston Finals**

CAR SHOW

Saturday, October 12, 1991

10:00 a.m. to 2:00 p.m.

(Gate Opens 8:00 a.m.)

Open To Pre 70 Cars Only
(Plus Selected Speciality Vehicles)

20 Trophy Winners Will Go To

Winston Finals
October 27

Winners will receive Award Plaque and 2 Tickets to Races
Dash Plaques to First 200 Cars

Here is your chance to be in the Winston Finals with your car. Imagine cruising down the quarter mile in front of 50,000 people, getting seen on television, and getting 2 Free Passes to the Final Day of The Winston Finals Drags (approx. value $90.00)

** HUGE RAFFLE!
Win Pairs of Tickets to Races, plus many other great prizes!
$5.00 Per Car Enrty (No Pre-Reg)
This event will be held at the location of Harvey's Cruise-Nite, 7447 E. Firestone Bl. Downey, CA
Some Vendor Spots available
(Call Lee for Details)
* PROCEEDS TO BENEFIT A LOCAL NON-PROFIT ORGANIZATION.

CRUISIN' RULES

- **NO ALCOHOL!**
- **NO BURN-OUTS!**
- **NO LOUD RADIOS!**
- **NO ANIMALS!**

FOR MORE INFO:

CALL

LEE OR JENNI

(213) 929-3811

Cantina La Vida

THE CARBON CANYON

ROADHOUSE

SINCE 1883

Pool Tables • Full Bar • Great Food • Dancing

Proudly Presents

The Best Kept Secret

THE HOT ROD SHOW

FRIDAY AUGUST 26
AND
FRIDAY SEPTEMBER 16, 1994

4:30 PM TO 8:30 PM
NO ENTRY FEE!!

OPEN TO ALL PRE-'75 SHOW CARS

• ANTIQUE	• SPECIAL INTEREST
• CLASSIC	• SPORTS CAR
• COMMERCIAL	• STOCK/ORIGINAL
• CONVERTIBLE	• STREET ROD
• CUSTOM	• HANDCRAFTED/EXOTIC
• FOREIGN	• ROADSTER/HOT ROD
• MUSCLE CAR	• T-BUCKET

LIVE BLUES BAND STARTING AT 9 PM
CATEGORIES – BEST OF SHOW, TOP 5 RODS, CLUB PARTICIPATION & BEST HARLEY.
WINNERS RECEIVE – TROPHIES, GIFT CERTIFICATES & CASH PRIZES
RAFFLE + 50/50 & CRUISERS • FOOD/DRINK SPECIALS
FOR MORE INFO: CALL ROD FRENCH – (909) 357-2578 OR
CANTINA LA VIDA – (714) 996-0720

714-996-0720

3RD ANNUAL CHAMBER OF COMMERCE

ARTESIA

INTERNATIONAL SUMMER STREET FESTIVAL AND GOOD OLD DAYS

CAR SHOW

PRE '75 CARS ONLY

SUNDAY, JUNE 5

10 AM to 4:00 PM

Pioneer Blvd. will be closed to thru traffic for 7 city blocks. Between Artesia Blvd. & 178 St. Show Cars will line both sides of street.

• Pre-Reg. Required (form below)	**Trophies, Best In Each Class**
• $10 Pre-Reg. Fee	
• NO! Day of Event Registration	• *ANTIQUE* • *SPECIAL INTEREST*
• 2 D. J.'s + Live Entertainment	• *CLASSIC* • *SPORTS CAR*
• Reserved Street Parking	• *COMMERCIAL* • *STOCK/ORIGINAL*
• Special Dash Plaque	• *CONVERTIBLE* • *STREET ROD*
• Giant Door Prize Drawing	• *CUSTOM* • *HANDCRAFTED/EXOTIC*
• Event T-Shirts Available	• *FOREIGN* • *ROADSTER/HOT ROD*
• Food & Refreshments Available	• *MUSCLE CAR* • *T-BUCKET*
• No Alcohol • No Refunds	• *PLUS CLUB PARTICIPATION*

FREE **SPECTATOR ADMISSION!**	STREET VENDOR SPACES AVAILABLE, CONTACT ARTESIA CHAMBER OF COMMERCE FOR DETAILS, (310) 924-6397

Registration is open to all Pre-'75 cars. Complete the registration form and mail to: Bob French, Box 622, Downey, CA 90241. Make check payable to ARTESIA CHAMBER OF COMMERCE, and include a SELF ADDRESSED, STAMPED ENVELOPE to receive confirmation, map & entry pass.

• *PRE-REG. DEADLINE MAY 30, 1994.*
FOR MORE INFO CALL BOB FRENCH (310) 869-4977

- *CLIP & MAIL* -

Register my vehicle in the ARTESIA CAR SHOW!

Name_____

Address_____City_____Zip_____

Phone (Day)__(____)_____(Night)_(____)_____

Vehicle (year, make, model)_____

In consideration of inclusion as a participant in the Artesia Car Show, the participant agrees to indemnify and hold harmless City of Artesia, Artesia Chamber of Commerce, its members, agents, employees, Bob French, and other volunteers, from and against all liability of loss that the participant and/or participant's guests, including family and relatives, may sustain or incur as a result of claims, demands, costs or judgments arising from participant's involvement in the Artesia Car Show

Participant's Signature _____ Date _____

BE SURE TO ENCLOSE REGISTRATION FEE AND A SELF-ADDRESSED, STAMPED ENVELOPE!!

ANTIQUE & CLASSIC CAR AND PARTS EXCHANGE • 1995

Car, Motorcycle, Parts
29th Annual San Diego Region Meet
February 18 & 19

BY THE
HORSELESS CARRIAGE CLUB
ANTIQUE AUTOMOBILE CLUB
EARLY FORD V-8 CLUB

**PUBLIC
ADMITTED FREE!**

Automobiles, Parts and Related Items Only!

No furniture, beverage or food products or fire arms to be sold.
Unlimited vendor stalls equal to approximately 4 parking spaces each. Stalls will be sold, Advance Reservation or available at the Meet at $30.00 each for both days. This event will be held, rain or shine! Friday setup okay. Overnight parking by vendors okay. Reservation confirmation mailed by January 1st.

FOOT TRAFFIC ONLY!

San Diego Big 3 Car, Motorcycle Parts Meet
San Diego Stadium

To reserve the stall you have this year for next year, go to Stall F-D 1 & 2 before noon Sunday during this event. After noon, all spaces are open!!!

LOCATION MAP

N

ENTRY FROM FRIARS ROAD
San Diego Jack Murphy Stadium is located in the heart of San Diego's Mission Valley, which abounds with hotels, fine eating establishments, shopping centers and some of San Diego's finest attractions.
For information call:
(619) 275-1872 or (619) 276-7135

ALL VEHICLES IN MEET AREA MUST DISPLAY OFFICIAL NUMBERED STALL PASSES
APPLICATIONS FOR RESERVATIONS BY MAIL NOT ACCEPTED AFTER **JANUARY 1ST.**
PLEASE **PRINT** OR TYPE INFORMATION BELOW.

NAME_____PHONE_____

ADDRESS _____

CITY _____STATE_____ZIP_____

PLEASE RESERVE _____VENDOR'S STALLS AT $30.00 EACH.   AMOUNT ENCLOSED: $_____
CHECKS AND MAIL TO: **BIG 3 EXCHANGE**, 2415 MORENA BLVD. J., SAN DIEGO, CA 92110-4150

No refund. Rain or Shine. Committee and Stadium Authority not responsible for theft, damage, loss or personal injury. Only old cars and motorcycles, parts and related items may be displayed and sold or swapped! Stalls are subject to official inspection. Vendors to observe all applicable state, local and BIG 3 Committee requirements relating to this event.
I ACCEPT THE ABOVE CONDITIONS _____DATE_____
Signature of Applicant

FEBRUARY 1995

INTERESTED CLUBS MAY REPRODUCE THIS INFORMATION FOR THEIR NEWSLETTERS AND MEMBERS.

LONG BEACH OLDIES

&

Pharaohs Car Club
South Bay

INDOOR
OUTDOOR

PEOPLE CHOICE AWARD WILL BE GIVEN TO MOST POPULAR OLDIES CAR AT SHOW (REAL CAR) CAR CLUBS WELCOME

PRESENTS

THE 1994 SUMMER FEST
SUPER MODEL CAR SHOW   SPECIAL GUESTS

July 30

AT
GONZALES PARK
1101 W. CRESSEY ST.
COMPTON, CALIF 90222
MAJOR CROSS STREETS
    WILMINGTON AND
ROSECRANS

FOR MORE INFORMATION
CALL THE LONG BEACH
OLDIES HOT LINE....
(310) 984-0913

ORLIE'S LOWRIDING PHOTOGRAPHER MAGAZINE

AIR DESIGNS

SPONSORED BY

MORRIS MODELS & RACEWAY
2100 N. LONG BEACH BLVD., #BX2
COMPTON, CA 90220

PHONE (310) 608-7099

2100 LONG BEACH BLVD
BUS: COMPTON. CA 90221
(310) 608-7227

Big Kids Enterprises

Hobbies • Models • Toys

Dennis
22025 South Figueroa Street
Carson, Ca 90745 U.S.A.
310 325-7758 Msg. Machine
310 328-9423 Bus. Ph. / Fax

VELVET UNDERGROUND
-ROCK AND ROLL COLLECTIBLES-
AND MUSIC MEMORABILIA-

5843 ATLANTIC AVE. Long Beach, 90805   Compact Discs   Tapes   Cool Concert Permits
(310) 429-3307   Music Videos   Record Awards   Picture Discs

I WANT
YOU
BACK
SHOW

Continental
Cablevision

Host: Angel Rodriquez   100 NE I   Roma Ave
                         Downe., CA 90241
                         862-9955

Johnies Broiler
Restaurant

7447 FIRESTONE
DOWNEY, CA 90241

Bus. (310) 927-3383

RAFFLING A 1975 CAPRICE CLASSIC GLASS HOUSE AND 1979 CADILLAC
PROVIDED BY TOY MANS HOBBY. ALSO SURPRISE DOOR
PRIZE FOR SOME LUCKY REGISTERED MODELISTS
DOOR PRIZE PROVIDED BY BIG KIDS ENTERPRISES.

Are you **BOARD** by **REGULAR CARS SHOWS?**

To Benefit HBISM

If so, come to the 1st Annual

"*SURF CITY, USA*"
ROD RUN

HUNTINGTION BEACH
INTERNATIONAL SURFING MUSEUM
411 Olive, Huntington Beach, CA

AUG. 27   **9 AM - 2 PM**

Open to 100 Rods, Customs, Stockers, Woodies, etc.
Pre-'70 Cars/Trucks Only • (Plus some specially invited vehicles)

✔ Unique Trophies!
✔ One of a kind Numbered Dash Plaques!
✔ FREE Entry to the Surfing Museum!
✔ FREE Entry to the Surfing Swap Meet!
✔ SHOP Downtown H. B. till you drop!
✔ Only two blocks from the pier!
✔ Bring your own shade & lawn chairs.
✔ Hey guys this show will fill up fast, so sign up Today!!!!!
✔ Remember only 100 CARS will be allowed at this Show!

COST: $10.00 Pre Registration • Day of Event $15.00

PRE-REG. INFO: Complete the registration form and mail to: **LEE, 13630 PIONEER BLVD., NORWALK, CA 90650.** Make check payable to **HBISM**, and include a **SELF ADDRESSED, STAMPED ENVELOPE!**

FOR INFO CALL LEE AT (310) 929-3811 • Pre Reg. Deadline AUG. 15, 1994

- - - - - - - - - - - - - - - CLIP & MAIL TODAY - - - - - - - - - - - - - - - - - -

Name_____

Address_____ City_____ Zip_____

Phone (Day)__(____)_____ (Night)_(____)_____

Vehicle (year, make, model)_____

In consideration of inclusion as a participant in the "SURF CITY, USA" ROD RUN the participant agrees to indemnify and hold harmless HBISM, City of Huntington Beach, its members, agents, employees, Lee McCullough, and other volunteers, from and against all liability of loss that the participant and/or participant's guests, including family and relatives, may sustain or incur as a result of claims, demands, costs or judgments arising from participant's involvement in the "Surf City, USA" Rod Run.

Signature_____ Date_____

VINTAGE & CLASSIC AUTOMOBILE
SWAP MEET
&
ANTIQUE FLEA MARKET

October 29 and 30
Kern County Fairgrounds
Bakersfield, California

Admission $2.00   Vendors $20.00

Spaces are 20 Ft x 20 Ft

Gates open for vendors 3 pm on Friday Oct 28
Buyers welcome at 7 am on both
Saturday Oct 29 and Sunday Oct 30

Bakersfield Model A Ford Club

(805) 328-1553
(805) 393-3112

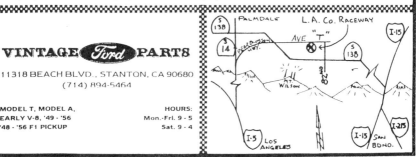

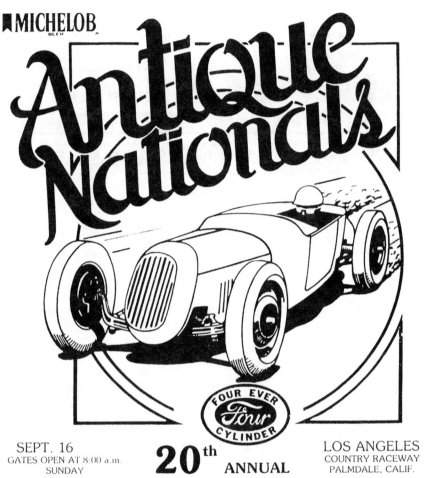

■MICHELOB
BEER

Antique Nationals

FOUR EVER
Four
CYLINDER

SEPT. 16
GATES OPEN AT 8:00 a.m.
SUNDAY

20th **ANNUAL**

LOS ANGELES
COUNTRY RACEWAY
PALMDALE, CALIF.

Race   1954 or earlier type vehicles, any engine.
13.99 and quicker open cars must have NHRA roll bar.
Tech information: (805) 944-2224

Show   Open to all — Lots of awards!

Parade   Dash plaques to all at noon

GENERAL ADMISSION: Adults $10, Children $1, no other fees.
INFO 4EVER4 (EVES, WKNDS) (818) 337-4827 / (714) 787-0672 "JIM" 605 FOXDALE, WEST COVINA, CA 91790

99¢ CAR SHOW

Pre-'75 cars only

Saturday, March 9
10 a.m. to 3 p.m.
Warren High School in Downey

99¢ Prereg
includes dash plaque & drivers drawing

Prereg Deadline:
March 4, 1991
no exceptions!!

*Grass parking   *DJ

$9.99 day-of-event reg
99¢ refreshments
99¢ door prize tickets

999+ cars expected

99¢ vendor spaces for details, call Bob (213)869-4977.

*Proceeds to local nonprofit organization

99¢ spectator admission —
kids under 9 free with paid adult

99+ TROPHIES

TROPHY SPONSORSHIPS AVAILABLE!

DOOR PRIZE CONTRIBUTIONS WELCOME!

Top 9 ANTIQUES	Top 9 CUSTOMS	Top 9 ROADSTERS/HOT RODS
Top 9 CLASSICS	Top 9 HANDCRAFTED/	Top 9 SPORTS CARS
Top 9 COMMERCIALS	REPLICARS	Top 9 STREET RODS
Top 9 CONVERTIBLES	Top 9 MUSCLE CARS	Top 9 T-BUCKETS

1st Registered
Shortest Distance (by prereg)

Longest Distance (by prereg)
Oldest Vehicle (by prereg)

Club Participation (by prereg)

---

*No alcohol   *No refunds

- - - - - - - - - - - - - - - - - - CLIP & MAIL -

Register my vehicle in the 99¢ Car Show!   Please print.

Name _____   Phone ( )_____

Address _____ City _____ Zip _____

Vehicle _____ Club Affiliation _____
(year, make, model)   Specify which class you are entering.

In consideration of inclusion as a participant in the 99¢ Car Show, the participant agrees to indemnify and hold harmless the 99¢ Car Show, the city of Downey, Warren High School, Downey Unified School District, Bob French, volunteers, members, agents, employees, and designated nonprofit organizations, from and against all liability of loss that the participant and/or participant's guests, including family and relatives, may sustain or incur as a result of claims, demands, costs, or judgments arising from participant's involvement in the 99¢ Car Show.

Signature of Participant _____   Date _____

BE SURE TO ENCLOSE 99¢ REGISTRATION FEE AND SELF-ADDRESSED, STAMPED ENVELOPE!!!
To receive confirmation and entry pass, mail check (payable to Bob French) to:
Bob French, Box 622, Downey CA 90241.

BRUNCH CReverse: CRUISE
BRUNCH
CRUISE

at

LA QUINTA INNS

Special Cruiser Brunch Available

Tia Juana's *

LONG BAR MEXICAN CAFE deluxe

(714) 551-2998

Sunday, August 19, 1990
10 a.m. to 2 p.m.

$5 per car entry
includes dash plaque
and trophies

*Located one block south of Santa Ana (5) fwy. at Sand Canyon exit.

PRE-70

▲ No alcohol   ▲ No animals
▲ No burnouts
▲ No loud radios

△ Live D.J. △

Brought to you by the

Cruise-Night Staff

For more information call:
Lee or Jenni at (213) 929-3811

CARS ONLY   △ Vendors spots available

Proceeds to benefit OCBA
Orange County Burn Assoc.   (OVER) ➤

August 4

SANTA FE SPRINGS

Drive-In Theater SINCE 1955

Drive-In Movie Cruise

GATES OPEN PROMPTLY AT 6:30 PM

Hey cruisers, get out your lawnchairs and your picnic baskets and enjoy a nite at the DRIVE-IN MOVIE, but be sure you have an AM RADIO on AM830. Bring your portable radio, and save your battery.

Proceeds to benefit the Orange County Burn Assoc.

Next summer date 9/22

$10.00
per carload
DONATION

PRE '75 CARS ONLY

FREE DASH PLAQUE TO EACH CAR.

ROOM FOR 1,000 OLD CARS!

A DRIVE-IN MOVIE SHIRT WILL BE AVAILABLE.

SNACK BAR WILL BE OPEN

Brought to you by the

Harvey's
Cruise-Night Staff

Take Valley View exit from I-5
Go North 1 Block to Alondra
Turn Left. Go ½ Mile!

For more information call:
Lee or Jenni at (213) 929-3811

Cruise Rules:
No Alcohol
No Burn-Outs
No Animals
No Mini's

DIXIE BELLE

RESTAURANT

AND

KUSTOMS
UNITED
CAR CLUB
Presents

* *

FRIDAY NIGHT CRUISE

AT
9559 EAST IMPERIAL HIGHWAY
DOWNEY

3RD FRIDAY OF THE MONTH

6:00 PM - 10:00 PM

PRE 1971 VEHICLES ONLY

PARKING $2.00 IN ATTENDED AREA

DOOR PRIZE DRAWING FOR PARKING TICKET HOLDERS

DANCE * D.J. ENTERTAINMENT * 50'S & 60'S MUSIC
BRING THE FAMILY TO THE BANQUET ROOM
BEST 50'S DRESS CONTEST
DANCE CONTEST * 50/50 RAFFLE * GAMES FOR ALL AGES

FOOD AND DRINKS AVAILABLE
FULL COURSE DINNERS IN NOSTALGIC DINING ROOM

FUN FOR ALL OF THE FAMILY
BRING THE KIDS AND PLAY TOGETHER

TO PATRONIZE THE BAR AREA YOU MUST BE 21 OR OLDER
NO ALCOHOLIC BEVERAGES WILL BE ALLOWED OUTSIDE
OF THE BUILDING OR IN THE VEHICLE AREA

NO EXCEPTIONS TO THIS RULE

ADDITIONAL INFORMATION
CALL HERMAN 213 925-3859 * MONTY 213 867-4112

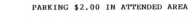

Cruisin Tuesday

PRE-70 CARS ONLY
EVERY TUESDAY NITE 6 PM TO 9 PM

FUDDRUCKERS

BUENA PARK

CRUISIN' RULES

<u>NO</u> Animals
Alcohol - Outside
Burnouts
Loud Radios

For more Information:
call LEE or JENNI at
(213) 929-3811 Daily

DIRECTIONS TO CRUISIN' TUESDAY

Located at the corner of Beach Blvd. and Orangethorpe in the city of Buena Park, **FUDDRUCKERS** is only 1 block north of the 91 fwy. at Beach Blvd.

Our **TUESDAY CRUISE** has a great parking lot, that is not only large enough for close to a hundred cars, but is well lit also!

I'm sure you know about the food, but mention that you're a cruiser and a 10% discount is offered. How can you top that? How about a raffle at 8:00 PM? Some of the nicest cars seen in the area. This makes this **CRUISE-NITE** the place to be on **Tuesday!**

Don't take our word on it, come out and try it for yourself, and see what we mean!!!

hosted by Vintage Iron Car Club

Starts at 5 p.m. till ???

HOT AUGUST NIGHT

End of Summer Cruise

SATURDAY - AUGUST 25

At Movieland Frontiertown in Colton, CA

Listen to the Sounds of the 50's & 60's

LIVE - IN PERSON

T. C. & THE SLICKS

Featuring:

Former Members Of:

The Soul Survivors (Expressway To Your Heart)

The Standells (Dirty Water)

Johnny Fortune of Santo & Johnny (Sleep Walk)

T. C. & THE SLICKS

Bring your Rod, Custom, Classic, Vintage Car or Specialty Car to **Movieland Frontier Town** - 1351 W. Valley Blvd., Colton, CA. North side of I-10 freeway between Rancho & Pepper Ave.

SPECIAL DRAWING: $100.00 First Prize - Winner Must Be Present. Portion of proceeds to MAKE A WISH FOUNDATION.

LOTS OF 50'S FUN

* 50's Dress Up Contest
* Hula Hoop Contest
* Bubble gum Blowing Contest
* Guest M.C. - Vic Slick of KBON Radio With Special Prize Giveaways.

TROPHIES PRESENTED FOR:

* Peoples Choice Car (Prizes   For 2nd & 3rd Also)
* Club Participation

KBON 103.9

"OLDIES FM"

FOR MORE INFORMATION

CALL: Jack (714) 886-7153

Im-Press Printing, 265 E. Baseline, San Bernardino, Ca. (714) 884-1121

NICKELODEON Pizza Pasta and Pleasin' Food

PRE-70 CARS ONLY

Join Us.... SUNDAY

Cruise Brunch

BRUNCH CRUISE

AUGUST 19TH. 10AM TO 2PM

14988 SAND CANYON AVE. IRVINE, CA.

PLENTY OF CARS, FUN AND GOOD FOOD!

SPECIAL SIT-DOWN MENU FROM $4.95 TO $6.95

$5 CAR ENTRY INCLUDES DASH PLAQUE AND TROPHIES

BIG BIG **BIG!** RAFFLE

LIVE D.J. DRAWING

OLD TOWN CRUISE SPONSORS

*Located one block south of Santa Ana (5) fwy. at Sand Canyon exit.

TIA JUANA'S
LA QUINTA HOTEL
SIRUS CELLERS WINE SHOP
ORANGE INN MARKET & CAFE
KNOWLWOODS HAMBURGERS
WEE HOUSE OF FINE GIFT'S

K-ORGE 1190 AM RADIO

PROCEEDS TO BENEFIT ORANGE COUNTY BURN ASSN.

FOR INFORMATION CALL:

JOE CARO

(213) 428-6972

Papa Cantella's
CRUISE NIGHT
EVERY WEDNESDAY
OF EVERY MONTH
FOR ALL CARS 1970 *or older*
(plus special invited vehicles)

6 P.M. to 9 p.m.

FREE COFFEE AND
SPECIAL BLUE PLATE PRICES

CRUISIN' RULES

<u>NO</u> *Animals*
Alcohol - Outside
Burnouts
Loud Radios

For more Information:
call LEE or JENNI at
<u>*(213) 929-3811 Daily*</u>

18065
GALE
AZUSA AVE.
FULLERTON RD.
POMONA FWY EAST

Approved *BY*
THE HARVEY'S CRUISE-NITE STAFF

Harvey's

PAPA CANTELLA'S DINER
18065 Gale Avenue
Industry, CA 91708
(818) 965-6953

THURSDAY
NITE
CRUISE AT

NORTHWOOD PIZZA

8956 KNOTT AVE. • LINCOLN CENTER • BUENA PARK • (714) 220-9400

PRE-70 CARS ONLY
EVERY THURSDAY-NITE 6 PM TO 9 PM

FOR MORE INFORMATION CALL:
LEE or JENNI AT (213) 929-3811 DAILY!

GREAT PARKING - ROOM FOR OVER 200 CARS

I'm sure you know about the f<u>ood,</u> but mention that you're a <u>cruiser</u> and a <u>10% discount</u> is offered. How can you top that? How about a raffle at 8:00pm? Some of the nicest cars in the area! This makes **NORTHWOOD PIZZA** the place to be on Thursday nite!!!

CRUISIN' RULES   **NO** Animals, Alcohol (Outside), Burnouts, Loud Radios, Mini-Trucks!!!!
ANY OFFENDERS WILL BE ASKED TO LEAVE!

DIRECTIONS TO NORTHWOOD PIZZA
Take the 91 Fwy. to the Knott Ave. exit go
south, approx. 2 miles to Lincoln,
northeast corner!

ASK FOR YOUR "CRUISER" DISCOUNT

TAKE A LOOK AT THE OTHERSIDE....

6 P.M. to 9 p.m.
CRUISIN' THRU THE WEEK

Approved BY
THE HARVEY'S CRUISE-NITE STAFF

These cruises are intended to allow you to enjoy a safe, well operated cruise in your area.

Pre - '70 cars only
(plus special invited vehicles)

Family-Oriented

Have FUN!!

Tuesdays	Fuddruckers in Buena Park	
Wednesdays	Basin Street in Lakewood	Papa Cantella's Diner in Industry 
Thursdays	Omega Drive-In in Orange	 Located at 309 West Chapman Only 1 Blk. West of the Circle in Orange

CRUISIN'

For more information, call Lee or Jenni at (213) 929-3811.

EVERY WEDNESDAY

CRUISE - NITE

At Johnnies Broiler • 7447 E. Firestone Bl., Downey, CA

OPEN TO PRE 70 CARS ONLY
(Plus Selected Specialty Vehicles)

ROOM FOR OVER 250 CARS
THE LARGEST WEEKLY CRUISE-NITE ON THE WEST COAST!!

HUGE RAFFLE EACH WEEK • HARVEY'S CHOICE AWARD • SPECIAL CAR ENTRY PRIZE • GREAT OLD TIME ROCK & ROLL MUSIC •

*RAFFLE TO BENEFIT FOR KIDS SAKE INC.
(HELP PREVENT CHILD ABUSE)

Get ready to travel back in time to the fabulous fifties, when Harvey's Broiler was the premier cruise spot on the west coast! See many of the finest Customs, Street Rods, and Muscle Cars ever assembled at one of the oldest and most famous Drive-Ins still in existance! Bring out your family and friends for a night you won't forget!

ONLY $2.00 PER CAR ENTRY

CRUISIN' RULES

NO Alcohol/Drugs
NO Animals
NO Burnouts
NO Speeding
*Any offenders will
be asked to leave!*

[map: Florence Ave. / L. B. Fwy (710) / Old River Rd. / Firestone Blvd. / 605 Fwy. / N]

**For more info. call
Lee McCullough or Jenni Peery
(213) 929-3811
Promotion Directors
Harvey's Cruise Nite**

The Cracker Barrel Buena Park
and
Lee & Jenni
presents:

THE NEWEST, GREATEST CRUISE NIGHT EVERY TUESDAY NIGHT!

LIVE
DISC JOCKEY

20% OFF
For all cruisers
at cruise night

RAFFLE & PRIZES

TROPHY NIGHT
EVERY FIRST TUESDAY
OF THE MONTH

PRE 70
CARS ONLY
6 P.M. TO 9 P.M.

Remember the days when you could go to a restaurant and feel the lumps in those real mashed potatoes, or those large portions for only few dollars? Well, now you can enjoy all those memories with our great shakes and homemade onion rings, plus much more. So cruise on down every Tuesday night with your family and cars to our all new Cracker Barrel Diner in Buena Park. Enjoy that fabulous 50's and 60's music with that real old fashion homemade food. We like to call this our "BLAST FROM THE PAST" night. *Fun! Fun! Fun!*

N

ORANGETHORP

BEACH BLVD.

WESTERN

91 FWY.

For more information call:
LEE or JENNI at (213) 929-3811 Daily

Brought to you by the

CRUISIN' RULES	
NO Animals	NO Burnouts
NO Alcohol	NO Loud Radios

Cruise Night Staff

EVERY WEDNESDAY

DOMENICO'S

ITALIAN RESTAURANT

CRUISE NITE

5:30 - 8:30 P.M.

Pre '70 Cars Only

10% Cruiser Discount

Fabulous Food

BRING THE FAMILY
SEE YOU THERE!

DOMENICO'S
7922 VALLEY VIEW, BUENA PARK

You Missa
This Cruise,
I Breaka
You Face!

	91 Fwy.
La Palma	
	Valley View

HUGE PARKING LOT! ROOM FOR OVER 200 CARS
(in rear of building)

FOR MORE INFO.
CALL LEE AT (310) 929-3811 DAILY

CRUISIN' RULES
NO ANIMALS   NO BURNOUTS
NO ALCOHOL   NO LOUD RADIOS

Brought to you by
Lee's Cruise-Night Staff

EVERY THURSDAY
SHAKEY'S®
CRUISE NITE

6:00 to 9 P.M.
Pre '70 Cars Only

Just a 1/4 mile north of Sonic

1422 AZUSA BL., COVINA • (818) 966-5819

ARROW HWY.			
	AZUSA BL	SHAKEY'S	SEARS SHOPPING PLAZA
10 FWY.			

FOR MORE INFO.
CALL LEE AT (310) 929-3811 DAILY

CRUISIN' RULES
NO ANIMALS   NO BURNOUTS
NO ALCOHOL   NO LOUD RADIOS

Brought to you by
Lee's Cruise-Night Staff

RODDERS AGAINST DRUGS

INVITES YOU TO JOIN THEM
EVERY THURSDAY
FOR THEIR WEEKLY "CRUISE NIGHT"
AT
RED ROBIN
1631 W. IMPERIAL HWY.
LA HABRA
50/50 — MUSIC — FOOD

*NO ALCOHOL IN PARKING LOT
* NO DRUGS
* NO CAR HOPPING

*NO BURNOUTS
*NO RAPPING OF PIPES
*NO EXHIBITION OF SPEED

BEGINNING IN JUNE, THROUGH AUGUST, WE WILL BE PRESENTING A WEEKLY "APPRECIATION TROPHY". A R.A.D. STAFF MEMBER WILL SELECT THEIR FAVORITE VEHICLE (CAR, TRUCK, MOTORCYCLE) OF THE NIGHT.

PROCEEDS BENEFITTING THE CHILDREN AT THE LOS ANGELES CENTERS FOR ALCOHOL & DRUG ABUSE (L.A. CADA).

REMEMBER
"YOUTH IS OUR FUTURE"

Any questions, call Jim LoBue (310) 696-7361

* PLEASE FOLLOW OUR SIMPLE RULES. THEY ARE FOR YOUR PROTECTION AND ENJOYMENT OR THE CARS.

If your club or organization needs to
create an effective flyer to promote
upcoming car events, help is
available — for layout, design,
art work, typesetting and printing.
Just call this number:

1-800-410-7766

Directory of America's Top Car Publications

These Magazines Will Help You
Know What's Hot, What's Not,
& What's Happening In The World
Of Vintage & Classic Cars

Personal Notes & Ideas

Top American Car Publications

All Chevy Magazine
2145 W. LaPalma
Anaheim, CA 92801

American Rodder Magazine
28210 Dorothy Dr.
Agoura HIlls, CA 91301

Automobile
888 7th Ave.
New York, NY 10106

Automobile Quarterly
Box 348
Kutztown, PA 19530

Auto Week
1400 Woodbridge Ave.
Detroit, MI 48207-3187

Car & Driver
1633 Broadway
New York, NY 10019-6741

Car Craft Magazine
6420 Wilshire Blvd.
Los Angeles, CA 90048

Cars & Parts Magazine
911 Vandemark Road
Sidney, OH 45367-9924

Classic Auto Restorer
P. O. Box 420250
Palm Coast, FL 32142-9486

Classic Cars National
 Buyer's Guide
14549 62nd St. N.
Clearwater, FL 34620-2328

Collector Car News
P. O. Box 2210
Palm Springs, CA 92263

Drive
3470 Buskirk Ave.
Pleasant Hill, CA 94523

Hemmings Motor News
P. O. Box 100
Route 9 W
Bennington, VT 05201

Hotline News
P. O. Box 2700
Huntington Beach, CA 92647

Hot Rodding Magazine
12100 Wilshire Blvd.
Los Angeles, CA 90025

Hot Rod Magazine
6420 Wilshire Blvd.
Los Angeles, CA 90048

Low-Rider Magazine
P. O. Box 648
Walnut, CA 91788-0648

Miss Information's
Automative Calendar of Events
1232 Highland Avenue
Glendale, CA 91202

Model A News & Restorers Club
24800 Michigan Ave.
Deerborn, MI 48124

Mustang & Fords Magazine
6420 Wilshire Blvd.
Los Angeles, CA 90048

Continued on next page —

Muscle Car Classics
8300 Santa Monica Avenue
Los Angeles, CA 90069

Muscle Cars
P. O. Box 1010
Denville, NJ 07834

Muscle Mustangs & Fast Fords
P. O. Box 1010
Denville, NJ 07834

Old Cars Price Guide
700 E. State Street
Iola, WI 54990-0001

Old Cars Weekly
700 E. State Street
Iola, WI 54990-0001

Popular Hot Rodding Magazine
P. O. Box 452
Mt. Morris, IL 61054

Road & Track
1633 Broadway
New York, NY 10019-6741

Rod & Custom Magazine
6420 Wilshire Blvd.
Los Angeles, CA 90048

Street Rodder Magazine
2145 W. LaPalma
Anaheim, CA 92801-1785

Super Chevy Magazine
12100 Wilshire Blvd., Ste. 250
Los Angeles, CA 90025

The Restorer Magazine
 (Model A Ford Club of America)
250 S. Cypress Street
Lahabra, CA 90631-5586

If you are aware of a good car publication that does not appear
in this directory, send us the details and we'll include it in the next
edition of *"The Mother of All Car Books."*

So You Think You Know Cars?

Classic Slogans I.Q. Test

Try This Test Out On Your Friends
At Car Shows, Cruise Nites & Parties

Personal Notes & Ideas

So You Think You Know Cars?
Classic Slogans I.Q. Test

The next time you're at a car event, or go to a party with people who think they know cars, see if they can name what makes used which slogans in their advertising campaigns. It's a lot of fun and will challenge the best of 'em. But first try taking it yourself and see how you do! On this page you'll find the Classic Slogans. See if you can name the make of each car before turning to the next page for the correct answers.

1 Low cost transportation.
2 The restful car.
3 The supreme combination of all that is fine in motorcars.
4 Ask the man who owns one.
5 The car that made good in a day.
6 Sleeve valve motors improve with use.
7 The car of silence.
8 The car with the 16 valve motor.
9 The car that has no valves.
10 .Solves the air-cooled automobile problem.
11 The car with the rotary air cooled motor.
12 It drives, it steers and brakes on all four wheels.
13 Champion of the world.
14 The hill climber.
15 Good everywhere.
16 A hill climber built in the hills.
17 The palace of the road.
18 Quality goes clear through.
19 A quality car.
20 Gets there and back.
21 The guaranteed car.
22 The car without a weakness.
23 The most for your money in a automobile.
24 The car you ought to own at the price you ought to pay.
25 The car too good for the price.
26 Legitimately high priced.
27 High grade at a modest price.
28 Made up to a standard, not down to a price.

29 More for the money than the price suggests.
30 Easily the best built car in America.
31 The super fine car.
32 Just a real good car.
33 Built for her majesty, the American woman.
34 Tested and proven in the south.
35 A chicago car for Chicago people.
36 The car of simplicity.
37 The simplest car.
38 Standard of the world.
39 The distinguished car.
40 The made to order car.
41 Choice of men who know.
42 The car of absolute exclusiveness.
43 Buy a _____ and keep your dates.
44 A car drives, a _____ glides.
45 Ride a _____ then decide.
46 The name that means something.
47 The most beautiful car in America.
48 There is a _____ in your future.
49 The goodness of automobiles.
50 All the name implies.
51 Gem of the highways.
52 Best car in the world.
53 The Beau K of the world.
54 No clutch to slip, no gears to strip.
55 Look for the white triangle.
56 When better cars are built.
57 It runs in silence.
58 The famous name.
59 For economical transportation.
60 Nothing to watch but the road.
61 _____ has a better idea.

HERE ARE THE CORRECT ANSWERS!

1	STAR	31	TEMPLAR
2	PACKARD	32	DURANT
3	PACKARD	33	PULLMAN
4	PACKARD	34	HANSON
5	STUTZ	35	BANKER
6	WILLYS KNIGHT	36	AUTO CAR
7	LYONS KNIGHT	37	CRESTMOBILE
8	DREXAL	38	CADILLAC
9	ELMORE	39	DANIELS
10	FROYER MILLER	40	SPRINGFIELD
11	EAGLE	41	HUEBERT A. LOZIER
12	F W D	42	NORWALK
13	PIOLET	43	BATES
14	MYTAG	44	FARMAN
15	BUICK	45	GLIDE
16	GLIDE	46	AUBURN
17	PULLMAN	47	PAIGE
18	DORT	48	FORD
19	MORSE	49	MINERVA
20	PRESCOT	50	PEERLESS
21	GARDNER	51	COLLIMBIA
22	MODOC	52	ROLLS ROYCE
23	CENTURY	53	YALE
24	MITCHEL	54	METZ
25	RELIANCE	55	HUDSON
26	LOZIER	56	BUICK
27	RUSSELL	57	IRIS
28	COVERT	58	PONTIAC
29	GRAY	59	CHEVROLET
30	LOCOMOBILE	60	OLDSMOBILE
		61	FORD

IF YOU GET 10 OR MORE CORRECT, YOU'RE A GENIUS!
(or, you're very, very OLD!)

If you are aware of other slogans used by vintage and classic cars,
send them to us and we'll include them in the next edition of
"The Mother of All Car Books."

Special Gift & Raffle Copies
Order Forms

*Use These Forms To Order Additional Copies
Of "The Mother of All Car Books"
To Use As Special Gifts Or Raffle Prizes*

Order Form

Please send me _____ copies of *"The Mother of All Car Books"* to use as gifts or as special raffle prizes at car events. I am enclosing my check or money order for $14.95 per book, plus $4 per book for postage and handling (California residents add 7.75% sales tax). Send to me at the following address: **(PLEASE PRINT)**

NAME _____ PHONE # _____

ADDRESS _____APT. # _____

CITY_____ STATE _____ ZIP _____

Fill out order form completely, include payment and mail to:

DUNCLIFF'S INTERNATIONAL
3662 Katella Ave., Dept. 226-CB
Los Alamitos, CA 90720

If you don't want to wait 3 to 4 weeks to receive your copies, just have your VISA or MasterCard handy and call TOLL-FREE 1-800-410-7766. Your order will be shipped to you within 48 hours!

NOTE: Special discount rates are available for quantity orders. Call the number above for more information.

— — — — — — — — — — — — — — — — — ✂ OR COPY — — —

Order Form

Please send me _____ copies of *"The Mother of All Car Books"* to use as gifts or as special raffle prizes at car events. I am enclosing my check or money order for $14.95 per book, plus $4 per book for postage and handling (California residents add 7.75% sales tax). Send to me at the following address: **(PLEASE PRINT)**

NAME _____ PHONE # _____

ADDRESS _____APT. # _____

CITY_____ STATE _____ ZIP _____

Fill out order form completely, include payment and mail to:

DUNCLIFF'S INTERNATIONAL
3662 Katella Ave., Dept. 226-CB
Los Alamitos, CA 90720

If you don't want to wait 3 to 4 weeks to receive your copies, just have your VISA or MasterCard handy and call TOLL-FREE 1-800-410-7766. Your order will be shipped to you within 48 hours!

NOTE: Special discount rates are available for quantity orders. Call the number above for more information.

Order Form

Please send me _____ copies of *"The Mother of All Car Books"* to use as gifts or as special raffle prizes at car events. I am enclosing my check or money order for $14.95 per book, plus $4 per book for postage and handling (California residents add 7.75% sales tax). Send to me at the following address: (PLEASE PRINT)

NAME _____ PHONE # _____

ADDRESS _____APT. # _____

CITY_____ STATE _____ ZIP _____

Fill out order form completely, include payment and mail to:

DUNCLIFF'S INTERNATIONAL
3662 Katella Ave., Dept. 226-CB
Los Alamitos, CA 90720

If you don't want to wait 3 to 4 weeks to receive your copies, just have your VISA or MasterCard handy and call TOLL-FREE 1-800-410-7766. Your order will be shipped to you within 48 hours!

NOTE: Special discount rates are available for quantity orders. Call the number above for more information.

— ✂ OR COPY — — —

Order Form

Please send me _____ copies of *"The Mother of All Car Books"* to use as gifts or as special raffle prizes at car events. I am enclosing my check or money order for $14.95 per book, plus $4 per book for postage and handling (California residents add 7.75% sales tax). Send to me at the following address: (PLEASE PRINT)

NAME _____ PHONE # _____

ADDRESS _____APT. # _____

CITY_____ STATE _____ ZIP _____

Fill out order form completely, include payment and mail to:

DUNCLIFF'S INTERNATIONAL
3662 Katella Ave., Dept. 226-CB
Los Alamitos, CA 90720

If you don't want to wait 3 to 4 weeks to receive your copies, just have your VISA or MasterCard handy and call TOLL-FREE 1-800-410-7766. Your order will be shipped to you within 48 hours!

NOTE: Special discount rates are available for quantity orders. Call the number above for more information.

Order Form

Please send me _____ copies of *"The Mother of All Car Books"* to use as gifts or as special raffle prizes at car events. I am enclosing my check or money order for $14.95 per book, plus $4 per book for postage and handling (California residents add 7.75% sales tax). Send to me at the following address: **(PLEASE PRINT)**

NAME _____ PHONE # _____

ADDRESS _____APT. # _____

CITY_____ STATE _____ ZIP _____

Fill out order form completely, include payment and mail to:

**DUNCLIFF'S INTERNATIONAL
3662 Katella Ave., Dept. 226-CB
Los Alamitos, CA 90720**

If you don't want to wait 3 to 4 weeks to receive your copies, just have your VISA or MasterCard handy and call TOLL-FREE 1-800-410-7766. Your order will be shipped to you within 48 hours!

NOTE: Special discount rates are available for quantity orders. Call the number above for more information.

— — — — — — — — — — — — — — — — — ✂ OR COPY — — —

Order Form

Please send me _____ copies of *"The Mother of All Car Books"* to use as gifts or as special raffle prizes at car events. I am enclosing my check or money order for $14.95 per book, plus $4 per book for postage and handling (California residents add 7.75% sales tax). Send to me at the following address: **(PLEASE PRINT)**

NAME _____ PHONE # _____

ADDRESS _____APT. # _____

CITY_____ STATE _____ ZIP _____

Fill out order form completely, include payment and mail to:

**DUNCLIFF'S INTERNATIONAL
3662 Katella Ave., Dept. 226-CB
Los Alamitos, CA 90720**

If you don't want to wait 3 to 4 weeks to receive your copies, just have your VISA or MasterCard handy and call TOLL-FREE 1-800-410-7766. Your order will be shipped to you within 48 hours!

NOTE: Special discount rates are available for quantity orders. Call the number above for more information.

Personal Notes & Ideas

Personal Notes & Ideas

Personal Notes & Ideas

Personal Notes & Ideas